The Fishmeal Revolution

The publisher and the University of California Press Foundation gratefully acknowledge the generous support of the Ralph and Shirley Shapiro Endowment Fund in Environmental Studies.

The Fishmeal Revolution

THE INDUSTRIALIZATION OF THE HUMBOLDT CURRENT ECOSYSTEM

Kristin A. Wintersteen

UNIVERSITY OF CALIFORNIA PRESS

University of California Press
Oakland, California

© 2021 by Kristin A. Wintersteen

Library of Congress Cataloging-in-Publication Data

Names: Wintersteen, Kristin A., 1979– author.
Title: The fishmeal revolution : the industrialization of the Humboldt
    Current ecosystem / Kristin A. Wintersteen.
Description: Oakland, California : University of California Press, [2021] |
    Includes bibliographical references and index.
Identifiers: LCCN 2020051325 (print) | LCCN 2020051326 (ebook) |
    ISBN 9780520379626 (cloth) | ISBN 9780520379633 (paperback) |
    ISBN 9780520976825 (epub)
Subjects: LCSH: Fish meal industry—Peru—History. | Fish meal
    industry—Chile—History. | Peru Current.
Classification: LCC HD9469.F52 P58 2021 (print) | LCC HD9469.F52 (ebook) |
    DDC 338.3/7270985—dc23
LC record available at https://lccn.loc.gov/2020051325
LC ebook record available at https://lccn.loc.gov/2020051326

30 29 28 27 26 25 24 23 22 21
10 9 8 7 6 5 4 3 2 1

CONTENTS

List of Illustrations   vii
Acknowledgments   ix
Abbreviations and Acronyms   xv

Introduction   1

1 · A Deep History of the Humboldt Current Ecosystem   15

2 · The New Industrial Ecology of Animal Farming in the Atlantic and Pacific Worlds, 1840–1930   30

3 · Protein from the Sea: The "Nutrition Problem" and the Industrialization of Fishing in Chile and Peru   45

4 · The Golden Anchoveta: The Making of the World's Largest Single-Species Fishery in Chimbote, Peru   59

5 · States of Uncertainty: Science, Policy, and the Bio-economics of Peru's 1972 Fishmeal Collapse   76

6 · The Translocal History of Industrial Fisheries in Iquique and Talcahuano, Chile   92

Conclusion   110

Appendix A. Glossary of Marine Species   127
Appendix B. Diagram of Humboldt Current Trophic Web   131
Appendix C. Map of Major Current Systems of Eastern and Central Pacific Ocean   132

Appendix D. Map of World Fisheries Management Zones 133
Appendix E. Graph of World Fisheries Landings and
ENSO Events, 1950–2014 135
Notes 137
Bibliography 189
Index 215

ILLUSTRATIONS

FIGURES

1. Huanchaco, Peru, in the late nineteenth century. *4*
2. View of Paita, Peru (1930). *23*
3. Iquique, Chile, in the late nineteenth century. *29*
4. Diagram of apparatus for producing fishmeal (front view). *39*
5. Man carrying sierras in San Antonio, Chile (undated photo). *48*
6. Women processing the catch, Chile (1960). *50*
7. Men aboard a fishing trawler, Chile (1958). *55*
8. Aerial view of Chimbote, Peru (1929). *62*
9. Men preparing to load anchoveta into a fishing vessel's hold, Chile (1964). *67*
10. People on the beach in front of fishmeal plants, Chimbote, Peru (2008). *74*
11. Humboldt Current reduction fisheries, 1950–2014. *87*
12. Industrial purse seiners in El Ferrol Bay, Chimbote, Peru (2009). *90*
13. Boats in Iquique, Chile, harbor (1907). *95*
14. Fish drying in Talcahuano, Chile (1930). *97*
15. Fishmeal plant in Arica, Chile (1965). *100*
16. Men hauling sacks in a fishmeal plant, Coquimbo, Chile (1964). *101*
17. Diagram of Humboldt Current marine ecosystem. *131*
18. World fisheries production and El Niño 1950–2014 *136*

MAPS

1. Physical geography and major fishing cities of the Humboldt Current system. *7*
2. Major surface current systems of the central and eastern Pacific Ocean. *132*
3. World fisheries management zones. *134*

ACKNOWLEDGMENTS

This book is the long-awaited product of many journeys. During more than eleven years of research and study, I resided in ten different cities and traveled to twenty-two others—in eight countries, on three continents—as I worked to conceptualize the intersecting layers of this global environmental and ecological history. Needless to say, the creative and intellectual debts I have accrued during this process are far more numerous than I could hope to articulate here. What follows is but a glimpse of the human and institutional synergies that contributed along the way.

Numerous institutions and funding sources facilitated my research and writing at both the postdoctoral and dissertation stages. These included major fellowships for writing, foreign travel, and fieldwork: a Residential Fellowship at the Institute for Historical Studies at the University of Texas at Austin, the Fulbright-Hays Doctoral Dissertation Research Award, the Graduate Academic Scholarship from the Organization of American States, the F. K. Weyerhaeuser Forest History Fellowship, and the Katherine G. Stern Dissertation Fellowship from Duke University. Short-term grants included the Samuel Hays Research Fellowship from the American Society for Environmental History, Faculty Research Awards from both the University of Houston and Tulane University, the Albert J. Beveridge Award from the American Historical Organization, and an Exploratory Travel and Data Grant from the Economic History Association. Without the generosity of these organizations, their benefactors, and their staff, this work would not have been possible.

Three readers for the University of California Press provided critical feedback on an earlier draft of the manuscript, although any errors herein are my own. For their invaluable insights, I heartily thank Greg Cushman, Daniel

Pauly, and John Soluri. Editor Kate Marshall has been supportive throughout the publishing process. Gray Kidd assisted with bibliographic entries. John D. French and Prescott B. Wintersteen Jr., provided helpful suggestions as I finalized the files.

I am deeply grateful to the people in Chile and Peru who shared with me their expertise, their histories, their libraries, and even their homes and families. In Lima, the late Hernán Peralta Bouroncle, founder of the *Centro Para la Documentación Pesquera* (CENDOPES), warmly shared his immense personal knowledge on countless occasions and allowed unfettered access to a lifetime of collected materials. This project and the methodology that has informed it originated in the memorable environmental history seminars and *terrenos* I attended with "El Profe" Fernando Ramírez Morales at the University of Chile in 2000–01. Also in Chile, Hernán Rojas Moraga and Patricia Sánchez shared the vast beauty of their favorite places—from Vitacura and Los Andes to El Colorado, Reñaca, and Linares—and I treasure the memories of our long conversations, *asados*, and hikes, which provided a welcome escape from the bustle of urban life. In Puente del Alto, Santiago, and Collipulli, Nicolás García Inostroza and his family received us with open arms whenever we showed up at their doorsteps. Ximena Saldivia, Mauricio Mora, and their extended family were generous hosts in Talcahuano. And thanks to the daily conversations I enjoyed with Juan "Marma" Fariña, I felt more at home in Santiago.

The inimitable conservation biologist Patricia Majluf—founder of the Center for Environmental Sustainability at the Universidad de Cayetano Heredia in Lima—enthusiastically supported this project from the beginning, facilitating contacts and opportunities to visit key industrial sites. Santiago de la Puente shared his extensive reference library. María Elena Foronda Farro and the late Óscar Díaz made my trips to Chimbote fun and informative. Alex Muñoz Wilson provided information and encouragement at several points along the way. Crucial assistance also came from scientists, administrators, and other fisheries professionals, including Contralmirante Hector Soldi and Renato Guevara at IMARPE in Peru, Leonardo Sasso at IFOP in Chile, and Enrique Anton, Jorge Csirke, Giuliano Fregoli, Luca Garibaldi, Richard Grainger, and Angel Gumy at FAO in Rome. Furthermore, the attentiveness of many archivists and reference librarians made the task of sifting through dusty trade journals and boxes of obscure ephemera easier and all the more pleasant.

Interviews, local outings, and samples of strange shellfish greatly enlivened the research process. The knowledge that locals shared with me enriched my understanding of the fishing industry beyond measure, including Elsa Baltodano, Cosme Caracciolo, Javier Castro, Oscar de la Puente, Juan Hernández, Arturo Huapaya, Ricardo Moranté, Héctor Olivares, Guillermo Risco, Arturo Saldivia, and Ricardo Ulloa, among others. Executives at several fishing companies in both Peru and Chile generously allowed me to visit their fishmeal and fish processing facilities: Austral, S.A.; Borsea, S.A.; CORPESCA, S.A.; Hayduk, S.A.; Mar Profundo, S.A.; Pesquera Camanchaca, S.A.; Pesquera San José, S.A.; Prisco, S.A.; Redes Netto; and TASA, S.A.

I thank my colleagues at the University of Houston, especially the conveners and participants of the Gulf Coast Food Studies Group, the Center for Public History Research Colloquium, and other individuals at UH and Rice University who have given their support, feedback, and collaboration in recent years. They include Keliy Anderson-Staley, Dominic Boyer, Francisco Cantu, Julie Cohn, Xiaoping Cong, Mark Goldberg, John Hart, Phil Howard, Cymene Howe, Karl Ittman, Wes Jackson, Susan Kellogg, Kairn Klieman, Keith McNeal, Marty Melosi, Natalia Milanesio, Rick Mizelle, Kristina Neumann, Cathy Patterson, Monica Perales, Raúl Ramos, Linda Reed, Todd Romero, Jimmy Schafer, Eric Walther, Nancy Young, and Leandra Zarnow.

During a year at the Institute for Historical Studies at the University of Texas at Austin, I enjoyed the camaraderie and collegiality of several outstanding individuals, among them Mitch Aso, Erika Bsumek, Emma Flatt, Seth Garfield, Mary Gayne, Neil Kamil, Mark Metzler, and Kerry Webb; I am also thankful to Jonathan Brown, Bruce Hunt, and Megan Raby for providing careful feedback on a previous version of this manuscript. Erin Gaines and Andy Gerhart shared their home, and even let me take care of their chickens on one or two occasions. Courtney Meador helped me to survive the travails of multiple relocations and to appreciate, with good humor, the "ugly beauty" of the Texas petrochemical landscape.

Three transformative semesters as a Zemurray-Stone fellow at Tulane University's Stone Center for Latin American Studies in New Orleans expanded my approach to teaching, research, and service learning, while giving me the opportunity to engage with many wonderful colleagues, among them Richard Campanella, Ana Margarida Esteves Fernandes, Guadalupe García, Jimmy Huck, Mattea Musso, Tom Reese, Jessica Rich, Federico Rossi, Edie Wolfe, and Justin Wolfe.

Several institutes provided opportunities to share works-in-progress with scholars from far and wide. Six months' residency in Berlin as a member of the desiguALdades research network (in affiliation with the Freie Universität and the Ibero-Amerikanisches Institut) deepened the transnational and interdisciplinary dialogues that inform my work. There I crossed paths with many bright scholars: André Cicalo, Sarah Fellmeth, Barbara Göbel, Maya Ishizawa, David Manuel-Navarrete, Raúl Matta, Renata Motta, Prem Poddar, María Fernanda Valdés Valencia, and not least, my precious friend Olga Piperi. Five different summer workshops—the RAND Faculty Leaders Program (2018), the National Center for Faculty Development and Diversity Faculty Success Program (2017), the National Endowment for Humanities Summer Institute in Flagstaff, AZ (2016), the Cornell Summer Institute on Contested Landscapes (2013), and the Global Labor History Summer Institute (2008)—have pushed me to rethink the practices of teaching and research. My virtual "pen pal," Jeanette Tran, helped me to stay grounded from week-to-week, always lending a thoughtful listening ear.

As a PhD student at Duke University, I found an unparalleled intellectual community and the freedom to pursue transnational and interdisciplinary research for my dissertation. Through his uniquely committed and passionate mentorship, John D. French has left many indelible imprints on my ways of thinking, learning, and knowing, and has supported me in countless ways throughout my professional development. Jan French's perspicacity has helped to keep me grounded over the years. Furthermore, I have welcomed the guidance and friendship of Jocelyn Olcott, as well as dissertation committee members Ed Balleisen, Gunther Peck, Tom Rogers, and Pete Sigal. Natalie Hartman, associate director of Duke's Center for Latin American Studies, was a kind and cheerful facilitator of many research trips, grant applications, and day-to-day life as a graduate student. Short-term research at the Center for Globalization, Governance, and Competitiveness under the direction of Gary Gereffi afforded me the opportunity to learn how to apply the methodology of global value chains to complex topics with real-world relevance.

Good friends and colleagues have helped to make these adventures more enjoyable; for this I thank Ben Best, Leigh Campoamor, Katharine French-Fuller, Ester Gaya, Reena Goldthree, Shaleyla Kelez, Jess Metcalf, Sean McMahon, Kinohi Nishikawa, Bryan Pitts, Christina Ramos, Liz Shesko, Varun Swamy, Felicity Turner, and Ivonne Wallace-Fuentes. André Boustany allowed me the unforgettable experience of observing a tuna-tagging expedition off the North Carolina coast. Lorien Olive, Beatriz Balanta, and Álvaro Jarrín hosted me during visits to Guayaquil and Rio de Janeiro. An ongoing source of comfort and hilarity, Caroline Yezer has shared her places of refuge in Lima, Taos, and elsewhere on more than one occasion.

I first encountered the fields that uniquely intersected to inform this project—Latin American history, fisheries science, and international studies—as a student, then employee, at the University of Washington in Seattle. The mentorship of Chuck Bergquist and Anand Yang, the friendship of Karam Dana, and the collegiality of many faculty and staff at the Jackson School for International Studies encouraged my intellectual curiosity in these areas during and after college.

Crucially, several "wonder-women" briefly shared their homes with me along the way, inspiring me with their sure-footed independence: Cindy Brown, Ximena Moraga, Gigi Peterson, and Ina Stengel. Professional cheerleaders who helped me to reach my goals were Kris Madorsky, Ronald Garb, Vanessa Joy, and Philip Spiro. Throughout these years, I have spent countless hours at my favorite coffee shops in Durham, Santiago, Austin, and Houston; I am ever grateful to the neighbors, baristas, servers, and managers who accompanied me through the daily grind, among them, Meredith Canada, Kent Childress, Tracy Gill, Tam Lo, and Daniela López.

Pittsburgh's postindustrial, park-filled hillscapes served as my earliest crucible of inspiration, and the city is still home to my dearest friends and family. The late Bill Milburn and Marilyn and Bill Martin deeply shaped my personal growth. Katherine Beattie, Ethan and Azi Block, Lauren Fleishman Mayer, Adrienne and Frank Izaguirre, and Ariel Jacobson—as well as long-time friends of both coasts, Colleen Stevenson and Gabe Yarra—have been consistent proof of the forces of good (and good humor) in this world. I owe the greatest debt to my family, especially my parents, Sigrid and Prescott, and sister Katherine, for their keen artistic sensibilities and, most importantly, their unwavering love and support.

For every dusty, windowless archive where I scoured boxes of documents and ephemera, I enjoyed as many amazing landscapes—Chile's Andean skyline, the oceanside bluffs of Lima, the Landwehrkanal in Berlin—where ideas could linger and take form. My Houston home floated above a toad-filled garden; their melodic songs, and the evening "coos" of an owl outside my window, offered reminders of nature's flourishing at unexpected moments. Finally, just as I was nearing the finish line of this globetrotting marathon, an extra-worldly creature tumbled joyously into my life: my own little Ziggy Stardust has shown me that there are many more adventures to be had.

ABBREVIATIONS AND ACRONYMS

ARNAD	*Archivo Nacional de la Administración* (National Archive of Government Administration, Santiago, Chile)
BNCH	*Biblioteca Nacional de Chile* (National Library, Santiago, Chile)
BP	before present (years)
CAG	*Compañia Administradora del Guano* (Guano Administration Company, Perú)
CalCOFI	California Cooperative Oceanic Fisheries Investigations
CENDOPES	*Centro para la Documentación Pesquera* (Center for Fisheries Documentation, Lima, Perú)
CONAPACH	*Confederación Nacional de Pescadores Artesanales de Chile* (National Confederation of Artisanal Fishermen, Valparaíso, Chile)
CORFO	*Corporación del Fomento* (Chilean Development Corporation, Santiago, Chile)
CPP	*Consorcio Pesquero del Perú* (Peruvian Fishing Consortium, Lima, Perú)
CPPS	*Convenio Para el Pacífico Sureste* (Convention for the Southeast Pacific, Guayaquil, Ecuador)

CRYRZA	*Comisión para la Rehabilitación y Reconstrucción de la Zona Afectada* (Rehabilitation and Reconstruction Commission for the Affected Zone, Chimbote, Perú)
DLA	*Deutsche Literaturarchiv-Marbach* (German Literary Archive, Marbach-am-Neckar, Germany)
ECLA	Economic Commission for Latin America of the United Nations (*Comisión Económica Para América Latina*, Santiago, Chile)
EEZ	Exclusive Economic Zone (Law of the Sea)
ENSO	El Niño Southern Oscillation
FAO	Food and Agricultural Organization of the United Nations
FEO	Fishmeal Exporters Organization
FPC	Fish Protein Concentrate
HCS	Humboldt Current System
IATTC	Inter-American Tropical Tuna Commission
IFFO	International Fishmeal and Fish Oil Organization
IFOP	*Instituto del Fomento Pesquero* (Institute for Fisheries Development, Valparaíso, Chile)
IMARPE	*Instituto del Mar del Perú* (Institute for Ocean Research, Callao, Perú)
IPC	International Proteins Corporation
ITQ	individual transferable quota
IVQ	individual vessel quota
IWC	International Whaling Commission
LME	large marine ecosystem
LOC	United States Library of Congress
MIPE	*Ministerio de Pesquería* (Ministry of Fisheries, Lima, Peru)
MSK	Mitsubishi Shoji Kaija, Ltd.

MTI	marine trophic index
NARA	United States National Archives and Records Administration (College Park, MD)
NGO	nongovernmental organization
NOAA	United States National Oceanic and Atmospheric Administration
ONI	Oceanic Niño Index
PDO	Pacific Decadal Oscillation
SCIPA	*Servicio Cooperativo Inter-Americano* (Inter-American Cooperative Service)
SIO	Scripps Institute for Oceanography at the University of California, San Diego (La Jolla, CA)
SNP	*Sociedad Nacional de Pesquería* (National Fisheries Society, Lima, Perú)
SOGESA	*Sociedad de Gestión de la Planta Siderúrgica de Chimbote y de la Central Hidroeléctrica del Cañón del Pato* (Management Society for the Chimbote Steel Mill and Cañón del Pato Hydroelectric Facility, Peru)
SPRFMO	South and Southeast Pacific Regional Fisheries Management Organization
SST	sea surface temperature
TURF	territorial use rights in fisheries
UNCLOS	United Nations Convention on the Law of the Sea
UNDP	United Nations Development Program
UNICEF	United Nations International Children's Emergency Fund
USAID	United States Agency for International Development
USDA	United States Department of Agriculture
USFW	United States Fish and Wildlife Service
UW	University of Washington (Seattle, WA)

Introduction

GAZING OUT FROM THE DECK of a steamer near the town of Huarmey, Peru, the ornithologist Robert Cushman Murphy stood in awe at the sight of "such multitudes of herrings as I had never previously beheld." He marveled at the dense school of "quivering, silvery creatures" swimming in the cold coastal current: they were "packed together like sardines in a tin ... as their legion, which somehow seems more like an individual organism than a conglomeration of millions, streams through the gauntlet of its diverse and ubiquitous enemies."[1] Eighteenth- and nineteenth-century seafarers traveling along the South American Pacific coast had often remarked on the tiny fishes that swam in schools so massive that they visibly darkened the sea surface against the distant horizon.

The immense, quivering schools Murphy described were anchoveta (*Engraulis ringens*), an endemic species that thrives in the cold, plankton-rich waters of the Humboldt Current ecosystem. Their abundant populations are integral to the diets of many other marine fauna, including tuna, seals, and the innumerable seabirds that nest on rocky islands off the arid coast between northern Peru and central Chile. Murphy recalled the frenetic battle that ensued at the encounter between predators and prey: "I estimated that a hundred schools of anchoveta were within sight. At times, when the bonitos attacked them from beneath, large areas of the surface would be so broken by the leaping of the little fishes that the ocean hissed as though a deluge of rain were descending upon it. The most remarkable sight of all was the manner in which whole herds of sea-lions were lolling and frolicking among the anchovetas, gorging themselves to the limit of their capacity."[2] The feeding frenzy was a dramatic, if apocryphal, display of the anchoveta's key role in this marine ecosystem.[3]

Observing the scene from his perch above the sea surface, Murphy had a mere human's-eye view of the watery tumult.[4] But in any case, it was the multitudinous flocks of sea birds that drew his keenest interest at the time. Since the late nineteenth century, this region of the Peru-Chile coast had been a key field site for European and US marine ornithologists due to the global economic importance of the guano trade.[5] "The long files of pelicans, the low-moving black clouds of cormorants, or the rainstorms of plunging gannets probably can not be equaled in any other part of the world," the zoologist Robert E. Coker wrote in 1908, after nearly two years of study on the Peruvian coast.[6] Three endemic birds comprised what Murphy called the "great guano-producing triumvirate" of this eco-region: the numerous and "wonderfully specialized" *piquero* (*Sula variegata,* or Peruvian booby); the large and "most conspicuous" *alcatráz* (a species of pelican, *Pelicanus occidentalus,* frequently encountered in huge flocks); and, finally, that which he deemed "first in importance" and efficiency as a guano-making "machine": the *guanay* (Peruvian cormorant, *Phalacrocorax bougainvillii).*[7] In 1913, two US ornithologists identified a single species of petrel (*Oceanodroma hornbyi*) that was common to the entire length of the coast between the Gulf of Guayaquil (3°S) to central Chile (30°S). Such a large latitudinal range highlighted the distinctiveness of this "special faunal zone," Murphy asserted.[8] The broad contours of this oceanic system had been recognized by indigenous peoples of the littoral and mariners sailing what they knew as the "South Sea" for centuries, if not millennia.[9]

Oceanic winds generally blow counterclockwise in this region, pushing surface waters from the west and south toward the Equator, along the continent's western edge. In contrast to the notoriously stormy Caribbean, the tranquility of these cold, deep-blue waters is rumored to have inspired the name "Pacific" when Ferdinand de Magellan passed through in 1520.[10] By the seventeenth century, the Pacific Ocean had become a subject of interest among European scientists who sought to theorize the interrelationships among tides, winds, and ocean currents.[11] The Prussian naturalist Alexander von Humboldt helped to popularize knowledge of the coastal current system among Euro-Atlantic intellectual elites upon returning from his voyage to the Americas, where in 1802 he had measured and recorded the ocean and atmospheric conditions off the coast of Peru. Since the surface-level current clearly flowed northward, Humboldt attributed the cold sea surface temperatures to the waters' apparent origins in sub-Antarctic latitudes, but this proved inaccurate.[12] Instead, a strong coastal upwelling was the defining feature of the marine ecosystem and its biogeography in these waters.

Together, these two intersecting realms—the oceanic-climatological, and the biotic-zoological—have comprised the driving forces of the Humboldt Current marine ecosystem.[13]

Coker, Murphy, and others documented the region's distinctive biogeography prior to the ravages of large-scale industrial fishing. Coker unequivocally declared the tiny anchoveta to be "the most valuable resource of the waters of Peru."[14] Murphy, who set out to investigate the ecological forces driving the extraordinary abundance of the marine ecosystem, reached a similar conclusion: finding only *Engraulis ringens* in the stomachs of the boobies (*piqueros*) he examined, he conceded that "this creature is probably the mainstay of [their] existence."[15] At the same time that these scientists recognized the importance of these fisheries and their food webs, however, their reports also promoted—in some cases explicitly—the industrial development of fishing in the areas they surveyed. Coker described indigenous Peruvians' practice of salting and sun-drying anchoveta as "an opportunity that is not now utilized" by fish-processing entrepreneurs: "This little fish of manifold uses is all the more significant because of the rare opportunity it offers for the preparation of an excellent preserved product."[16] In a 1923 article in *The Scientific Monthly*, Murphy also emphasized the underdevelopment of commercial Peruvian fisheries, reporting that there was "not a single organized fishing industry" in operation along the entire coast. "Few littoral waters of the globe teem with fish and with other edible products as do those of Peru," he remarked, "and yet in no other enlightened country are fisheries more restricted to methods which ... are such as the Indians have followed from immemorial times."[17] Locals typically used wooden boats (*lanchas*) or traditional craft, such as reed rafts (*los caballitos de totora*), woven from the tall grasses of Peru's north coast wetlands near Huanchaco. These vessels were adequate for subsistence fishing and small-scale commercial activity, given the near-shore abundance of large fish shoals in this region prior to World War Two.

The experts' enthusiastic assessments of the potential for commercial production and export of Humboldt Current marine proteins had not been overstated: in the late 1950s, Peru and Chile emerged as two of the top-producing industrial fishing nations. Their primary export product, however, was not ultimately fillets or canned goods made from high-grade "table fish," but rather concentrated proteins in the form of fishmeal and fish oil—critical ingredients in the specially formulated animal feeds that fueled the rapid expansion of intensive poultry, hog, and fish farming during the second half of the twentieth century.[18] Expanding agricultural economies of scale and

FIGURE 1. Huanchaco, Peru, in the late nineteenth century. Mateo Paz Soldán with Mariano Felipe Paz Soldán, eds., *Geografía del Perú* (Paris: F. Didot, 1862), Plate XIV. Prints and Photographs Division, United States Library of Congress.

"just-in-time" production models increased the demand for fishmeal and other high-protein feed commodities, one of the sector's most costly inputs.[19] Between 1950 and 2010, approximately 27 percent (an average of twenty million metric tons annually) of global marine fisheries landings became fodder for nonhuman consumers, and 90 percent of those fish were classified as food-grade.[20] During the same period, Peru and Chile together accounted for an average of 48.7 percent of total fishmeal and oil produced annually (33.8% and 14.9%, respectively).[21] Worldwide, fishmeal and oil producers have primarily targeted "forage fish"—small, oily species that form large schools and are important food sources for foraging marine predators—for industrial-scale "reduction" to more easily digestible, nutrient-rich substances. Cooked, pressed, and pulverized, they traveled across the oceans in jute sacks or cargo ships' bulk holds, ultimately arriving at the troughs of industrially farmed animals and fish, primarily in the United States, Northern Europe, and increasingly by the twenty-first century, China.

Global fishmeal and fish oil production became major components of what fisheries biologist David H. Cushing has called the "second industrialization" that occurred in world fisheries between 1950 and 1977, as the application of new technologies and the expansion of traditional fishing grounds exponentially increased the rate at which humans extracted biomass from marine ecosystems.[22] While the first phase of fisheries industrialization occurred in three relatively more limited areas—the North Sea, the North Atlantic (between Cape Hatteras and the Gulf of St. Lawrence), and off the Northwest Pacific Coast of the Americas—the second phase increased pressure on fish stocks worldwide.[23] During the second phase, European, Japanese, and Russian long-distance factory trawlers incorporated refrigeration and freezing technologies to process their catch on-board (and away from land-based regulations). Sonar, echo-sounding, hydraulic power blocks, and nylon nets further revolutionized humans' ability to detect, observe, and extract underwater resources, delivering seemingly endless supplies of cheap fish to ever-hungry consumers, both animal and human. Equipped with these tools, purse seine fleets depleted stocks of herring, sardines, anchovies, and mackerel between the 1940s and late 1960s in multiple ocean regions.[24] They included the coasts of British Columbia, California, Japan, the US Atlantic and Gulf Coasts, South Africa, Namibia, and in the North Sea.[25] As humans traversed the maritime "techno-frontier" in the second half of the twentieth century, the world's oceans became more legible—and their resources more accessible—to scientists, governments, and industrialists on a planetary scale.[26]

Central to this emerging global industrial food web, the humble anchoveta became "the most heavily exploited fish in world history" after a rapid period of expansion in Peru and northern Chile during the 1960s.[27] Seafood, agribusiness, and pharmaceutical concerns invested in fishing vessels and processing plants in both countries during the boom years. Overall, schooling fishes of the Humboldt Current supplied an estimated 55.8 percent of all fishmeal produced between 1950 and 2010, including the anchoveta (*Engraulis ringens*, at 33.7%), sardine (*Sardinops sagax,* at 16.6%), and jack mackerel (*Trachurus murphyi*, at 5.5%).[28] In the early twenty-first century, this region continued to yield up to 10 percent of the total world marine fisheries catch in an area spanning less than 1 percent of the world's ocean surface.[29]

The variabilities of the Humboldt Current marine ecosystem have punctuated the global history of this commodity, most notably in 1972, when an incursion of unusually warm waters coincided with a decades-long peak in the intensification of industrial fishing and fishmeal production in Peru. The remarkable impact caused by this ocean-atmospheric phenomenon, known as El Niño, attracted great attention from international scientists and industrialists alike. The ensuing collapse in the fishery severely disrupted global flows of marine proteins, impacting farmers in distant markets. Without the anchoveta, supplies of fishmeal and oil dried up almost overnight, wreaking havoc for brokers with contracts to fill.[30] But Chilean industrialists continued to produce and export fishmeal using newly abundant sardine and mackerel species, incorporating technologies that created a higher-grade product with less raw material, while Peru struggled to restructure the industry and its gigantic bureaucracy. Along with the estimated 35 percent of the world's land-based agricultural harvest that is used to feed livestock, oceanic ecosystems and littoral societies have been key suppliers of nutrients to the industrial food web during the past century.[31] Their histories are therefore crucial to understanding the environmental and human dimensions of modern food production.

THE GLOBAL ENVIRONMENTAL SIGNIFICANCE OF THE HUMBOLDT CURRENT ECOSYSTEM

Between 5,800 and 3,600 years ago, in the desert valleys of what is now the northern coast of Peru, humans built what were once the largest settlements in the Western Hemisphere. In addition to cultivating several food crops (including beans, squash, avocado, sweet potato, and peanuts), along with cotton, in irrigated fields, they subsisted on protein taken from the sea, and kept no domesticated animals. This society lived a "unique evolutionary experiment," adapted to the particular ecological conditions of the desert coast, which was carved by episodes of severe flooding and tectonic shocks. The ridges such events formed in the land are discernible today to paleoarchaeologists in several locations offshore, including near the mouth of the Santa River (9°S), just north of Chimbote.[32] The west coast of South America was (and remains) one of the most seismically active regions on Earth.

Oceanographically, three major characteristics broadly shape the Humboldt Current System (HCS): its coastal flows and counterflows; a strong upwelling of nutrient-rich water; and the inherent variability of these conditions, both spatially and temporally. Under normal conditions, the surface-level current sweeps northward along the western edge of the South American continent, "literally bathing the shores" from southern Chile (45°S) to equatorial latitudes near Guayaquil (4°S), before turning sharply

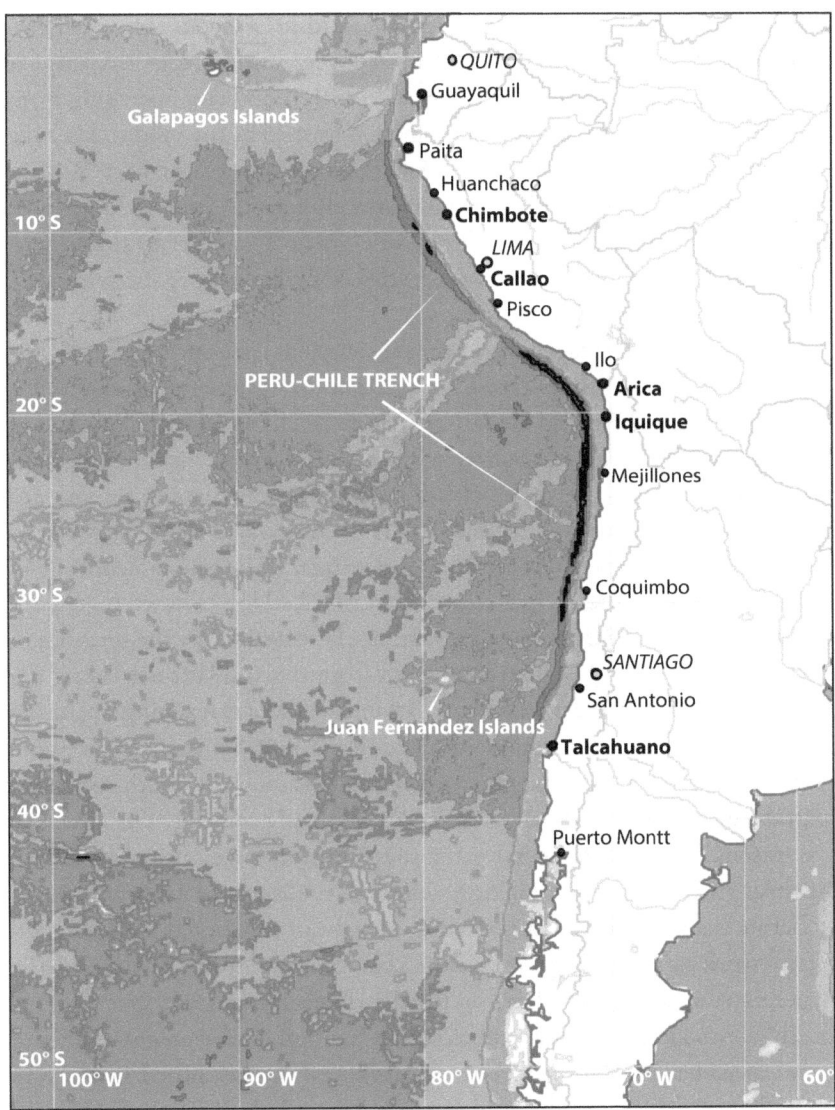

MAP 1. Physical geography and major fishing cities of the Humboldt Current system. Map by the author. *Sources:* ESRI, DeLorne, HERE, MaomyIndia, OpenStreetMap; GRID Arendal.

west toward the Galapagos Islands.[33] A poleward coastal countercurrent also flows beneath the sea surface, carrying warmer waters from the tropics. Parallel to the coast, these currents collide with the strong upwelling from the depths of the Peru-Chile Trench, which is formed by the subduction zone offshore where the Nazca and South American tectonic plates meet. Within the larger HCS, there are three smaller upwelling subsystems—located off the coasts of Peru (5–18°S), northern Chile (18–30°S), and central-southern Chile (30–42°S)—within which the cycles of biological productivity shift according to local conditions.[34]

Cycles of warming and cooling ripple throughout the Southeastern Pacific at varying intervals of time—intra-seasonal, annual, inter-annual, and multi-decadal—driving local and global-scale shifts in climate, precipitation, and interspecies relationships (trophodynamics).[35] The spatial distribution, size, density, and reproductive cycles of fish populations fluctuate in response to short-term, localized oceanographic shifts, as well as longer-term, trans-Pacific variations in sea surface temperature and winds.[36] The phenomenon of El Niño, so-named by the Peruvian fishermen who had long known of its periodic recurrence every three to seven years, is characterized by the presence of warm surface waters that flow southward from tropical latitudes along the coast of Ecuador and Northern Peru.[37] Its impacts are far-reaching, spanning the entire Pacific Basin (thus denominated the El Niño Southern Oscillation, ENSO), and cause a significant increase in rainfall across the South American coastal region. The development of El Niño typically coincides with the normal seasonal warming of coastal waters, beginning in December and continuing through February, thus making it difficult to discern in its early stages.[38]

Before the 1972 El Niño attracted significant international attention, scientists working along the Peru-Chile coast noticed shifts in the oceanic current system and their effects on the distribution of marine species. "It is locally assumed that the current has certain swinging movements, and these are of considerable significance to the fisheries," Coker noted in his 1918 study.[39] Marine ornithologists began to associate the presence and behaviors of certain bird species in this region with shifting oceanic conditions, which they recognized as recurring on a cyclical basis, with alternating intensity.[40] Murphy reported that the arrival of El Niño in 1925—an unusually strong and highly localized event—raised the sea surface temperature off northern Peru as much as 5°C and caused "vast numbers" of bird carcasses to wash ashore.[41] The unwelcome intrusion of warm waters caused the anchoveta schools to shrink or disappear, starving those species that depended upon it for sustenance.⁴² Farther south, Chilean fishermen noticed other local variations within the Humboldt Current in which coastal currents flowed strongly toward the shore, shifting the usual locations of fish schools and endangering unsuspecting fishermen, particularly if they encountered foggy conditions.⁴³ These recurring but unpredictable phenomena have continually altered the spatial distribution of energy and nutrients along the South American littoral, reshaping ecosystems, population dynamics, and the trophic webs that integrate them.⁴⁴

With a total surface area of 2,468,858 square kilometers (1,543,042.5 square miles), the Humboldt Current is one of the planet's sixty-six large marine ecosystems (LMEs), but its boundaries are neither static nor impervious.⁴⁵ The mixing of water masses of different densities and organic compositions creates a marine environment with abundant plankton, and thus food for anchoveta and other schooling fishes, despite a low concentration of oxygen. These species in turn attract migrating predators such as tuna, sea birds, and whales. The Humboldt Current forms one of four eastern boundary current upwelling systems in the world, in addition to the California Current in the North Pacific, the Benguela Current off southwestern Africa, and the Iberia/Canary Current in the eastern Atlantic.

Each of these upwelling ecosystems is characterized by nutrient-rich waters that rise to the sea surface, supporting voluminous quantities of anchovies (*Engraulidae*) and sardines (*Sardinops*). The populations of these fish alternate in abundance every few decades in correlation with cooler (anchovies) or warmer (sardines) oceanic phases. Scientists describe these multi-decadal events as "regime shifts," which "restructure the entire ecosystem from phytoplankton to the top predators."⁴⁶ Interconnected at the global level and strongly influenced by climate, fisheries regime shifts are not driven by ENSO, but they do lead to migrations and fluctuations of sardine and anchoveta populations within the marine ecosystem. Catch data from the second half of the twentieth century clearly indicate several distinct alternations of anchoveta- and sardine-dominated regimes.⁴⁷ For earlier periods, geoarchaeological evidence also documents such shifts, including one circa 1480–1540, from an anchoveta- to a sardine-dominated regime.⁴⁸ Similar events likely occurred in the nineteenth century.⁴⁹ Combined with the spectacular density of marine life in the coastal ecosystem, the impacts of these historic cycles have been as evident in the sediment accumulated on the rainless coastal desert as they have in the short-term fluctuations of global commodity prices.

WRITING THE HISTORY OF INDUSTRIALIZATION IN THE HUMBOLDT CURRENT ECOSYSTEM

The biogeographical contours of the Humboldt Current marine ecosystem frame this history of the "fishmeal revolution" and its impact on the global food industry. Distinct from the iconic tales of large predators such as the North Atlantic cod (*Gadus morhua*) or the Atlantic bluefin tuna (*Thunnus thynnus*), the anchoveta and other forage fish followed their own meandering paths toward the "reduction" factories of late twentieth and early twenty-first century seashores. The history of this region, like that of the Pacific world more broadly, is "episodic, a collected set of characters, and experiences" whose worlds are intricately and inextricably interconnected. It is also translocal, a term this study uses to underscore the ways in which "the stories take on full meanings only when linked to other stories and places."[50] The fishmeal industry followed the ebbs and flows of fish populations, whose successive collapses and renewals occurred at different sites along the Peru-Chile coast. Oceanographic shifts occurred at decisive moments for postwar national and international economic development, as well as for urban growth in Peruvian and Chilean cities (most importantly for this study, in 1965, 1972–73, 1982–83, and 1997–98), interrupting life cycles and periodically crippling the fishmeal industry and its captive global market.[51]

Yet this history did not follow a unilinear path toward ecosystem collapse, nor one of simple boom and bust: in the fishmeal revolution, ecological variability and interspecies relationships—including humans—were key. The cyclical fluctuations of the Humboldt Current become increasingly evident by broadening the analytical frame, not only spatially but also temporally: "a long-term historical perspective is essential to fathoming anthropogenic and other effects in marine ecosystems."[52] It is furthermore crucial to take into account the food webs, and their "entwined trophic forms," within and among these ecosystems, and the ways in which these relationships have been shaped by recurring oceanographic shifts over time.[53] To understand the forces shaping the twentieth-century development of the fishmeal industry in Peru and Chile thus requires an analytical approach that accommodates multiple scales of time and space.

This study examines the global and transnational history of fishmeal as a commodity, in part by tracing the interconnected histories of the industrial fishmeal epicenters of Chimbote, Iquique, and Talcahuano—translocal connections across a single "spatial category," the Humboldt Current ecosystem.[54] Throughout this region's modern history, ecological shifts, alongside the impacts of sustained, intensive resource extraction, have yielded unintended consequences for both human and nonhuman communities.

Catastrophic impacts from climate events have required scientists, policy makers, workers, and industrialists to try to adapt to the uncertainties of oceanographic oscillations.[55] Peruvian and Chilean industrial fisheries developed just after successive collapses decimated other industrial pelagic fisheries between the 1940s and the 1960s: herring and mackerel in the Northeast Atlantic, herring and sardines in the North Pacific, mackerel in the Southeast Atlantic, and sardines in the South Atlantic off southern Africa. This trend accelerated rapidly following the introduction of new technologies during those decades.[56]

This industrial history in the Southeast Pacific in some ways appeared to echo the classic "fisherman's problem" of overfishing followed by collapse. The experience of the US West Coast sardine industry after the 1940s loomed large among experts who theorized this scenario—the first industrial fisheries collapse to be a subject for "large-scale scientific investigation" in the era of the second industrialization.[57] Historian Arthur F. McEvoy described the history of Peru's anchoveta fishery as having "reprised in practically every detail that of its California progenitor."[58] The industrial history of California fisheries was indeed inextricably linked to the atmospheric cycles of the greater Pacific world. However, the Peruvian and Chilean "fishmeal revolution" occurred within the unique historical-environmental context of the Humboldt Current region during a time of rapid transformation in the industrial production, distribution, and consumption of food.

Twentieth-century marine sciences were also shaped by the dynamics of the Humboldt Current during particular moments in its long climatological history. Each El Niño cycle is distinctive in its intensity, geographical distribution, and temperature variation. The strong events of 1982 and 1997 were more ecologically significant for the marine ecosystem as a whole, while the moderate events of 1965 and 1972 had more severe and localized economic consequences. Furthermore, contemporary interdisciplinary understandings of this region are the product of decades of collaborative research, much of which was undertaken by multinational teams of scholars in a context of significant inter-American Cold War tensions. Indeed, as environmental historian Gregory Cushman has aptly noted, "Modern science co-evolved with modern global networks of trade and influence characterized by immense concentrations of wealth and power."[59] In Chile, Peru, and other industrializing coastal nations, scientists often worked under the sponsorship of national governments, private industry, and/or postwar international organizations to assess possibilities for industrial development.

In the early 1940s, following separate requests by the Peruvian and Chilean governments, the US Fish and Wildlife Service (USFW) sent experts to survey the fisheries resources located along their coasts.[60] These teams completed two of the most comprehensive surveys of this region's fisheries in the decades prior to industrialization. While such studies facilitated the intensification of commercial fishing pressure by increasing the knowledge of exploitable species, the data they collected was also an important contribution to the evolving understandings of this marine ecosystem in the United States and international communities of fisheries scientists.

Since 1950 the FAO has systematically collected and published annual catch data for all reporting countries, building the first comprehensive historical-statistical database for fisheries. This tool has facilitated ongoing research and collaboration at the transnational, global, and comparative levels. However, the FAO datasets also have known limitations, including reporting bias and a tendency to underreport small-scale fisheries.[61] With this in mind, fisheries scientists at the *Sea Around Us* Project (University of British Columbia) have created new models that recalculate total fish landings by taking into account the estimated discarded or unreported catch, thereby better representing the total impact of fishing effort in terms of *biomass* extracted from the marine ecosystem between 1950 and 2015.[62] These adjusted data are the basis for the world fisheries landings figures included in this study, along with food commodity consumption estimates extracted from the FAO Fisheries Statistical Series (FAOSTAT), available for the period 1976–2013.

In six distinct but chronologically overlapping chapters, *The Fishmeal Revolution* examines the translocal, regional, and global forces that shaped fisheries development in the Southeast Pacific. It explores the multiple connections between marine ecological cycles, transnational systems of food production, and fundamental questions of oceans governance that have emerged from the industrialization of the Humboldt Current ecosystem. Chapter 1 places the ecoregion's colonial and early postcolonial history in the perspective of "deep" (geological) time and the spatial and temporal frame of pre-Columbian indigenous cultures of coastal Peru-Chile. Paleoceanographical and bioarchaeological evidence shows that warm and cool climatic cycles shaped the features of the littoral and its societies long before European mariners arrived in the Southeast Pacific in the fifteenth century. Creole scientists, Spanish colonialists, and, later, European naturalists such as Alexander von

Humboldt and Charles Darwin helped to bring the flora, fauna, and oceanography of this region into the imaginations of post-Enlightenment Westerners who sought to understand natural ecosystems from a planetary perspective.[63]

Fishmeal and oil became increasingly important and valuable commodities during the late nineteenth and early twentieth centuries. Chapter 2 examines the incorporation of marine proteins into the process of agricultural modernization, particularly in the United States and Germany, first as fertilizer and later as a feed ingredient for swine and poultry production. It weaves together details from US consular reports, US and German fisheries bulletins, and other specialized studies of animal nutrition, as well as records of the Japanese brokerage firm Mitsubishi Shoji Kaisha, Ltd., in explaining the emergence of this new global commodity.

After the 1920s, the Humboldt Current region was also a site of national and international nutrition interventions that sought to improve public health by promoting the consumption of fish proteins, through both home cooking and institutional feeding programs. While quantitative data, gray literature, and scientific journal articles provide a top-down view of the fishmeal revolution after 1950, other sources better illuminate the human dimension of the institution-building and policy making process during the mid-twentieth century. The Peruvian Marine Research Institute (Instituto del Mar del Peru, IMARPE, 1960) and the Institute for Fisheries Development in Chile (Instituto de Fomento Pesquero, IFOP, 1964) were established jointly by United Nations and national government funds, but their leadership eventually transferred to local scientists. Chapter 3 draws from correspondence among FAO field officers, fisheries scientists, and other policy makers whose accounts highlight the tensions between social welfare goals and profit seeking that shaped the institution-building process in Peru and Chile.

Chapter 4 traces the rapid development of Peru's single-species fishmeal industry, centering on the city of Chimbote. Studies by experts working for FAO, IMARPE, and private fishing interests, as well as newspaper articles, personal interviews, and a singular work of fiction by the novelist José María Arguedas inform this historical portrait of the city and its legacy of having once been the world's most important fishing port. With the entire Peruvian fishing industry dependent on the anchoveta, this species, along with the oceanographic forces that shaped its life cycles, had a distinctive causality in the history of the modern food system, as well as in Chimbote's urban landscape, which was rapidly transformed during the first major fishmeal boom (1957–1972).

During the course of my archival research in Peru and Chile, semi-formal personal interviews with individuals representing multiple perspectives of the industrial and artisanal fishing sectors, as well as with experienced scientific researchers from both local and international organizations, helped to inform my understanding of more recent events. Chapter 5 explores the debates, both public and private, that surrounded Peru's emergence as the dominant producer of fishmeal, as well as the attempts by the Peruvian government to regulate the anchoveta fishery in a context of uncertainty and growing concerns about overfishing. The 1972 anchoveta fishery collapse brought catastrophic consequences for Humboldt Current fishmeal production that rippled through global commodity markets and shaped international scientific debates about the interactions between climate and fisheries.

Yet the industry in this region was not simply characterized by a short-lived period of over-investment followed by ecological and economic downturn: the history of industrial fisheries in Chile brings to light the multifaceted nature of fishmeal production in the Humboldt Current ecosystem. Chapter 6 demonstrates the ways in which interconnected cycles of abundance and decline differently shaped the dynamics of human fishing activity and industrial growth in the two Chilean cities of Iquique and Talcahuano. Scientific and international agency reports, press articles, and records from Chile's Ministry of Agriculture and the US National Archive shape this portion of the study. Utilizing smaller quantities of multiple species for their sources of raw material, Chilean fishmeal industrialists avoided the extreme impact of the 1972 collapse, eventually concentrating on the production of higher-quality, "special" grade fishmeal. By the late 1990s, as Peruvian anchoveta stocks recovered and Chilean producers solidified their niche position in global markets, the strongest El Niño event of the twentieth century sent another shock through Humboldt Current food webs, generating new discussions about the importance of climate variability in the tropical Pacific for societies and policy makers worldwide.[64]

Considered as a whole within the changing land- and seascapes of our modern global food system, the historical trajectory of fisheries industrialization in the Humboldt Current ecosystem intersects with pressing issues in twenty-first-century policy making. In recent years, policy makers have continued to refine the institutional mechanisms put in place as societies contend with the depletion of ocean resources. In closing, this study briefly considers some of the lessons *The Fishmeal Revolution* holds for contemporary debates surrounding fisheries management, food production, and environmental and social sustainability.

ONE

A Deep History of the Humboldt Current Ecosystem

FOR CENTURIES, RESIDENTS OF COASTAL Peru and Chile have encountered a curious phenomenon during certain seasons. Occasionally, a foul smell invaded the atmosphere; the hulls of ships blackened, and locals complained of headaches and the tarnishing of their silver.[1] In the English-speaking world this was known as the "Callao Painter" because of its occurrence to the west of that Peruvian port. One sailor pondered the sight of it in this 1921 poem:

> Silent artist of the sea,
> Tell us why this mystery ...
> Callao Painter, tell us, pray,
> From whence comes your pigment gray?
> Plant or fish, or mineral salt
> Acting on the cruiser's vault; ...
> Mystery of old Peru,
> Callao Painter, what are you?[2]

It was a sign of large-scale shifts in the ocean's chemistry, but early twentieth-century mariners did not then know that lead in the ships' paint was reacting with hydrogen sulfide, resulting from unusually low-oxygen conditions in the seawater.[3] The presence of warm waters in the coastal zone that later became associated with El Niño created a "red tide" (*el aguaje rojo*), resulting in massive mortality among marine organisms, and changing the usually chlorophyll-saturated waters from emerald green into a dark red hue.[4] These events, remarkable in their aesthetic drama, were visible reflections of the Humboldt Current ecosystem's climate-driven cycles.

Along the Peru-Chile coast, the movements of organisms are not only latitudinal and longitudinal, but also vertical, within the oceanic realm. Oscillations on multiple spatial and temporal scales have shaped not only the oceanography, but also the geomorphology of the littoral and seafloor, which are themselves subject to dramatic seismic events. This dynamic historical ecology anchors the long history of human settlement and, later, industrialization in this region. Since the initial human settlement of the South American Pacific coast, which archaeologists now date to over 14,000 years BP, the littoral that early coastal societies inhabited has undergone major shifts in climate and population.[5] Despite the degradation of many archaeological sites in coastal Peru, this region has been a site of primary importance to scholars studying some of the field's major questions in the twentieth and twenty-first centuries: When and how did the first humans arrive in the Americas? What role did agriculture play in the creation of complex, hierarchical societies? How did early human groups organize themselves to exploit the available resources in a shifting climate? And what caused the apparent demise of once-thriving cultures thousands of years ago (after 3800 BP)?[6] When Europeans arrived in the late fifteenth century, they encountered a landscape that had long been altered by ancient peoples and their hydraulic systems.

Colonial-era mariners had strategic reasons to observe and interpret ocean currents, and by the late nineteenth century their cumulative knowledge had contributed significantly to the emerging multidisciplinary world of marine sciences.[7] By the late 1800s, the extraordinary, complex, and highly variable climatic system of the Southeast Pacific attracted the attention of many European and North American botanists, zoologists, archaeologists, oceanographers, and geologists. The interest that Alexander von Humboldt (1769–1859) took in this region was but one catalyst for its recognition as a distinctive oceanic zone.

Humboldt spent several months of his Spanish American voyage (1799–1804) in Peru, between August and December 1802, where he recorded a series of measurements of sea and air temperatures.[8] He undertook this voyage in a context of transoceanic imperial struggles for power and resources in the Americas. New republics were just beginning to free themselves of European colonial rule, and Humboldt's privileged access to the far limits of the Spanish American empire derived from his membership in the Prussian aristocracy. Scholars debated contentiously for decades over whether or not Humboldt deserved attribution for his observations of the currents off the Peruvian coast.[9] However, his endeavors in the measurement and quantification of this cold-water system were "far from being [a mere] blueprint for the exercise of distant empire:" they contributed broadly to his theories on the unity of nature and its mysterious forces—a Humboldtian "global physics" that ascribed due importance to this region within the greater ocean-atmospheric circulatory system on a planetary scale.[10] Likewise, the deep history of this oceanic region builds upon an "architecture of likenesses" that is integral to the story—not just facts, dates, and documents, but "a domain of inquiry that extends millions of years into the past."[11] At the same time, the dynamism of the marine ecosystem that is evident at different spatial and temporal scales has continued to shape debates in archaeology, fisheries science, and marine policy well into the early twenty-first century.

THE PERU-CHILE COAST IN DEEP TIME

Rising sharply from the Peru-Chile Trench, the western edge of the South American continent features a narrow, hyper-arid coastal plain that stretches from northern Peru to the central Chilean coast (5°S to 30°S). The Sechura and Atacama Deserts form one of the driest regions in the world.[12] Seasonal Andean snowmelts and cycles of torrential rains have periodically carved through the arid landscape, resulting in fleeting veins of green, salt lakes, and desert blooms. "Extensive beaches and endless deserts, dominated by barren hills, would be devastating if not for the rivers that, like torrents, flow out of the mountains and cut, now and then, the overwhelming aridity."[13] Green oases dot the dry earth above subterranean aquifers, and vegetation thrives in the river valleys. From a contemporary perspective, the apparent austerity of the expansive, sparsely inhabited coastal desert belies the fecundity of its earth. Studies of the geology, paleoceanography, and archaeology of the Peru-Chile coast reveal that warm/cold cycles on multiple timescales created a particular symbiosis between marine productivity and early agricultural practices.

Layers of sediment on the ocean floor document geological change along the western edge of the South American continent. Formed by the convergence of the Nazca and South American Plates, the world's second-longest ocean trench parallels the Peru-Chile coast, and the Andes Mountains—the world's second-highest range—rise dramatically to the east.[14] With sediments dating from the Eocene Epoch (between 56 and 33.9 million years ago), the subduction zone along this continental margin creates one of the most seismically active regions on Earth.[15] Although detailed historical records for western South America extend back only a few hundred years, geologists have tallied at least 165 tsunamis of varying intensity that struck the Peru-Chile coast between 1562 and 2019, usually triggered by earthquakes or volcano activity. The most catastrophic event ever recorded in the region began with two strong earthquakes in 1868, centered near Arica, which generated waves up to twenty-one meters high and affected populations all along the coast (from Trujillo, Peru, to Chiloé, Chile), reportedly resulting in twenty-five thousand deaths in South America alone, and registering at tide gauges across the Pacific Rim for two to three days thereafter.[16] Tectonic shifts have not only inflicted devastating mega-earthquakes and tsunamis on littoral societies; the physical geography of the coast—most importantly, the deep Peru-Chile Trench—also influences the upwelling of nutrient-rich waters offshore.[17]

Climate oscillations further shape this region's coastal landscape. Geologists have found evidence of alternating warm and cold periods throughout the Pleistocene (2.58 million–11,700 years ago), recurring every 100,000 years.[18] Precipitation and river runoff carried iron from the Andes to the waters of the Pacific, nourishing the productive cycles of the marine ecosystem.

Fluctuations in climate throughout the Holocene Epoch (11,700 BP to the present) have also been linked to major shifts in coastal human populations.[19] Although the precise timing and process of "peopling" the Americas remains controversial among archaeologists, in Monte Verde, Patagonia, Chilean archaeologists have found some of the oldest human evidence in the hemisphere: a footprint dating to approximately 14,600 BP.[20] In the Atacama Desert, initial human occupation apparently coincided with a shift from a very arid to a very humid regime. Hunters lived in campsites around paleo-lakes in the high-altitude Altiplano, but when these lakes dried up (around 9500 BP), the human population vanished, not to return for another five thousand years.[21]

Geoarchaeological evidence suggests that the El Niño phenomenon began to recur around 5800 BP, after a millennia-long hiatus. At the same time, the northward-flowing current appeared along the Peru-Chile coast, along with the marine ecosystem dominated by small schooling fishes. A complex fishing and agricultural civilization—centered in Caral, the first urban center in the Americas—flourished in the Supe Valley. Caral was the social, cultural, and economic hub for a thriving population whose settlement stretched eastward from the coast, across the Andes and to the jungle, bounded to the north by the Santa River (9°S) and in the south by the Chillón River (12°S).[22]

For nearly two millennia, this society had adeptly combined the cultivation of cotton and food crops with net fishing in this arid environment, before abruptly disappearing in 3800–3600 BP.[23] Archaeologists believe that a series of severe disaster events—including earthquakes, flooding, and landslides— likely played a strong role in the sudden demise of this Late preceramic society. Recent excavations at Vichama, a site about 150 kilometers (90 miles) north of Lima, revealed a mural portraying human faces and a toad. This ancient scene (c. 3800 BP) seems to depict the arrival of the rains that would replenish the coastal valleys, hinting at the significance of climate oscillations for cycles of human life.[24]

Relatively little is known about the maritime technologies used by the earliest human groups living along the South American Pacific coast, or about the geographic extent of their movements and migrations. Archaeologist Agostín Llagostera proposed several distinct dimensions of the ancient economic conquest of the sea in this region, with a hunter-gatherer ("longitudinal") phase in which early humans subsisted by collecting mollusks and fish along the coast, followed by a "bathytudinal" phase in which fishhooks allowed them to expand their exploits to deeper waters.[25] The diversity of terrestrial environments—in particular, the varying availability of fresh water—and the heterogeneity of archaic-era archaeological sites along the Peru-Chile coast have complicated scholarly efforts to ascribe generalized temporal classifications to these subsistence phases across the entire region.[26] In Patagonia, southern Chile, one of the last areas of the coastal Americas to be populated, excavations have revealed dugout canoes dating to 4500 BP.[27] Scant comparative evidence suggests that a sea route could have connected Peru to Central America and western Mexico after 4000 BP.[28] But archaeologist Ruth Shady Solís concluded that the Peruvian civilization of Caral lived "in total isolation not only from other societies of the Old World but also of the New World, since theirs were more advanced by at least fifteen hundred years than those of Mesoamerica, the other "pristine" center of American civilization."[29]

Whether rapid or gradual, changes in the coastal climate were transformative for the land- and seascape as well as for its coevolving human geography.[30] Desert environments in the Peru-Chile coastal zone displayed a great degree of diversity, with major distinctions between the civilizations of northern and southern Peru, as well as among the groups that inhabited more temperate areas farther to the south.[31] In the northern regions, a shifting climate easily destabilized the fragile ecosystems that formed in the dense coastal fog, but also periodically replenished coastal soils and aquifers, allowing for agricultural production to supplement the harvest of marine proteins.[32] In the Supe Valley (c. 5800–3600 BP), networks among settlements facilitated an "economic complementarity" between fishers and farmers, connecting people and products from coast, mountains, and rainforest.[33] Four thousand years later, farther to the north in the Moche Valley, extensive complexes of canals and aqueducts extended from the rivers to irrigate Chimú agricultural lands (c. 0–1470).[34] *Huaca* (sacred site) construction coincided with periods of strong rains, which carried mineral-laden sediment across the dry plains and into the sea, where it nourished coastal ecosystems.[35] With this in mind, it is clear that "ceramic-based chronologies" are inadequate to account for the relative advancement of ancient societies in coastal Peru-Chile, and the discontinuity of their settlements in both time and space, nor do they indicate the causes driving major population shifts.[36] Remains of ancient adobe constructions such as those at the city of Chan Chan—carved by torrents of rain linked to a strong El Niño circa 1300–1350—further confirm that the ancient world was deeply shaped by warm-cool, wet-dry cycles of the Southeast Pacific Ocean's climate-atmospheric system.[37]

Notwithstanding ongoing debates within these fields of knowledge and localized differences among archaeological sites, there is little doubt that marine resources were centrally important in the diets of indigenous Peruvians and Chileans living along the Pacific coast. Ancient Peruvians' cultivation of wild cotton plants (*Gossypium barbadense*)—one of the earliest identified plants in the region's archeobotany—led to a "Cotton Revolution" that increased the efficiency of their net-making and their ability to capture the dense schools of tiny anchoveta.[38] Fish, nets, and marine fauna were common motifs in the ceramic, textile, and architectural iconography of the pre-Columbian cultures of southern Peru.[39]

Although its center of government was not located on the coast, the sea was also an integral part of the later Inca empire (c. 1438–1533). Some historians posit that Túpac Inca Yupanqui (c. 1441–1493) "discovered Oceania" by the late 1400s, reaching Mangareva, west of Easter Island, as leader of a maritime expedition consisting of as many as twenty-two hundred men in 148 *balsas*.[40] Archaeological studies have shown that inhabitants of Cerro Azul, Peru, dedicated themselves to procuring anchovies and sardines for shipment to inland communities, thereby contributing to the empire's vertically organized trade and tribute regime.[41] Excavations at Lo Demás, another

Inca-period fishing site, evince a distinctive shift from a cooler anchovy-dominated regime to a warmer sardine-dominated regime, as well as a period of increasing frequency of El Niño events beginning around 1500.[42]

COLONIAL AND POST-COLONIAL LITTORAL ENCOUNTERS (1532–1855)

By 1532, when Francisco Pizarro's expedition arrived in northern Peru with plans to conquer the territory, the region was under the control of the Inca, who ruled from Cuzco in the interior highlands. Stretching from the Patía River in present-day Colombia to the Maule River in Chile at its greatest extent, the Inca empire comprised a "vertical archipelago," integrating villages across multiple ecological zones via an extensive network of roads.[43] In 1553 Pedro Cieza de León recalled the "many irrigation channels, green and so beautiful" that Juan de la Torre, traveling with Francisco Pizarro, had described.[44] In a climate system with scarce and seasonal rains that carried water from highlands to coast, control of the irrigation system was intricately tied to local politics.[45]

In the Andean world, land, sea, and atmosphere were interconnected through a cycle in which flora and fauna evolved to capture water from the vapor-heavy air. A thick fog often formed as cool air moved from the ocean surface across the hyper-arid coastal desert. The haze of saturated air—*la garúa* in Peru; *la camanchaca* in northern Chile—hung low over the mostly barren landscape, rarely yielding any rain. When this moisture settled on the hilly dunes (*las lomas*) it formed a cloud forest, a microclimate providing unique habitat for plants, animals, and humans. Spanish botanist Hipólito Ruiz López (1754–1816) observed that, "in the time of the *garúa* or of water the hillsides bloom with many and diverse plants that when flowering provide a delicious carpet."[46] Of the Chincha Valley, Cieza de León recounted: "It is a beautiful thing to behold its groves, channels [*acequias*] and the innumerable fruits all around and the delicious and fragrant melons."[47] The rhythms of the lomas were seasonal and highly susceptible to climate change. La garúa (or la camanchaca) could persist for six to eight continuous months (May through November), hovering near eight hundred meters above for most of the day and sinking to the ground at night, saturating the environment with moisture.[48]

The lomas had a particular role in the pre-Hispanic coast-sierra ecosystem, providing, among other things, wild game to hunt, including viscacha, foxes, puma, guanaco, and deer.[49] Frequently the object of political struggles, these regions were typically controlled by coastal peoples, though during drought in the highlands the *serranos* (indigenous and mestizo Andeans) were known to descend to graze their animals. Under Spanish colonialism, the increased demand for meat and wood depleted the lomas of their native flora and fauna. Said Cieza de León: "Of the sheep of this land [Chincha] almost none remains, because the wars among the Christians did away with the many they once had."[50] Deforestation and desertification intensified around human settlements along the coast.

Marine resources were an integral part of agricultural as well as political practices within the Inca Empire. Both Cieza de León and Bernabé Cobo mentioned the custom of placing sardine heads together with each grain of corn when planting, for fertilization.[51] Prior to the arrival of the Spanish, a chiefdom of thirty to thirty-five fishermen had been sent to live in Chancay in order to attend to the Inca ruler and provide fish and shellfish whenever he visited.[52] Fishermen of Quilcay reported also working as messengers, carrying information from Arequipa all along the coast, as far as Guayaquil in the north and Valdivia in the south. Peruvian historian Maria Rostworowski described this practice among pre-Hispanic Peruvian fishermen—"unlike those who work on land, toward a freedom of movement and the habit of navigating with great facility all along the coast"—as "longitudinality" (*longitudinalidad*).[53]

European explorers and naturalists arriving on the South American coast by sea commonly remarked on the current and winds they had endured during their travels—conditions that intensified during the Austral summer (January–March). When Pizarro and his men wanted to sail southward to Lima, they were reportedly delayed for more than fifteen days due to the coastal gale. "The South wind and none other reigns much of the time as I have said in the Peruvian provinces, from Chile until almost near Tumbes," wrote Cieza de León. He recommended that expeditions travel by land, preferably during the months of January through March, when conditions were more favorable.[54] Agustín de Zárate, whom the king of Spain sent to Peru (1525–37?) shortly after Pizarro's conquest, similarly described the gusts that blew continuously from the southwest, as well as the "vapours" (garúa, or coastal fog) that lingered over the land without releasing rain: "This constant wind and current render the navigation exceedingly difficult, from Panama to Peru for the greater part of the year; so that vessels are obliged always to tack to windward against wind and current."[55] British pirates

FIGURE 2. View of Paita, Peru (1930). From the American Geographical Society Library, University of Wisconsin-Milwaukee Libraries.

traveling south from Paita often sailed out to sea to avoid the coastal current, a tactic probably also used by the pre-Hispanic peoples of the region.[56]

Despite mariners' observations of the climatic features of this seascape, the state of European scientific knowledge about the oceanography of the Southeast Pacific and its southerly cold current advanced relatively little during the eighteenth century.[57] "The Want of understanding Natural Philosophy among Sailors, is a greater Evil than is imagined," French explorer Amedée François Frézier noted in 1716, complaining that the "tedious" voyage from Lima (Callao) south to Concepción (Talcahuano) was taking some ships six to seven months "because they only advanced by the Help of some small Northern Blasts and the Land-Breezes."[58] Antonio de Ulloa (1748) noted a rather comical illustration of the excruciating pace of the "disagreeable and fatiguing" southward voyage along the coast: "They relate here a story . . . that the master of a merchant ship, who had been lately married at Paita, took his wife on board with him, in order to carry her to Callao. In the vessel she was delivered of a son, and before the ship reached Callao, the boy could read distinctly."[59] As the oceanographer E. R. Gunther noted, however, data collection on British vessels at sea during this time was impeded not only by the ongoing war with Spain, but also by the lack of instruments: traveling in the South Sea in 1740, British explorer Richard Walter specifically mentioned his need of a thermometer.[60]

While mariners did not customarily take scientific measurements of ocean conditions prior to the nineteenth century, they did make detailed qualitative observations of the abundant marine life and the ways in which indigenous fishers utilized coastal resources. "All along the coast there is much fish to be caught, and the *indios* make rafts for their fisheries from large reeds, or from the skins of sea lions," wrote Cieza de León in 1553.[61] He also described an encounter between Pizarro's men and "an infinite number of sea lions, of whom there are many and very large ones along that coast," which they came upon near Paita after hearing their "frightful snorting and roaring."[62] Bernabé Cobo noted the great number of anchovetas that washed up on the beaches, which the *indígenas* had only to collect—a phenomenon that occurs when predators press a mass of these tiny fish against the shore (*varazón*). Once during a voyage from Lima to Trujillo in 1627, Cobo's ship collided with an enormous school of anchoveta, dense enough to instantly fill a basket dipped into the sea.[63] During his voyage to Peru and Chile (1777–1788), the botanist Ruiz saw "many bonitos, dolphins, and seals."[64] He was far more impressed, however, by the phosphorescence he observed in the sea, which one night "was so much in evidence . . . that the prow and the helm of the ship, as well as its wake, seemed to be on fire as if with burning sulfur or spirits."[65] The sight intrigued Ruiz, who wondered whether insects or "oily substances" might be present, and so, "we repeatedly took numerous samples of water in buckets or tubs and studied them under good lenses, but found nothing. We stirred up the water with various instruments in dark places, but very rarely observing a weak, transitory sparkle."[66] This bioluminescence was evidence of the ocean's productivity, likely caused by a phytoplankton bloom—the opposite of the massive mortalities caused by *aguaje rojo*, which was likely what turned the sea "as red as Blood to as great a distance as we could see" during the voyage of British sailor W. Funnel in 1729.[67] Such phenomena lent an aesthetic of mystery to these waters—which were typically of a green hue, in contrast to the warmer blue waters of the tropics—due to the high concentration of chlorophyll. Across three centuries, these visions of the Pacific seascape offered momentary glimpses of the dynamic marine ecology hidden beneath its surface.

By the end of the eighteenth century, hunters and traders had developed commercial enterprises that commoditized the skins, flesh, and oils of the marine animals that lived and reproduced along the South American Pacific coast. In May 1788, the *Columbia Rediviva* under Captain John Kendrick and the *Lady Washington* under Captain Robert Gray sailed from Boston

Harbor, two ships whose voyage would open a new commercial era in the Pacific.[68] Captain Gray's report of the voyage inspired a wave of seal hunting in the south of Chile. British and US whaling vessels also operated in the Pacific after 1787–1788.[69] During the 1790s, the Spanish Crown's Real Companía Marítima de Pesca hunted large numbers of seals on the southern Patagonian coast.[70] The wide range of these animals meant that their hunters pursued them along the entire west coast of the Americas, and indeed throughout the Pacific. The Pacific Bank of Nantucket, founded in 1804, and US ships named *Lima, Peru,* and *Chile,* signaled the territorial expansion of commerce that was taking place. However, trade with the Spanish colonies was forbidden, so US sealers and whalers endured the "ever-present threat of seizure" prior to the independence of Chile (1810) and Peru (1824).[71]

Between the sixteenth and eighteenth centuries, the Southeast Pacific was traversed not only by fishermen, but also sailors, merchants, hunters, naturalists, and explorers from other world regions. The impact of invasive species, mineral extraction, and agricultural production during the Spanish colonial era further interrupted the cycles of fragile coastal ecosystems, leaving many terrestrial faunas extinct by the early nineteenth century.[72]

NINETEENTH-CENTURY MARINE SCIENCES AND THE NAMING OF "HUMBOLDT'S CURRENT"

In November 1802, while sailing from Callao to Guayaquil, the Prussian naturalist Alexander von Humboldt dipped his thermometer into the Pacific Ocean off Trujillo, measuring the temperature of the surface current that flowed northward along the South American continent. The current had long been known by local fishermen and long-distance mariners, as Humboldt himself observed, but the opportunity to shape emerging theories of ocean circulation titillated the indefatigable naturalist, who reportedly traveled with six thermometers, two barometers, two chronometers, and a cyanometer, among numerous other instruments, all of which he employed to measure and record unique details of the maritime, atmospheric, and terrestrial realms.[73]

By the late 1700s, European scientists had only recently begun to employ thermometers to study sea surface temperatures. In 1776 Benjamin Franklin made the first thermometric measurement of the Gulf Stream, a warm Atlantic current system flowing west to east between North America and the

European continent. Humboldt knew that the existence of a complementary cold current in the Southern Hemisphere—and the ability to reliably measure it—would be of great significance for Western scientific understandings of oceans and atmosphere on a planetary scale. As he later told an audience at a lecture in Berlin: "It was my... pleasure to fulfill Franklin's wish and to quantifiably verify the thermal qualities, which seafarers have long known, of the South-North current of a large and important area in the South Sea."[74] Humboldt's study of this phenomenon, while flawed in some of its conclusions, likely contributed to his theory of isotherms, which conceptualized the global distribution of climate and temperature.[75]

Humboldt studied the interconnections between oceanic and atmospheric processes at a time when new technologies such as the thermometer, and the growing number of ships whose captains recorded valuable data, fueled European scientific debates about ocean circulation. At just over 15°C, the Peruvian sea was indeed remarkably cool, despite the ship's position near the Equator. But outside the boundary of the cold current, Humboldt measured the temperature at 25°C.[76] In *Cosmos,* Humboldt later described the conditions he observed: "It brings the cold waters of the high southern latitudes to the coast of Chili, follows the shores of this continent, and of Peru, first from south to north, and is then deflected from the bay of Arica onwards from south-south-east to north-north-west.... On that part of the shore of South America, south of Payta, which inclines furthest westward, the current is suddenly deflected in the same direction from the shore, turning so sharply to the west, that a ship sailing northward passes suddenly from cold into warm water."[77] His theory that these low temperatures were evidence of polar water flowing north from the Antarctic was contrary to the reigning theories about wind-driven ocean circulation.[78] (Humboldt's theory was inaccurate; the cold surface temperatures were later shown to result from the intense upwelling of waters from deep offshore.) During his American voyage, Humboldt also spent considerable time studying conditions in the Gulf of Mexico, in order to learn more about its role within the larger Atlantic and global oceanic system. Although Humboldt did not discern all the features of the cold current from his observations at the sea surface, he recognized its scale and significance for theories of oceanic circulation and climatology in contrast to the warm Gulf Stream, which flowed across the cooler Atlantic and impacted climate patterns across Europe.[79]

Amid the voluminous scholarly literature devoted to Alexander von Humboldt in recent decades, his contributions to marine sciences have received scant attention.[80] This is due in part to the fact that many of his writings in the field were never published at all or were scattered in bits and pieces in some of his longer published texts. Yet his consuming interest in the subject led him to work for decades collecting information about the maritime world by enlisting ship captains to record data and by collaborating with other oceanographers in order to share and discuss findings—but these were never fully completed.[81] In the second half of the nineteenth century, Humboldt's name nonetheless became associated with the current system whose temperature he measured in 1802.[82] When he arrived there, three years into his American voyage, he had journeyed by land from Quito, passing through the lush upper Amazon on the way to Lima. In Quito he had learned that his plans to circumnavigate the Earth with the Baudin expedition would not come to fruition because the ships had taken another route.[83] Depressed by the monotony of the coastal desert and the "sad remains" of canals and aqueducts that his team encountered, Humboldt imagined that its barrenness had resulted from the exploits of colonial rule.[84] More than simply a record of anthropogenic impacts on climate in the modern era, however, this desertscape and the cold current offshore reveal a deep, multilayered history of climate and ocean cycles linked to the ebb and flow of human histories.

The Southeast Pacific Ocean was an unexplored frontier for most European scientists at the turn of the nineteenth century. Although the Spaniard Ponce de León made the first recorded mention of the Atlantic Gulf Stream in 1513, scientists entertained little discussion of global theories of ocean circulation prior to 1800. Notable exceptions were the German geographer Bernhard Varen (1622–1650), who first described the concept of boundary currents, and English astronomer Edmond Halley (1656–1742), whose theory of atmospheric circulation provided a way to understand the forces driving ocean currents. Humboldt's intervention in oceanography came just before a new wave of theories on circulation, as well as new techniques to quantifiably measure oceanic conditions. Such data collection constituted the first step toward the mathematization of the field that would follow in the next century.[85]

After about 1850, writers began ascribing this famous name to the current system off the South American Pacific coast, even though Humboldt had failed to recognize one of its key features: the upwelling of cold water from the deep. In some cases, authors misrepresented or took for granted Humboldt's theories without regard for their acceptance among specialists.[86] One disputed detail in these discussions concerned the relative importance of the north-flowing coastal current versus the upwelling in determining the cold-water temperature. In 1844, the French oceanographer Urbain Dortet de Tessan (1804–1879) suggested that an upwelling of the lower layers of seawater led to the low surface temperatures off Peru, a phenomenon that Humboldt had postulated only for certain areas of the Atlantic.[87] Humboldt believed that the cold temperatures of the Southeast Pacific came from waters originating in the Antarctic region. Although he did not advocate naming the current system after his own work, in 1855 Humboldt remarked contentedly on the "great and flattering honor" bestowed upon him, now that on British and French maps the chilly, north-flowing river within the South Sea would be called "Humboldt's Current."[88] Throughout the nineteenth century, several French and German oceanographers contributed to the theory of upwelling, but Humboldt's celebrity following his return to Europe attracted additional attention and fanfare, even after some of his ideas were disproven.[89]

Other notable scholars developed their studies of biology and ecology in the waters of the South and Southeast Pacific, including the British naturalist Charles Darwin, who sailed there aboard H.M.S. *Beagle* (1831–36). As a laboratory for European natural scientists, the Peru-Chile coastal zone offered an emporium of unknown marine species. Darwin intended to collect specimens and eventually to publish an account similar to Humboldt's upon his return. His expedition shipped hundreds of specimens back to England for study, no small feat given the logistical difficulties of preserving and transporting them.[90] In 1784, Spanish botanist Hipólito Ruiz had suffered the catastrophic loss of fifty-five boxes of specimens gathered in the mountains and countryside around Lima, along with eight hundred color drawings, thirty-three potted plants, and all his equipment, which the crew threw overboard during a severe storm they encountered off the coast of Chile.[91] Such occurrences dramatically heightened the stakes for scientists charged with studying the territories and ecosystems of the Southeast Pacific frontier.

Significantly, Darwin's voyage to the region coincided with a significant shift in the global climate at the end of the Little Ice Age. Schooling fishes such as the anchoveta respond dramatically to changing oceanographic conditions. Twenty-first-century fisheries scientists identified a probable "regime shift" beginning around 1820 in the Southeast Pacific, although primary productivity had been low during the previous four hundred years. Subsequently, in the nineteenth century, oceanic conditions (high primary productivity, low oxygenation) in the world's boundary current marine ecosystems began to favor a much greater abundance of anchovies and sardines.[92] During

FIGURE 3. Iquique, Chile, in the late nineteenth century. Mateo Paz Soldán with Mariano Felipe Paz Soldán, eds., *Geografía del Perú* (Paris: F. Didot, 1862), Plate LII. Prints and Photographs Division, United States Library of Congress.

his five-year voyage in South America (1827–1832), the German botanist Eduard Friedrich Poeppig (1798–1868) noted "clouds of seabirds" floating in the skies off Chile—visible evidence of the intensely productive upwelling ecosystem that then flourished beneath the sea surface.[93]

During the early 1840s, the English naturalist Leonard Jenyns classified the fish specimens that the *Beagle* had brought back to Europe. Among the samples, Jenyns identified the anchoveta, *Engraulis ringens* (1842). Noting its similarity to the European anchovy, he described its color as "silvery, with the back and upper part of the sides deep dusky blue." The specimen itself was not so noteworthy on its own, but Jenyns believed it was a heretofore undescribed species of *Engraulis*.[94] In their natural environment, furthermore, it was the sheer scale of the anchoveta schools and their frenzied encounters with predators that made this species so amazing to behold. This unusual abundance was the key to its becoming, a century later, the most commercially important marine protein in the Southeast Pacific.

TWO

The New Industrial Ecology of Animal Farming in the Atlantic and Pacific Worlds, 1840–1930

ONE OF THE GREAT PREOCCUPATIONS in emerging industrial societies during the late nineteenth and early twentieth centuries was the adequate and reliable provision of food for their rapidly urbanizing human populations. Food riots had notoriously threatened the social order in newly industrialized societies of England and France, and in 1905, residents of Santiago, Chile, rebelled against rising prices of staples amid meat shortages.[1] The application of science to agriculture supported new methods that aimed to increase crop yields and animal husbandry, increasingly separating the cycles of food production from the constraints of the natural environment and its climatic cycles. Industries emerged to supply and distribute the organic, and later chemical, inputs these experts recommended to enhance the productivity of the soil. Agricultural modernization revolutionized the practices of crop cultivation and consumption, as chemical fertilizers and mechanization intensified farm production, particularly on large estates in Europe and the United States.[2]

Animals raised for meat assumed an increasingly important role within this landscape. Between 1870 and 1938, worldwide production of livestock grew faster than that of crops, reaching an estimated 35 percent of the total estimated agricultural output in 25 nations.[3] The growing herds of farm animals also occupied vast swaths of land—by the early twenty-first century, more than twice as much land was used for pasture as for arable and tree crops—and they consumed an increasing proportion of the world's food crops, a problem that was particularly acute in the densely populated nations of Northern Europe.[4] As animal feedstuffs became one of the largest and fastest growing expenditures for farmers across the industrializing world, agricultural scientists and entrepreneurs turned their attention to the search for the most bio-economically efficient means of satisfying the nutritional requirements of cattle, sheep, hogs, and poultry. This meant, above all else, finding a cheap source of protein.

Like all crops, the production of traditional feed crops—cereals, hay, and grass—followed seasonal and inter-annual climate cycles and required sufficient water and fertile soil. Farmers incorporated a wide array of organic substances into the cultivation of their crops in order to replenish the nitrogen required for plant growth prior to the advent of chemical fertilizers. From 1845 to 1870, Peruvian guano (the nitrogen- and phosphorous-rich accumulations of seabird droppings) was the most valued and sought-after fertilizer by European and US farmers.[5] Guano was costly, but agriculturalists preferred it to other mineral-laden by-products, such as oil cake (the dry mass left over after pressing the oil from linseed, cotton seed, or similar), or the bones, blood, feathers, or manure of farm animals. Dried fish scrap (also called "fish guano"), which included cannery waste as well as quantities of whole fish that exceeded local market demand, was also a fertilizer traded on international markets. Peruvian guano was expensive, but the use of these by-products recycled nutrients back into the agro-ecosystem while also providing a profitable outlet for organic industrial waste.

Yet when these commodities proved insufficient in quantity to meet the needs of US and European agriculturalists, they turned to the oceans to fulfill the deficit of nitrogen, phosphorous, and protein. By the early twentieth century, new research on feedstuffs suggested that animals more efficiently digested these essential nutrients and could thus better utilize them if they consumed them directly as fishmeal (fish scrap in ground form). US farmers began experimenting with fishmeal for feeds in the mid-nineteenth century in coastal regions that relied heavily on fish for food. On the other hand, in 1892, scientists in Germany demonstrated that the phosphates and nitrogen that fishmeal contained were more readily available to plants in the form of manure, after passing through the animals' digestive systems.[6] As livestock gained importance within global agriculture, industrial fishing thus became increasingly essential to the farming economy. By the end of the nineteenth century, many of the world's farm animals consumed a steady diet of fish-derived nutrients, and in 1930, the US Bureau of Fisheries declared, "'Fish meal is probably the most valuable source of efficient protein and the essential mineral [sic] now to the feeding trade today.'"[7] Despite their tenuous understanding of the chemical composition of fish proteins and the biophysical processes driving animal nutrition, by the early decades of the twentieth century, agriculturalists had begun to recognize fishmeal's potential as a feedstuff.

To examine the industrial ecology of animal farming not only requires us to blur the boundaries between food and non-food industries, and between their land- and ocean-based extraction, but also to reflect upon the meaning and value of waste within human and natural bio-ecological cycles. As environmental historians have pointed out, the nitrogen cycle and its modification through industrial chemistry were fundamental to the processes of agricultural modernization since they aided humans' ability to bypass ecological limits.[8] Plants and animals require nitrogen to synthesize proteins as part of their basic life cycle; when they die and decompose, or excrete excesses in the form of urine and manure, nitrogen returns to the soil, water, or atmosphere, in the form of gaseous ammonia. The goal of industrial livestock farming was "to produce the maximum salable animal protein relative to what is fed to animals"—in other words, the basic equation was to use the least possible ratio of feedstock to marketable quantities of meat.[9] Ruminants (cattle, sheep) can subsist on grasses and grains, but monogastric animals (those with single-chambered stomachs, including swine, poultry, and humans) require specific amino acids in their diets, particularly lysine, which are not available in sufficient quantities in plant-based feedstuffs like corn, oats, wheat, or barley.[10] In intensive farming, these animals thus require the addition of costlier high-protein commodities to their diets.

This chapter explores the commodification of marine-based proteins during the nineteenth and early twentieth centuries, most importantly the products of fishmeal and fish oil produced along the Atlantic and Pacific coasts of North America, as they transformed the industrial ecology of animal farming in Germany and the United States. Atlantic-coast farmers had been using menhaden to fertilize their depleted croplands since at least the seventeenth century, but the earliest published reference to the practice in the United States appeared in a 1792 trade press article, which touted the fish's potential as an abundant source of "manure."[11] Following the first dedicated experiments using fish oil as an animal feed source in 1833, decades of research and small-scale industrial production helped to build consumer demand for these commodities, both locally and on global markets. Traditional fishmeal-producing areas such as the North Sea, Japan, and the US Atlantic, Gulf, and Pacific coasts, processed fish harvested from local waters, but the protein trade followed the dynamics of those fish populations, fluctuating over time.

THE "CHOICEST GLUE FOR POSTAGE STAMPS": MARINE PRODUCTS IN NORTH ATLANTIC INDUSTRIES BEFORE 1850

Marine-based oils were important to the ecology of the industrial revolution. The mélange of products for which they were used prior to the introduction of synthetic replacements attest to versatile organic properties of marine animals' bodies. US Fisheries Commissioner Charles H. Stevenson outlined five general classes of non-food aquatic products commonly utilized in "the arts and industries": (1) oils, fats, and waxes; (2) fertilizers; (3) skins, furs, and leathers; (4) hard substances such as shells, bones, and scales; and finally a fifth group of (5) miscellany, including glue, salt, sponges, and isinglass, a substance derived from fish swim bladders and used as a preservative, an adhesive, a stabilizer in some desserts, and an ingredient to refine beer.[12] Thus, fish and marine mammals underwrote a wide range of specialized crafts and manufactures in the United States and Northern Europe during the early industrial era.

Whales yielded the first marine-based oil commodity to gain substantial commercial value in local and global markets. The small-scale trade of whale oil dates from at least the sixteenth century. While indigenous coastal communities traditionally practiced whale hunting, most did not have the means to travel long distances to follow their migrations prior to about 1600.[13] Prior to the introduction of new industrial methods after the 1860s, traditional whale hunting focused on species that swam slowly and close to the littoral.[14] Astonishingly, the weight of a single blue whale (*Balaenoptera musculus*)—the largest and most commercially important whale species hunted in the modern industrial era—equaled that of twenty-five elephants or 150 oxen; one particularly large specimen could measure up to 106 feet in length and yield as many as fifty-two tons of oil.[15] Producers rendered their blubber into fuel, soap, and other derivative products used for a variety of endeavors such as sizing yarns, dressing leather, washing fruit trees, and smearing sheep (a traditional Scottish practice of applying grease and tar to the animal's wool in order to protect it from parasites).[16]

A second but chemically distinct type of whale oil, made from the blubber of sperm whales (*Physeter macrocephalus*), was commercially important for US fleets as early as the seventeenth century.[17] Sperm oil was used for purposes such as candle making, medicinal ointments, "producing a polish on linen in laundering," incense, and perfume.[18] By the mid-nineteenth century, rapidly declining whale populations led fleets to adopt new, long-distance methods in order to hunt species that migrated through the open ocean.[19]

Industrialists also sought alternative sources of marine-based oils, such as the waste from food-fish processing: Codfish skins, wrote Stevenson, produced the "choicest glue for postage stamps" and other adhesives.[20] However, the available quantities of waste products were insufficient to supply the growing market demand for industrially rendered animal fats.

Beginning in the early nineteenth century, the oil of menhaden (*Brevoortia tyrannus* and *Brevoortia patronus*)—schooling fishes that inhabit nearly the entire length of the US Atlantic and Gulf coasts, respectively—augmented whale oil supplies, both by mixture and by replacing it altogether.[21] Menhaden oil was particularly well suited for the manufacture of paints for exterior surfaces and in industrial facilities (boiler fronts, smoke-stacks), because after drying it was resistant to moisture and heat. Miners in Pennsylvania and West Virginia also used menhaden oil to illuminate their lamps, and tanners used it to fill and prepare leather.[22]

Yet unlike whales, whose majestic silhouettes inspired visions of epic battles among their masculine sea-hunters, the shoals of scrawny menhaden were often described as "trash" by prospective consumers on the US Atlantic coast. "[Menhaden] is not considered a food-fish and is rarely eaten, owing to the abundance of bones, although the flavor is not unpleasant," Stevenson wrote.[23] Fishermen used menhaden as bait for catching other fish before the industrial production of oil and meal created a steadier and more lucrative market for the fishery. In times when more palatable species were available for consumption and the exhaustion of the ocean's abundant fisheries seemed impossible, people designated them unmarketable, instead channeling them toward (and providing rhetorical justification for) non-food uses within the industrial economy.

Each spring, Atlantic-coast farmers harvested menhaden using shore seines, often jointly owned by several individuals, made of cotton twine. In this "farmer-fishery" regime, farmers initially applied the fish directly to their fields; they preferred to use rotten fish whose nutrients were more readily available. When they discovered the utility and profitability of the oil itself, agriculturalists devised an artisanal method for separating it: "Some of the farmers would provide a few casks or hogsheads which they partly filled with fish, adding water to cover them, and with weighted boards placed on top to keep the mass down. On the disintegration of the fish through putrefaction they were occasionally stirred with a long pole to break up the mass and liberate the oil, which floated to the surface of the water and was skimmed off from time to time. After several weeks the oil ceased to flow, and the residuary mass was used as fertilizer."[24] Another method for producing fertilizer from fishery by-products involved digging a five- to six-foot-deep hole, layering wood ashes, fish scrap, and lime to fill it, and finally covering it with earth and weighted boards—this yielded a potent fertilizer in a few months' time.[25] The farmers thus employed the natural process of decomposition to break down the fish proteins, releasing the nitrogen and phosphorous compounds necessary for plant growth.

The earliest known reference to the *industrial* manufacture of menhaden oil suggests that this process began commercially as early as 1811 on the Northeast Atlantic coast of the United States. That year, Rhode Island entrepreneurs John Tallman and Christopher Barker established a plant near Portsmouth.[26] Technological innovations during the mid-nineteenth century supported the intensification of fish oil and fertilizer production. Fishers adapted their purse seine nets to harvest the schools of menhaden, greatly increasing the supply of fish to a growing number of industrial facilities. Tallman and Barker began using steam to cook the fish in their Rhode Island plant in 1842, and in 1855 a Long Island plant incorporated the first fully mechanical press. As demand grew, entrepreneurs built more plants along the New England coast that utilized the new steam cooking and hydraulic pressing procedures, thus extracting greater quantities and higher-quality oil from the flesh of the fish.[27] After 1860 traders offered menhaden oil on the New York market, and the industry experienced a brief surge; it expanded rapidly into the Southern states following the Civil War, concentrating in Virginia and North Carolina and eventually expanding to the Texas Gulf Coast. "Floating factory" boats operated off the coast after 1876, although problematic processing and storage conditions aboard limited the success of this method.[28]

The industry emerged partly in response to direct demand from the growing US agricultural sector, where farmers used various grades of menhaden oil and guano products to add nitrogen to grass, grain, and maize crops.[29] The boom in menhaden landings peaked in 1884, only to decline precipitously by 1892 due to overfishing. But by the turn of the twentieth century, dried fish scrap contributed an estimated 25 percent of the total volume of compound fertilizer in the United States and contained an average of 8 percent nitrogen and 8.5 percent phosphoric acid, values comparable to those they found for Peruvian guano.[30] Fish proteins were thus an integral part of rural economies as well as the emerging agro-industries in the United States. Although World War One interrupted global commodity trade flows, demand for these products began to increase soon thereafter with the reorientation of the industry toward animal feeds.

Menhaden was by no means the only fish species of commercial importance to be rendered into scrap, meal, and oil for industrial purposes. While the US Atlantic menhaden fishery was one of the most significant in terms of its size during the nineteenth and early twentieth centuries, other centers of fish oil and fertilizer production formed in coastal areas with dense populations of *Clupeidae* fishes (mainly sardines and herrings), including the North American Pacific coast, Japan, Norway, India, and South Africa.[31] While demand for fish meal and oil seemed to increase steadily, the populations of these fish oscillated between abundance and rapid decline, causing a pronounced ebb and flow in fertilizer and oil production that rippled through local economies and global trade flows.

THE INDUSTRIAL ECOLOGY OF ANIMAL FARMING IN GERMANY AND THE UNITED STATES, 1840–1914

The economic growth of any industry is largely dependent on the fullest exploitation of its by-products.

GEORGE C. CARR
"International Trade in Fish Meal," 1931

Germany was the site of path-breaking agricultural research during the nineteenth century that fueled the technological transformation of farming.[32] Many historians credit the German chemist Justus von Liebig with founding the field of agricultural chemistry, particularly with the 1840 publication of his influential book, *Organic Chemistry in Its Applications to Agriculture and Physiology*.[33] While Liebig's work laid out an early theoretical framework for academic study, the German state institutionalized the production of agricultural knowledge in part with the 1847 establishment of a special faculty position, whose responsibility it was both to train students as well as to advise the national government, and to help direct agricultural experiment stations after 1852.[34] Researchers established the first state-supported agricultural experiment station on the Möckern estate near Leipzig.[35] The purpose of such stations was to develop new methods for increasing crop yields by testing scientific theories through controlled, practical applications. This intentional dialogue (or tension) between theory and practice became a model for similar stations established elsewhere in Germany and in the United States in the 1870s and 1880s.[36]

From the beginning, the production of fertilizer and animal feeds was among the top research priorities in German agricultural chemistry. In 1852, the Möckern station's first statute listed six topics of particular interest, of which the first was to study plants and their environmental and nutritional requirements for growth, and the second was to understand "the constituents of plants, and their effect on animal organisms, especially on feeding, through the analysis and evaluation of feeds, and several other goals related to animal nutrition."[37] The station's board was particularly concerned with testing the profitability of various types of manure as fertilizer.[38] Agricultural historian Frank Uekötter has noted that, in Germany, "there was hardly anything that was not advertised as a fertilizer: bones and ground stones, minerals and organic substances, slaughterhouse and fish waste, and later even electromagnetic rays and radioactivity."[39]

The newly established field of agricultural chemistry forged strong connections between research and supporting industries in Germany.[40] However, in the emerging science of nutrition, synthesizing plant-based substitutes for organic proteins in animal feeds proved to be a formidable challenge. Among the first studies at the Möckern station, codirector Emil von Wolff examined the effect of nitrogen-rich and nitrogen-poor feeds on sheep.[41] Additional research in the following decades confirmed the superiority of "fish guano" in animal feeds, although the earliest research focused only on ruminants, making no pronouncements for its use in feeding hogs and chickens.[42] In 1891, the first German fishmeal plant was constructed in Pillau, after which a cluster of factories emerged outside Hamburg, mainly in Altona, Cuxhaven, and Bremerhaven.[43] These plants relied primarily on fish waste from processing plants, however, and so had a limited supply of raw material. German agriculturalists thus relied largely upon herring and herring meal imported from Norway to satisfy the growing domestic demand for this commodity.[44]

The agro-chemical industry's research priorities in part reflected the high price of imported fertilizers and feedstuffs for German agriculturalists, since these commodities were not readily available domestically. Using fish to feed farm animals effectively adapted the nitrogen cycle to that of industrial meat production. Fishmeal was among other organic additives that veterinarians recommended for domesticated animals by the early twentieth century as a means of promoting their ability to grow and reproduce.[45] In 1910, German chemists Fritz Haber and Carl Bosch revolutionized the science of agricultural chemistry with their method for producing ammonia by fixing atmospheric nitrogen—now known as the Haber-Bosch Process—which enabled the development of synthetic, chemical fertilizers.[46] Industrial production of these substances soon created new alternatives to the costly and limited supplies of guano and nitrates mined from the coastal regions of Peru and Chile.[47] Synthetic fertilizers were effective replacements for fish-based nutrients in explosives and agriculture, and they had displaced South American nitrates in global markets by the 1930s. Crucially, however, researchers were unable to find an equivalent substitute for fishmeal and oil in animal feeds.

Despite numerous studies demonstrating the effectiveness of fish-derived products in farm animal nutrition, large-scale production and trade of fishmeal for feeds remained relatively limited until the first decades of the twentieth century. By the time US researchers started establishing their own agricultural experiment stations in the 1870s, farmers had long experimented with using fish for feed for domestic animals. The earliest known reference to such experiments in the United States dates to 1833.[48] Some reports noted the concern among farmers that using fishmeal in feeds would taint the flavor of the animals' flesh after slaughter. Others insisted, however, that the taste of the meat was unaffected, provided that farmers limited the proportion of fish in the animals' diets and ensured that their fishmeal derived from only unspoiled raw materials.[49]

Fishmeal became a way to profit not only from by-products, but also from the harvest of species not otherwise marketable for food—"waste fish" that could furnish "a reserve supply of protein" to animal farmers.[50] As one USDA expert wrote, "It would seem that in this new field for the use of fish meal for feeding purposes an outlet may have been found for the use of this outcast of the fish tribe [dogfish (*Mustelus canis*)] and that it can at last be turned into material having a commercial and economic value."[51] Highlighting the nutritive potential of reincorporating waste streams into the farm economy, agriculturalist J. W. Turrentine stressed, "We have every reason, from practical experience, from actual experiment, and from what we know of the nature of the case, to believe that the immense amount of animal waste produced in this country from our slaughter houses, and especially from our fisheries, can be utilized with the greatest ease and profit to supply the most pressing need of a most important part of our agriculture, nitrogenous food for stock."[52] Other researchers emphasized that the nitrogen in fishmeal would reappear in the animals' manure, thereby creating greater overall efficiency in the application of these limited resources.[53] "There is every reason to favor the view that fish meal should not be spread on the land until it has been passed through the digestive apparatus of farm stock," wrote USDA junior animal husbandman Frank Ashbrook in 1917.[54] These boosters saw fishmeal as a way to take advantage of the unutilized by-products from meat and fish processing by reincorporating the leftover protein sources back into the food system, feeding them directly to the animals, whose manure would, in turn, recycle nitrogen into phosphorous back into the soil.

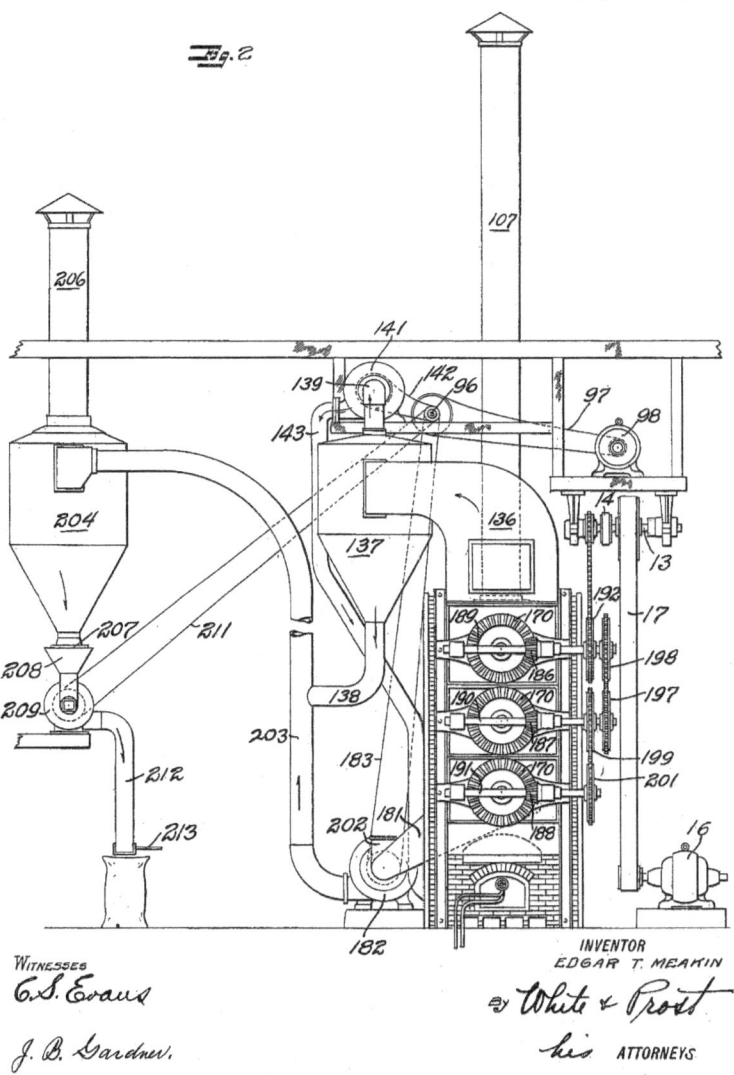

FIGURE 4. Diagram of apparatus for producing fishmeal (front view). E.T. Meakin. U.S. Patent No. 1,421,283 (1922).

Raw materials for fishmeal came not only from the refuse of cannery and other edible fish processing, but increasingly from fish harvested exclusively for this purpose. Often the demand for fishmeal outpaced the demand for canned fish, increasing the profitability of landings in the case of oversupply. Along the North American Pacific coast, from Alaska to California, the production of sardines (*Sardinops sagax*) and anchovies (*Engraulis mordax*) for food went hand-in-hand with the reduction of cannery by-products and surplus fish into fishmeal. With no limits on sardine extraction in the early twentieth century, harvests fast outpaced demand for canned products, creating a profitable surplus if transformed into fishmeal.[55] As US fisheries biologists Edward Ueber and Alec MacCall explained, "Investing in a plant that reduced sardine was one way for fishing families to get rich."[56] Canneries not attached to fishmeal plants could scarcely compete: at one point, California industrialist F. E. Booth "had no choice but to make as much fishmeal as he could or abandon his business to competitors."[57] The market for fishmeal was both local and international: in early twentieth-century Japan, where the existing facilities were also unable to meet local demand, Pacific Coast industrialists found a ready market for their wares.[58]

California authorities opposed the reduction of edible fish into fertilizer and animal fodder, however, and the state enacted legislation after 1919 limiting the use of whole fish for this purpose.[59] The new regulations frustrated brokers: "So rigid are the fishing laws of the State of California for the sake of the conservation of the fish, that not nearly enough fish meal is produced in the sardine canneries (reduction plants) in this state to supply the ever increasing demand for meal."[60] Fishing companies resisted the state-imposed limits, with many operating factory boats just outside the state's jurisdictional area. In this context, US West Coast brokers were unable to supply fishmeal to Japanese buyers. In the early decades of the twentieth century, steadily increasing demand signaled the shift from fishmeal's use as fertilizer to a commodity highly coveted for farm animal nutrition.

COMMODIFICATION AND THE INTERNATIONAL TRADE OF FISH PROTEINS, 1914–1930

Global supplies of fish meal and oil ebbed and flowed with fish population dynamics in the producing regions. The overlapping seasons for herring, menhaden, and sardine fisheries provided a more or less continuous year-round flow of fish proteins to Germany, the Netherlands, and the United States. Brokerage firms contracted in advance of the fishing season for a specified quantity of fishmeal with a stipulated range of values for protein and other mineral content. As global commerce of these commodities increased during the 1920s and '30s, business networks developed and producers consolidated into lobby groups, determining policies, standards, and procedures for the trade.

Two world wars disrupted these global protein flows. As the first country to use fishmeal in feeds on a large scale, Germany relied strongly on imports and thus faced significant difficulties when traditional supplies were unavailable during and after World War One.[61] German hog farmers in the country's northern and western regions used an estimated 60 percent of the imported fishmeal, which totaled eight to ten thousand metric tons per month in the early 1920s. Although German scientists engineered much of the technology to process fishmeal, without immediate access to a nutrient-rich marine ecosystem such as the California Current, there were insufficient raw materials for local industrialists to produce it locally.[62]

Shortages of food and feedstuffs persisted in the interwar period. Fat and protein were the two most important "supply gaps" in the German food system during the 1930s.[63] In 1931, Germany was Europe's largest consumer of fishmeal, and Hamburg was the central port for its brokerage.[64] English, Swedish, Canadian, US, and South American fishmeal products competed in German markets, but farmers there were often unable to afford it for their feeds. German fishmeal buyers began dealing directly with producers in order to avoid intermediary brokers.[65] In search of a good deal, the Hamburg-based entrepreneur Carlos Ludewig, who claimed to own the biggest fishmeal factory on the European continent, traveled to Korea in 1931 to inspect the sardine cake on offer there.[66] Meanwhile, German and UK engineers created new processing technologies that increased the speed and efficiency of fishmeal rendering while also reducing odors, but these advances could not overcome the supply problem.

Growing demand for fish protein commodities led to a surge in global production capacity. Industrialists constructed fishmeal plants in new coastal regions, such as South Africa, and looked toward South America both for raw materials and as a potential market for fertilizers. India had an estimated six hundred fish scrap factories in 1920 and exported significant quantities to Indian Ocean markets.[67] But production still depended heavily on local marine environments. When sardines moved away from the coast of San

Pedro (a fishing port near Los Angeles, California) in 1926, most of the small boats in the sardine industry could not safely travel as far as Santa Barbara to fish and were left unable to fulfill their contracts.[68] Farmers sourced fishmeal from British Columbia and Japan to supplement that which was produced along the US West Coast, from Washington to California. With herring, menhaden, and sardine populations responding strongly to oceanographic conditions, local shifts in climate and ecology strongly influenced these trade flows.

Japan was important in international fertilizer markets as both a producer and importer of sardine oil and fish scrap. In the 1920s, Japanese demand for imported fish proteins was so strong that firms on the US West Coast based their prices on those in the Japanese market.[69] But as the global requirements for animal feedstuffs grew, Japan also became an exporter of fishmeal. The multinational structure of the brokerage firm Mitsubishi Shoji Kaisha, Ltd. (MSK), illustrates the nature of global sourcing and trading networks for these economically and environmentally important, but otherwise invisible, protein commodities. MSK offices in Tokyo, Kobe, Osaka, Seattle, San Francisco, New York, London, and Berlin sent regular communications regarding market conditions during the 1920s and '30s, as brokers sought to bridge the supply gap by connecting distant ocean ecosystems to the new industrial ecology of animal farming in the United States and Europe.[70] Such an institutional structure helped brokers to maneuver within the bureaucracy of interoceanic shipping, for example, by importing and reexporting in order to avoid certain freight tariffs and thus sell their products at a lower rate in European markets.[71]

International shipping was an important arena through which buyers and sellers established, monitored, and contested industry standards. Fishmeal for livestock feed received a separate classification in US customs returns in 1920, and by 1927 both the United States and Germany had implemented feedstuffs laws specifying the range of acceptable materials to be sold as feed commodities.[72] Traders and customs houses soon established rules to deal with the increasing flow of fishmeal in international shipments. Certain markets had more specific requirements for the product's characteristics. Purchase and freight contracts for fishmeal usually stipulated its quality (based primarily on the chemical analysis of protein and moisture content) and instructions for stowage during transport. In 1931, the Nippon Gyoryo Kaisha (Japan Fish Products Co.) formed the Export Fish Meal Association in order to ensure uniform quality, in the wake of negative publicity stemming from some of their shipments of fishmeal to Europe having deteriorated during the voyage.[73]

Fishmeal presented special hazards to shippers due to its organic properties. This cargo, usually packed in gunny sacks stacked in the ship's hold, was subject to internal heating due to the oxidation of the fishmeal—a process that sometimes led to spontaneous combustion during shipping. MSK held an insurance policy that defined spontaneous combustion as "the ignition of a body by the internal development of heat, without the action of an external agent, such as takes place frequently in heaps of rags, wool or cotton cooked with oil, or wet coal."[74] Shippers eventually adopted rules for fishmeal stowage, stipulating that it have a limited moisture content and that sacks be stored with sufficient ventilation to maintain a cool temperature and prevent mold and oxidation.[75] Stevedores were required to check the conditions of the fishmeal periodically during shipment and storage at terminals. The continuous chemical reactions occurring in the fishmeal also released ammonia, along with odors so powerful that some ships refused to transport the commodity because its stench penetrated the other cargo aboard.[76] While sacks of fish proteins sat on ships for weeks during their transoceanic voyages, the chemical process of decomposition marched inexorably forward.

The new industrial ecology of animal farming that coalesced by the 1930s redirected massive quantities of marine proteins from the northern Atlantic and Pacific Oceans to the feeding troughs of US and European farms in a large-scale adaptation of the nitrogen cycle. "The food problem of the world is intimately bound up with the use of several farm animals as converters and as producers of foods," as one scientist aptly observed.[77] Schools of small, oily "trash fish" became increasingly popular sources of protein for farmers' growing herds and flocks. The nineteenth-century experiments that applied science to agriculture, transforming theory into practice, helped to lay the foundations for the international market for fishmeal and oil that later emerged: nearly a century after the first experiments using fish as feed, fishmeal was a global commodity with large-scale production, circulation, and international demand. Fishmeal was so highly desired as a feedstuff, as one German study later put it, that one could scarcely imagine modern agriculture without it.[78]

In the coming decades, as food companies increased their scale and scope of production, they also increased their exposure to the risk of the naturally occurring dynamics of climate and weather patterns.[79] At the same time, the mass production of cattle, hogs, and poultry stimulated major changes in the industrial ecosystem in order to sustain the increasing numbers of animals that no longer grazed or foraged on open land. Situating themselves as purveyors of proteins to both animals and people, US and European feed producers—dependent on commodity crops whose prices and availability often fluctuated wildly due to environmental and other factors—thus integrated vertically and horizontally in order to stabilize the supplies and markets on which their profits depended.[80] They also relied on advanced mathematical models (for example, linear programming) to calculate the nutritionally and economically optimal feed ratios, weighing shifting costs against predicted rates of growth and/or death among the animals.[81] Fishmeal was an ingredient that poultry and hog producers could scarcely remove from the equation of their specially formulated feeds, since it provided the so-called "unidentified growth factor" (also called the "k-factor") that competing commodities like soy and peanuts could not match. With no equally effective synthetic substitute for fishmeal available, poultry and hog farmers grew more dependent on the dynamics of distant oceans—and increasingly, after the late 1950s, on the Humboldt Current.

THREE

Protein from the Sea

THE "NUTRITION PROBLEM" AND
THE INDUSTRIALIZATION OF FISHING
IN CHILE AND PERU

DURING THE MIDDLE DECADES of the twentieth century, US and European leaders established international institutions and policies that included among their primary goals the stabilization of commodity flows, especially food supplies. At the same time, agencies such as the League of Nations (1919–1946) and later the United Nations Food and Agricultural Organization (FAO, est. 1945) employed an expanding global network of scientists and technocrats who sought to improve general nutrition and public health through consumer education and community outreach.[1] Agribusinesses also began to scale up their production of food crops with the aid of new chemical inputs and the mechanization of farm labor, rapidly increasing their capacity to produce greater quantities at a lower cost. Firms vertically integrated across their supply chains, often investing in the production of fishmeal and other feed commodities. Latin American nations, meanwhile, looked to build up domestic industries amid rhetoric about economic growth and improving the nutrition of hungry populations. Yet lingering tensions played out among these overlapping agendas, as leaders weighed the long-term costs of social welfare programs against the short-term profits that industrial fisheries generated, especially when producing fishmeal and oil for export.

For nations like Chile and Peru, which sought to expand their economies through industrial development, ocean fisheries provided a seemingly abundant source of raw materials that could be harvested to serve social as well as economic ends. As this chapter shows, fisheries remained primarily local prior to 1950. After surveying the state of local fisheries prior to 1950, this chapter examines the intersection of nutrition debates and the role of FAO technical assistance programs in Chile and Peru, as global market demand for fishmeal and oil expanded in the postwar era. While FAO officials proffered advice on technological and policy interventions, leaders of Chilean and Peruvian industry and government—reluctant to cede autonomy to foreign technocrats and aware of the value of their marine resources—expressed mixed reactions to these gestures. Rather than foreign-led technical interventions, they clearly preferred direct economic aid and access to credit in order to import and upgrade their fleets and machinery. US fishing firms expanded into the Southeast Pacific following the collapse of sardine and menhaden populations, as the profitability of fish protein commodities on global markets soared. By the 1960s, the "reduction" of Humboldt Current species to proteins and oils for use in specially formulated animal feeds had become the primary focus of the industrial fishing sector in both countries.

EARLY INDUSTRIAL FISHERIES AND THE "NUTRITION PROBLEM" IN CHILE AND PERU

Flanking the dynamic upwelling ecosystem, communities along the Peru-Chile coast had nearby access to a wide variety of marine species for food and industry. Nonetheless, fishing remained primarily a localized, subsistence-oriented activity in both countries until after the 1940s. Travelers from the sixteenth-century Spanish chronicler Pedro de Cieza de León to the nineteenth-century British geographer William Bollaert had remarked on particular traditions among littoral societies, such as the use of sea lion hides (*Otaria flavescens*) to create fishing rafts in the Atacama Desert region of Tarapacá (now part of northern Chile). While some indigenous coastal communities of the South American Pacific coast had practiced whaling for subsistence, long-distance fleets designed for the high seas began to peruse these cold waters after the first sperm whale was harpooned there by British whalers in 1789—an industry that intensified during the following century.[2]

US ornithologists Robert Coker and Robert Cushman Murphy made important contributions to the marine biology of the Humboldt Current ecosystem during the early 1900s through their studies of guano birds and their feeding behaviors along the Peruvian coast. Their reports also assessed the state of the local fisheries in detail.[3] Murphy "could not fail to be impressed by the unrealized opportunities for the development of desiccating, canning, and packing plants in Peru," not only due to the diversity of species along the coast, but also because of their similarity to products that were already being marketed in other world regions, including Florida (United States), Chile, and Japan.[4]

German scientific commissions also played an active role in oceanographic and biological research in the Humboldt Current ecosystem. At the request of the Chilean government, Hamburg's director of fisheries traveled there to conduct some of the earliest studies with experimental trawling in the late 1920s.[5] At that time several German scientific commissions were also actively studying other ecological and technical questions affecting their domestic food economy, including the relationship between ocean currents and herring population movements in the North Sea, international policy issues surrounding whaling, as well as methods for improving quality and reducing the cost of fishmeal (much of which Germany imported from Norway).[6] Between 1924 and 1935, German industrialists developed a new type of herring trawl, increasing their access to waning stocks.[7] In Chile, however these initial efforts to address the "fisheries problem" fell short: Pedro Golusda, advisor to the Department of Fish and Game (Departamento de Pesca y Caza), noted that following the Lübbert commission's study, the state had contracted two "European specialists," but upon arrival in the country they discovered that their funds had been reappropriated for other purposes.[8]

Industrial-scale commercial fisheries faced significant barriers both in Chile and Peru, not only in terms of scientific research and access to capital, but also in their ability to reach consumer markets. Local infrastructure was inadequate for the preservation and distribution—whether foreign or domestic—of highly perishable fish products. Even if fish stocks were plentiful, canneries often lacked the materials they required to operate; in other cases, a lack of cold storage or poor sanitation resulted in spoilage or contamination. Murphy reported in the 1920s that Peruvians imported quantities of "stockfish" from "countries within the northern hemisphere" for local consumption.[9] In Chile, consistent deficits in local supplies of beef throughout the early twentieth century presented a food supply issue that policy makers hoped to address in part through improved fish distribution. Invoking memories of violent food riots that had occurred several decades before, a resident of Santiago described a "homeric struggle" involved with his attempt to procure fish at the local market, where only by pushing and shoving (*"a fuerza de empujones"*) could he purchase a few kilos of fish before speculators resold the remaining supplies at prohibitive prices on the black market.[10]

Economic development goals in support of fisheries expansion also complemented the emerging interest among physicians and public health experts in so-called "protective foods" during the 1930s. New ideas about the relationship between health and diet saw foods that provided "minerals,

FIGURE 5. Man carrying sierras in San Antonio, Chile (undated photo). Unknown photographer. Donación Blanca Tejos M., Colección Museo Histórico Nacional, Santiago, Chile.

vitamins, and 'good' protein" as a key deficiency among low-income populations worldwide.[11] In 1937, the League of Nations Mixed Committee on the Problem of Nutrition identified this as a "national problem," linked closely to poverty and lack of education, that was to be solved through a coordinated policy involving agricultural, economic, and educational interventions based on technical expertise.[12] Chile was one of twenty countries that established national nutrition committees within a year of the report's release.[13] National and intergovernmental agencies would subsequently organize periodic nutrition campaigns to change the dietary habits of Chileans and Peruvians, many of which promoted the consumption of fish as an economical and healthful food, while others attempted to create programs that utilized "fish protein concentrate" (FPC) powder to enrich breads, pastas, and other foods.

Throughout the 1940s, the Chilean and Peruvian governments each continued to sponsor research that explored the possibilities of expanding industrial fisheries along their coasts. Building on more than a decade of research collected by scientists of the state-led Guano Administration Company (Compañía Administradora del Guano, CAG), in 1941, Peru requested a commission of scientists from the US Fish and Wildlife Service (USFW) to study the resources of its coastal waters.[14] The Peruvian government then purchased the *Pacific Queen*, a new purse seiner built in Tacoma, Washington, from the research team, as well as at least two other US-built vessels.¹⁵ Chile commissioned a similar USFW study in 1943, and within two years, at least one US firm had invested $200,000 in an Antofagasta-based company, supplying it with fifty US-built fishing vessels.¹⁶

Both countries were among Latin America's fastest growing producers of canned goods during this time, with Chile reporting a steady increase in production from 1939 to 1946 and Peru's exports of canned goods growing rapidly from 1942 to 1947.¹⁷ Particularly in Peru, an important US supplier of canned bonito, salt fish, and liver oil during the war, US agencies and firms played a significant role in the sector's growth. Canneries were concentrated around Callao and Lima, the country's main port and adjacent capital city, as well as Pisco, a smaller port on the central coast south of the capital; the sector reported a threefold increase in fish production between 1940 and 1942 with little additional investment.¹⁸ After 1943, the Inter-American Food Production Cooperative (Servicio Cooperativo Inter-Americano de la Producción de Alimentos, SCIPA, an organization partly funded by the US government) supported ongoing efforts to improve production and distribution of fish products in Peru, which culminated in the construction of the largest fish cannery in South America two years later.¹⁹

By the end of the decade, scientists and technical experts from the United States and Europe had completed preliminary surveys of the fisheries resources and their utilization all along the Peru-Chile coast, unanimously emphasizing the potential for larger-scale extraction by a more modernized fleet. Although the vast bounty of the sea presented an imagined, theoretical solution to the "nutrition problem" in terms of food supply, both capital cities and smaller towns were generally ill-equipped to provide the transportation, cold-storage, and distribution infrastructure required for highly perishable proteins to reach consumers at their local grocers.

External wartime demand for canned fish temporarily provided a limited market for these nascent industries to export bonito to the United States. With relatively little capital investment, Peruvian canneries helped to meet the global need for protein from the sea during and immediately after World War Two. The market advantages afforded to Peruvian canneries by wartime trade disruptions were, however, soon overcome by other economic and political considerations. Firstly, supplies of tin—an essential commodity for this subsector—were limited, unreliable, and expensive. At the same time, US West Coast fishing firms were eager after the war to defend their business while capitalizing on access to new fishing grounds on the new

FIGURE 6. Women processing the catch, Chile (1960). Unknown photographer. Archivo Zig-Zag/Quimantú, Colección Museo Histórico Nacional, Santiago, Chile.

Pacific fisheries frontier of the Central-West and Southern regions.[20] As US producers recuperated their production flows, they faced competition from not only Peruvian but also Japanese canned tuna imports, and they began to pressure policy makers to pass restrictions on imported tuna and bonito. The US government implemented a series of measures aimed at restricting bonito imports, beginning with a 1949 prohibition on the sale of bonito as "tuna" in US markets, and followed by a series of tariffs on bonito imports in subsequent years. These measures dealt a harsh blow to the Peruvian sector, which had depended heavily on US markets for the sale of its products.[21]

THE FOOD AND AGRICULTURAL ORGANIZATION (FAO) IN PERU AND CHILE, 1949–1955

Building on the groundwork laid by League of Nations researchers, the formal establishment of the United Nations Food and Agricultural Organization (FAO) in 1945 institutionalized the dialogue among agriculture, health sciences, and economics that would shape the organization's nutrition interventions in the impoverished world regions.²² From its inception, the FAO was plagued by tensions among member nations and between its experts and local politicians—as the institution's leadership struggled to determine the precise method for accomplishing its goals on the ground in member countries (whether to act as a regulatory agency, intervene economically by stimulating agricultural production and stabilizing prices, or simply to collect and distribute information in an advisory role). Most strategies ultimately focused on providing technical assistance, and Chile and Peru were among their most important target clients in the area of fisheries development.²³

When FAO officials conducted a comprehensive study of Latin American fisheries in 1949, they found that Peru and Chile possessed a fleet comparable in size and technology to the rest of Latin America: almost 10 percent (267) of Peru's approximately 2,789 vessels had motors in 1946; of Chile's 3,795 boats, about 16 percent (589) were motorized. By comparison, the US fishing fleet eclipsed these figures by a factor of twenty to one, with 66,528 boats, over half of them (33,814) equipped with motors.²⁴

In Peru, FAO technician Mogens Jul interviewed many individuals in 1949—including US-born industrialists, a US diplomat, and several Peruvian entrepreneurs—who expressed frustration and disdain for the prevalence of traditional subsistence-oriented, small-scale fishing methods. Such operations were unable to produce large quantities of surplus fish for commercial sale, due mainly to barriers of capital, technology, and infrastructure: the unrefrigerated holds of their boats transported the fish haphazardly to shore, where they transferred the fish to market in large baskets without ice or any other form of preservation.²⁵ Charles Bridgett, assistant commercial attaché to the US Embassy in Lima, lamented that the disorganized industry received little support from government other than the modest regulations designed "to force the fishermen to fish."²⁶ Except for the Frigorífico Nacional at Callao for distribution to markets in Lima, there was almost no infrastructure in the 1940s to support the storage, transport, and sale of fresh fish beyond the coastal towns.²⁷ With a limited supply of ice, a dearth of storage facilities and fresh water near the wharves, and only two refrigerated trucks operating in all of Peru in 1949 (total capacity six tons), it was impractical, if not impossible, to supply the growing city centers with fresh fish for local consumption.²⁸

Jul's research in Chile highlighted many of the common and persistent issues that both countries had faced, including affordable supplies of tin, a need for refrigeration facilities, and general underdevelopment of needed infrastructure. Here, too, the primary concern of most industrialists was the need for loans and foreign exchange in order to upgrade their harvesting and processing technology. Chilean interviewees also stressed that low prices of fish and poor retail distribution were a significant problem for producers, since a lack of profitability dis-incentivized private investment, while middlemen often capitalized on the demand for meat by reselling the fish at higher prices.[29]

The director of fisheries, Rodolfo Ravanol, reported the existence of a school in San Vicente (a *caleta* near Talcahuano) with fifteen teachers and approximately 160–180 students enrolled, that educated youths from age fifteen in a four-year course of study on boat building and fishing methods. The Instituto de Biología Marina in Montemar also had an active research staff of ten.[30] Chilean interviewees projected a more positive image of the local labor force and its technical capacity than US executives had in Peru.

These contrasting dispositions between the governments of Chile and Peru by no means eliminated the frequent tensions between European or North American "experts" and their Chilean or Peruvian counterparts. One FAO technician reported that Chilean fishermen "work in very primitive and sad conditions" despite the abundance of Chilean seas.[31] Another complained about a lack of cooperation and even distrust between fishermen and the Chilean technicians and deplored their ignorance of "modern" fishing gear and motors, the absence of capitalist-style "competition" in the marketplace, and the existence of tariff barriers that limited access to adequate equipment. He urged the FAO to "use its influence to persuade the government to do something about the situation."[32] But the reception of FAO officials themselves was somewhat mixed among Peruvian and Chilean leaders.

Bibiano Fernández Osorio y Tafall, the first director of the FAO Regional Office for Latin America in Santiago, was also palpably disappointed by his first tour of Latin America. Having completed his doctoral research on the nutritional potential of phytoplankton in Mexico's Mar de Cortés, the Spanish-born biologist complained to his superiors in Rome that "biology is a hobby of little consequence" among those he met and lamented that there was little emphasis on fish as a protein source:[33] "[T]he Fisheries Service officials in these countries agreed that increased production should be at the disposal of the population to provide abundant and cheap food. However, they did not seem interested in the promotion of scientific knowledge of marine resources based on international cooperation."[34] Such tepid reactions among fishery-sector representatives, which Osorio Tafall noted were especially strong in Chile and Peru, were not entirely surprising given that previous attempts to develop such relationships with the international organization had been unsuccessful. Two years prior, when Mogens Jul questioned the planning of an upcoming international fisheries congress without the inclusion of the FAO, Chilean Fisheries director Ravanol explained that his colleagues "felt that progress in this activity was too slow." Since the organizational initiative had been local, there was "no reason why Chile should contact FAO about it, or invite FAO's observance."[35] Ravanol's comments suggested that local officials resented the expectation that foreign technical assistance be unilaterally welcomed, regardless of their disrespect toward local expertise or denial of requests for credit.

Institutional cooperation and social welfare goals clashed with local industry's primary interest in the expansion of fishmeal production as an export commodity. The director observed a marked reticence among Humboldt Current industrialists to gear development toward domestic nutritional programs and markets: "When it was explained that the role of the FAO is not to concede loans and that the development of fisheries activities within each country must first satisfy the domestic market and improve the nutrition of the natives, they did not hide their disappointment. This reaction was particularly noticeable in Chile and Peru among industry representatives."[36] Instead of access to the credit they needed to import expensive fishing and processing equipment, FAO offered foreign-led technical assistance, whose terms would be dictated by technocrats with lofty ideals they judged impractical and unprofitable.

Nonetheless, believing that the promotion of regional cooperation within the sector was one of the agency's most important objectives, Osorio Tafall ultimately recommended that the plans for the first meeting of the Latin American Fisheries Council proceed.[37] Arturo G. Sandoval, then the technical assistance liaison officer for Latin America, traveled to Lima in June 1951 to discuss the possibility of holding such a meeting there. His report noted that fisheries was both "a popular and delicate subject" for Peruvians—in part "because of certain nationalistic problems connected with the industry." After attending a meeting with the minister of agriculture and director of fisheries, Cristóbal Vecorena Olivares, he reported that because of the government's "defensive" and "repelling attitude," he had to "do a little convincing talking" to promote the international partnership that was to be spearheaded by FAO. The explanation that Sandoval received for this posturing, as he described it, was: "The Minister does not believe in inactive councils or councils of nations without power to act; Perú, according to the Minister, has had some rather sour experiences in connection with whaling and its control or supervision through a council."[38] Whaling was still an important economic activity in Peru at the time, which produced tensions with the International Whaling Commission (IWC) because of Peruvian whalers' impact on populations migrating out of the Antarctic region, where quotas were in place. By 1951, approximately one-third of the world's total production of sperm whale oil came from the waters off Peru and Chile (two hundred thousand barrels from 6,414 whales that year alone), primarily from foreign-led expeditions.[39] Peruvian officials were not only interested in controlling access to their offshore resources, but also in demonstrating national sovereignty on the global stage, where they had previously been marginalized from the center of power.

Global demand for fishmeal continued to rise throughout this period, as the field of industrial chemistry made advances in large-scale agriculture and animal nutrition. Studies confirmed the recommendation that marine proteins be included in poultry diets in the absence of a satisfactory synthetic or plant-based alternative.[40] Osorio y Tafall noted disapprovingly that approximately half of the hake (*Merluccius gayi gayi*) caught by the Arauco Fishing Company—"the most important supplier of cheap fresh fish for the Santiago market"—was used to produce fishmeal.[41] Established by the state-run Chilean Development Corporation (Corporación del Fomento, CORFO) in 1938, Arauco was operating industrial trawlers in the central-south region. By the late 1940s, the company had a formidable fleet of four sixty-five- to seventy-five-foot trawlers, with a combined capacity of up to ten thousand metric tons of fish.[42] Although Mogens Jul described the company as "primarily devoted to the fresh fish trade," it is likely that a significant portion of the catch—if not the majority—never reached consumers in that form.[43] Echoing claims made in the United States about the palatability of menhaden, the company's fleet captain (*capitán de fragata*), Julio Luna Sauvat, explained that consumption of the "very cheap and abundant" hake (a white-fleshed species similar in texture to cod) was "not very liked by the population." Trawling for hake, which dwell in deeper waters than pelagic schooling species like anchoveta and sardines, involved dragging a large net through the middle or bottom portion of the ocean, yielding enormous quantities of bycatch along with the target species. The company's fishmeal plant absorbed this excess production. Given that two additional trawlers were under construction, and the company planned to expand further and acquire up to three more,

FIGURE 7. Men aboard a fishing trawler, Chile (1958). Unknown photographer. Archivo Zig-Zag/Quimantú, Colección Museo Histórico Nacional, Santiago, Chile.

evidently the company's leaders saw their principal economic opportunity in the production of farm animal fodder.

Fishmeal made from hake was a nutritionally inefficient use of "'good' protein" in the context of the local population's food supply needs, even though half or more of the total fishmeal produced in Chile was consumed by the domestic poultry industry, and by the end of the 1950s, demand had increased tenfold.[44] At the same time, Chile was more receptive overall to FAO's nutritional interventions than officials in Peru. Some of the first cooperative projects the agency sponsored took place in Chile during the early 1950s.

Danish fisheries economist John Fridthjof worked from 1951 to 1953 studying local markets and organizing public education campaigns, including a "Fisheries Extension Program" in the coal mining town of Lota.[45] Not unlike marketing strategies employed by the US Fisheries Association to build consumer markets there decades earlier, the Lota campaign included advertisements in print, radio, and theater productions; improvements in the construction of market stalls; distribution of fish via trucks; the formation of a local fishermen's union; neighborhood-based "Local Fish Committees" (fifty of them in 1954) charged with teaching people to "[seek] in the sea what the soil cannot give them"; and an educational campaign consisting of lesson plans to be taught in company schools.[46]

The FAO claimed a 45 percent increase in fish consumption in one district of Santiago following similar campaigns.[47] A review of the project described it as a "very successful undertaking," in part because of the "excellent cooperation" with more than five Chilean government agencies.[48] By the mid-1950s, although fish had not necessarily become the preferred cuisine of most Chileans, the high rates of fish consumption during Lent every April required the government to mobilize the nation's entire fleet capacity from Iquique to Puerto Montt to supply Santiago for the holiday using airplanes.[49]

The FAO also collaborated with the Chilean Nutrition Institute to develop recipes enriched with "fish flour" (also called fish protein concentrate, or "FPC"), a type of fishmeal made from fresher raw material and using additional technologies to remove the fishy odor and flavor.[50] In 1953 the FAO awarded fellowships to two Chileans to study "scientific baking" in the United States, and the Chilean Nutrition Institute conducted fish flour "acceptability tests" using a 150 kg sample produced by a South African firm, with reportedly positive results among those who sampled the recipes.[51] Five years later, the United Nations Children's Fund (UNICEF) established a plant at Quintero on the central coast.[52] That plant produced approximately fifteen tons of FPC, which were used in trials in Chile and in Peru, where Dr. George Graham treated children and infants at the British Hospital in Lima suffering from protein-deficiency diseases (marasmus and marasmic kwashiorkor).[53]

Despite the demonstrated evidence of the nutritional potential of fish proteins for direct human consumption, however, none of the four separate projects to test or produce FPC in Chile during the fishmeal boom years resulted in its large-scale, commercial production.[54] Instead, the potential for quick profits through fishmeal eclipsed such small-scale efforts to direct these marine resources toward resolving the problem of domestic hunger and malnutrition. By the middle of the 1950s, international demand for fishmeal—and thus its price—was so strong that Chilean poultry producers complained in 1954 that they could not afford domestic feedstuffs and were forced to import an inferior replacement protein source, based on beef by-products, from Argentina.[55]

NEW HORIZONS: CALIFORNIA, FAO, AND THE SOUTHEAST PACIFIC FISHERIES FRONTIER

Fishmeal and oil had long provided fishermen and industrialists in the North Atlantic a certain market for surplus fish catch—and this outlet proved wholly profitable on its own when the demand for both meal and oil expanded rapidly in the postwar period.[56] Even prior to the mid-1950s, when fishmeal production was concentrated in the Northern European countries of Denmark, Germany, Iceland, Norway, and the United Kingdom, the proportion of the world's total fish landings that were transformed into fishmeal had been increasing.[57] Between 1948 and 1959, world production of the commodity more than tripled, with over 20 percent of total fish landed destined for fishmeal "reduction" plants.[58]

Since feeds were the most significant cost for livestock farmers, consistent access to a reliable, high-quality supply of fishmeal was a competitive advantage that many of the new agri-businesses sought to secure for themselves, particularly as the scale of production increased.[59] California poultry producers had immediate access to fishmeal produced from North Pacific sardines before the 1940s, while along the US Atlantic and Gulf coasts, farmers relied primarily on fishmeal produced from whole menhaden or cannery waste. During the same period, the pet food industry became another growing source of demand for industrial fishery products.[60]

US firms engaged in vertical integration to gain more control over the supply chain, creating their own specially formulated feeds that yielded larger chicks (or piglets) in a shorter time, and reducing their vulnerability to price swings based on fluctuating fishmeal production.[61] These formulations took into account the emerging scientific understandings about animal nutrition that confirmed the importance of proteins for the health and survival of mass-farmed animals. They also incorporated the latest mathematical models (linear programming) in order to calculate least-cost rations.[62] These interventions afforded animal growers greater flexibility to respond to market shifts, as they could easily alter their formulas based on the variable costs of specific commodities.[63]

For fishermen and processors across all of these regions, fishmeal not only provided a welcome market for their surplus and by-products, but also encouraged them to fish for un-depleted species deemed undesirable to local (human) consumers. Manuel Lima, the first president of the New England Trash Fishermen's Association, explained in 1951 that they could make better returns "by quick offshore sweeps for trash fish" than they could going farther out to sea for "edible" species.[64] Producers in the United States discovered the profitability of this enterprise at the same time that they were forced to contend with the ecological impact of overfishing on their former target species. In 1948, US fisheries scientist Milton Lobell wrote to the newly appointed US undersecretary of fisheries, Wilbert Chapman, asserting his belief that the California fishing industry would soon need to rely heavily on resources extracted from the Latin American Pacific region.[65] Lobell's assertion proved correct. By that time, executives of the California-based Van Camp Sea Foods, who enjoyed close relationships with the most prominent marine biologists of the era, had already established four offices along the coast between San Diego and Lima, Peru.[66] Facing a growing crisis, the apparent opportunities for expanding tuna and anchovy fishing grounds to the south became increasingly irresistible.

During the course of the next decade, the introduction of new materials and technologies such as nylon fishing nets, power blocks, pumps, and winches allowed vessels to haul ever-increasing loads across greater distances, while offsetting the economic impact of local resource depletion. The San Diego tuna fleet had almost completely converted from bait boats to purse seiners by the early 1960s—a level of modernization (and attendant capital investment) that far outpaced most enterprises based along the South American Pacific coast.[67] Meanwhile, the priorities of short-term profits drove the agendas of international agencies, whether overtly or covertly. One prominent California tuna executive joked cynically about how they might use the rhetoric of social welfare to promote their cause in public fora: "A clever man might get in a paragraph or two about the value of fish as a resource, [and] the need of underprivileged peoples of the world for sources of protein food."[68]

FOUR

The Golden Anchoveta

THE MAKING OF THE WORLD'S LARGEST
SINGLE-SPECIES FISHERY IN CHIMBOTE, PERU

> Anchovetas, stars of the Peruvian sea, shiver and shimmer on all the horizons.
>
> EMILIO ROMERO, December 2, 1964

AS THE MODERN INDUSTRIAL WORLD took notice of the rich fishing grounds in the waters of the South American Pacific, Peruvian writers proudly exalted the species centrally important to their coastal ecosystem. "It amazes us with its abundance and vitality. With its multimillionaire persistence," noted Emilio Romero in the Lima daily, *El Comercio*, evoking the mysteriousness of the anchoveta's fluctuations: "Sometimes they vanish into the depths and are lost. Other times they appear with immense phosphorescence, trembling through the waters like sequins in the sun."[1] Peruvian geographer Víctor Pezet described the Ferrol Bay of Chimbote as "excessively rich in fish," conveying his "hope of seeing it converted into a great industry in the future, destined to feed many of the working classes who dedicate themselves to that pleasant trade."[2] This elusive treasure became newly redeemable to industrious pioneers as global demand for fishmeal grew during the mid-twentieth century, as the once unpretentious (if unpredictable) anchoveta—"gold that comes from the sea"—seemed to promise a prosperous future for Peru.[3]

Chimbote was the epicenter of the Peruvian fishmeal revolution at its peak during the 1960s. Between 1940 and 1961, the urban population increased fifteenfold, from four thousand to nearly sixty thousand inhabitants.[4] Migrants poured in from the Andean highlands and the North Coast in search of work on fishing boats, in canneries, or in the Siderperú steel mill that opened in 1956. But then the fishmeal boom took hold of the city: between 1956 and 1962, the total installed capacity of Chimbote's fishmeal plants multiplied by a factor of nineteen, and the registered tonnage of its industrial fishing fleet increased thirty-nine times.[5] The total number of plants increased nearly fourfold in the same period, bringing the total to twenty-seven by 1962.[6] The fast growth of fishmeal processing capacity created a steady appetite for the teeming shoals offshore.

If Chimbote was the heart of the post-war "reduction" fisheries in Peru, the anchoveta was the industry's golden apple. Even as fishmeal production expanded to at least a dozen ports along the Peruvian coast, none could rival the ecological advantage that Chimbote had, with its position adjacent to the northernmost region of the Humboldt Current upwelling, where the nutrient-rich waters persist year-round.[7] There, above the slightly widened continental shelf, the *Engraulis ringens* congregated in their greatest numbers, attracting whales and other foraging predators during their trans-oceanic migrations.[8] Located about sixty kilometers (fifty-six miles) north of Lima, Chimbote sits just south of the outlet of the Santa River (9°S), possessing one of the only protected harbors on the South American Pacific coast.

In the early 1960s, a public outcry over the unpleasant smells emanating from the fishmeal plants along Avenida Argentina (between Lima and Callao) led authorities to implement local regulations on atmospheric emissions. But whereas well-heeled *limeños* had succeeded in passing legislation to control the polluting odors, lax or nonexistent policies in Chimbote—which soon surpassed Callao as the main center of the industry—facilitated the installation of factories at a dizzying rate.[9] With all of this came a distinctive notoriety, as foreign reporters who visited the town described a noxious atmosphere which, "distasteful and penetrating, hovers incessantly over the metropolis, leaking into the remotest corner of the tightest building."[10] Yet observers and residents alike often linked this stinking smellscape to the price of progress. As one *Los Angeles Times* reporter put it, repeating an oft-cited maxim among local residents, "the smell of fish meal is the smell of money for Peru."[11]

So began the most notorious chapter in the story of the world's largest single-species fishery: with Chimbote leading the fishmeal revolution, Peru ascended from its position as twenty-eighth in the world in 1953 to the top-producing fishing nation in less than a decade.[12] This chapter explores the unprecedented expansion of the fishmeal industry in Peru during the 1950s and '60s—with Chimbote at its center—as governments, international agencies, scientists, business executives and workers, both foreign and domestic, navigated the conflicting social, economic, and environmental consequences of rapid industrial development. This remarkable expansion—at its peak between 1958 and 1964—was based almost entirely on the production and export of anchoveta fishmeal, quickly dwarfing the modest bonito canning industry. But the boom trajectory was halted by numerous challenges, both human-caused and ecological, by the mid-1970s, after an earthquake devastated Peru's central region and the catastrophic collapse of the anchoveta fishery brought the era of unbridled growth to a rapid close.

"THE SMELL OF MONEY": TRANSFORMING CHIMBOTE INTO PERU'S FISHMEAL BOOMTOWN

Since the nineteenth century, there had been several efforts to organize Chimbote into a modern center of industry and commerce. Its initial layout was designed by the Boston-born engineer Henry Meiggs, a railroad tycoon who built a network of railroads in Chile and Peru, including the first to cross the Andean Cordillera, in the decades before his 1877 death in Lima.[13] In the early decades of the twentieth century, this small settlement on the Peruvian North Coast had the makings of a US-style company town, with neat, square residential blocks, a plaza, church, market, and administrative offices. The Pan-American Highway, running parallel to the coast, traversed the town center and connected it to the capital city of Lima.

On the eve of World War Two, Peruvian policy makers had approved a Regional Development Plan that aimed to transform it into the site for Peru's premier iron, coal, and steel industry.[14] Foreign consultants who visited the area immediately noted its suitability for such activities. US engineer E. J. Clearly declared that Chimbote possessed "the best natural bay that exists on the west coast of South America."[15] The Santa River, which flows down from the mountains just north of the populated area, carries the highest volume of water of any South American river flowing into the Pacific Ocean.[16] Extensive deposits of anthracite coal east of Chimbote in the Huaylas Valley eventually supplied fuel for Peru's first steel mill, Siderperú (inaugurated in 1956), which processed iron ore from the Marcona mine in the southern province of Ica.[17] Soon various projects were under way to establish the infrastructure that would transform this small farming and fishing town into, as E. J. Clearly put it, the "Peruvian Pittsburgh."[18]

Yet the international experts who arrived in Chimbote to take part in this "vast program of industrialization" during the 1940s had a jaundiced view of Chimbote as a dramatically inhospitable setting. The rainless climate of the Peruvian coastal desert created a landscape largely devoid of vegetation.

FIGURE 8. Aerial view of Chimbote, Peru (1929). From the American Geographical Society Library, University of Wisconsin–Milwaukee Libraries.

Chimbote was uncivilized, a "place that possesses few comforts." Aside from the lack of basic data and qualified personnel, he went on, "it is hard to imagine how a population of 4,000 inhabitants . . . has been able to survive under these conditions."[19] For foreign visitors, mid-century Chimbote thus described an insufferable place on the frontier of Peru's vast Sechura Desert.

Ultimately, the city's infrastructure was unprepared for the rapid demographic growth of later decades. In 1948, commissioned by the Peruvian government, the world-renowned architects Josep Lluís Sert and Paul Lester Wiener created a master plan for Chimbote that envisioned a population of forty thousand inhabitants.[20] But this number was surpassed by nearly 30 percent by the time the next census was taken: between 1940 and 1961, the urban population of Chimbote jumped from 4,243 to 58,990.[21] In 1961, 93 percent of *chimbotanos* self-identified as migrants.[22] But indigenous Andeans who arrived as part of this wave faced discrimination: "The growing indigenous migration from the interior of this department towards the coast has been causing alarm to the inhabitants of this city," wrote one columnist, "where entire families arrive daily."[23]

Many families built their homes with adobe bricks and reeds harvested from what remained of the nearby wetlands. Meiggs's company-built wooden housing from the turn of the twentieth century, it turned out, did not ultimately supersede the reed huts of earlier generations, as Victor Pezet had imagined in 1912. Made from locally available materials, the adobe-and-reed constructions were far more practical for cash-strapped newcomers, and since the region receives almost no rainfall, they were surprisingly well-suited to the climate of the area. To most international observers, however, such modest structures were the unmistakable symbols of underdevelopment.

Chimbote's role in the advance toward industrialization and economic independence gained substance with the new Siderperú steel mill, the presence of which was in turn dwarfed by the growing fishmeal sector. Nevertheless, in 1957, columnist Wilfredo Peláez Gularte disputed claims that Chimbote was Peru's "port of the future." Writing in the Lima newspaper *La Prensa*, Peláez declared it a "problem city" with a "tragic and devastating panorama," overpopulated with slums and neglected by public officials. Chimbote, he believed, should not be considered "a point of reference for the future of the country. It is a poor city, and without the resources that would allow it to live independently."[24] Perpetually dependent on Lima for capital and expertise, Chimbote had hardly lived up to its image as a "promised land."

ADAPTING TO THE ANCHOVETA: TECHNOLOGIES OF FISHMEAL PRODUCTION IN PERU

Early twentieth-century Peruvian political and business leaders were well aware of the nearly untapped wealth of their offshore shoals, particularly since they were a subject of ongoing research as the primary source of sustenance for the guano birds. By the time Robert Cushman Murphy published his studies in the 1920s, US scientists had studied the coastal fish populations in relation to the life cycles of the guano-producing seabirds for almost two decades, most significantly under the auspices of government officials and the state-owned Compañía Administradora del Guano (CAG).[25] Despite the protests of those like Murphy, who warned that industrial fishing would lead to the same fate for the anchoveta as it had for the California sardine, the biological research undertaken by these "conservation technocrats" ultimately played a key role in the sector's development.[26]

Commercial-scale fishmeal production in Peru began haltingly. In 1923, a Japanese engineer named Nakashima received permission to establish a fish-canning plant in order to study the possibilities for further industrial development. Nakashima's endeavors led to plans to "produce fish meal and also obtain fish oil for industrial purposes," but it would be nearly two decades before the government made systematic efforts to establish operations.[27] CAG scientists had been studying fishmeal production since at least the late 1930s, and forged commercial ties with US firms in California and New York, including arrangements for equipment and vessel purchase, credit, and shipping.[28] The company later imported one of the first fishmeal processing plants, although its ownership apparently transferred to private entrepreneurs prior to producing any fishmeal.[29]

By 1940, CAG's extensive marine-biological research included studies of the North Atlantic menhaden fishery between Virginia and the North Carolina border, as well as the fisheries of Seattle, Anacortes, and Tacoma, Washington; San Francisco, Los Angeles, Monterrey, and San Pedro, California, in the North Pacific.[30] Following the US Fish & Wildlife Service (USFW) commission's 1943 report, the Peruvian government purchased several US-built vessels, including the *Pacific Queen*, a Tacoma-built purse seine that had been used by the research team during their study.[31] The introduction of the purse seine vessel, whose net encircles the school and closes at the bottom to form a purse-like shape, was decisive in the acceleration of industrial-scale fishing along the Peruvian coast.[32] Before the fishmeal boom, tuna and bonito canneries dotted Chimbote's shoreline, but during the 1960s, fishmeal quickly surpassed canning as the primary locomotive of industrial productivity.

Peruvian engineers and entrepreneurs soon adapted boats, gear, and equipment designs to suit the specific conditions of the Humboldt Current anchoveta fishery. Enrique del Solar, the first Peruvian marine biologist, had trained in Japan; he worked with Peruvian and German engineers to update the vessels to accommodate the anchoveta's small body size and dense schools. The first Peruvian fishing boats adapted to this species—called *bolicheras*—were tuna clippers outfitted with larger holds, which utilized nets with smaller openings.[33] In 1947, Peruvian naval engineer Augusto Maggiolo completed the first locally constructed bolichera, the *CONSA I*, for the fishing entrepreneur Carlos Otero Lora.[34] Although shipbuilding and plant construction along Peru's coast did not take off until later in the 1950s, these initiatives were among the earliest steps in reconfiguring the national fishing effort toward the industrial extraction and processing of a single species, the anchoveta (*Engraulis ringens*).[35]

FAO officers who visited Peru during the late 1940s and early 1950s encountered an enthusiastic private sector, even if their reception by government leaders was icy.[36] Fishing sector representatives had complained to FAO's Mogens Jul in 1949 that the CAG-owned plant for the most part sat idle, lacking raw material, only occasionally processing fish scrap from canneries or other surplus fish deemed unsuitable for direct human consumption.[37] The Comité Nacional de Pesca (National Fisheries Committee), a private sector interest group, embraced the opportunity to establish partnerships with foreign fishing concerns. Two Peruvian entrepreneurs, Arturo Madueño and Manuel Elguera McParlin, entered into a venture with the San Francisco-based firm Wilbur Ellis Company to establish the country's first fishmeal plant dedicated specifically to the reduction of whole anchoveta: the Pesquera Chimú in Chimbote went into production in 1955.[38] The official opening of this plant came just as a new law, passed in April of that year, reduced the export tax on fishery products.[39]

Soon thereafter the Peruvian fishmeal industry entered its first major period of expansion with a major influx of capital to the sector. Fourteen new fishing companies formed during 1955–56 alone.[40] During the early years of the boom, more than half of the newly installed plants were small-scale operations that sought to supply their facilities with whole anchoveta (rather than cannery offal from bonito processing) in order to produce fishmeal directly for export.[41] The industry's on-shore processing capacity grew even more rapidly than the rate of new plant construction, as Peruvian producers expanded existing plants and built ever-larger new ones. Between 1956 and June 1962, the total installed capacity of *active* Peruvian processing plants skyrocketed from 139 tons per hour to 2,729 tons per hour—nearly a twentyfold increase in less than seven years.[42]

As the industry grew, those who could afford it upgraded their equipment in attempts to outpace competitors in the "race for fish." After 1954, nylon nets replaced those made of cotton, which were vastly heavier and required frequent repairs, and mechanization allowed crews to fill their holds with greater ease.[43] But the local fleet could not supply sufficient quantities of fish to keep the plants consistently in operation. Excess plant capacity stimulated a boom in the import and construction of fishing vessels, as larger, lighter boats replaced many of the small, wooden ones.[44]

Local shipyards established new facilities and expanded their operations to service an expanding fleet of bolicheras. Bolichera construction reached a peak in 1963, with 489 boats built that year alone, which nearly doubled the total number of vessels operating in Peruvian waters at that time.[45] Four years later, researchers estimated a total of 1,536 operable fishing boats along the Peruvian littoral. Significantly, more than two-thirds (72%) of the fishers surveyed in 1967 classified as industrialists, who often also owned the processing plants they supplied.[46] In most Peruvian ports, wooden vessels far outnumbered those of metal construction, though the latter were preferred because of their greater speed, longevity, and lower maintenance costs.[47]

The largest bolicheras operating in Peru at this time could haul up to 350 tons, but in the anchoveta fishery, crews rarely filled the hold in a single day, and the unrefrigerated catch needed to be unloaded as soon as possible. These conditions made somewhat smaller vessels (two hundred tons) generally more efficient to operate.[48] However, many industrialists complained of a shortage of credit in order to finance the construction of boats, and a lack of government incentives for the fisheries sector. They noted the comparatively favorable conditions their competitors in Chile enjoyed, where from 1953 to 1960 fishmeal exports were granted a special exchange rate in order to promote the industry's rapid development.[49] Capital-rich, vertically integrated firms employed a variety of vessel sizes in order to adapt to the fluctuating anchoveta schools and their proximity to their onshore processing facilities.[50]

Struggling to meet the demand for new bolicheras, some Peruvian firms resorted to enlarging the holds of their preexisting vessels in order to increase their capacity. Many undertook these modifications without adequately updating the vessel design, as informal shipbuilding operations clogged the streets of Callao. This scenario contributed to a high rate of accidents at sea as dozens of overloaded bolicheras sank before they could reach port. *La Prensa* reported a rapid increase in such accidents during the peak of the first bolichera construction boom: the number of sunken vessels catapulted from 31 sunken vessels in 1959, to 192 in 1963.[51] The newspaper cited criticisms by non-Peruvians, including one unnamed "European expert" who commented that such vessels were not actual fishing boats but simply "motorized holds" (*bodegas con motor*) that lacked engineering integrity. This led insurance firms to refuse contracts with Peruvian vessels, exacerbating the problem of limited capital and credit. More and more fishers sought to enter the game, although neither the shipyards nor the fishmeal industrialists could pay the construction costs in the short term.[52]

While technological modernization was not uniform, the very abundance of anchoveta during the boom years allowed less efficient vessels to continue

FIGURE 9. Men preparing to load anchoveta into a fishing vessel's hold, Chile (1964). Unknown photographer. Archivo Zig-Zag/Quimantú, Colección Museo Histórico Nacional, Santiago, Chile.

operating profitably. Crews on the significant proportion of vessels not yet updated (up to 23% of the fleet in 1967) faced highly differentiated working conditions that depended on the proprietor's specific investments in equipment and maintenance. By the end of the decade, FAO fisheries expert Hellevang noted that most Peruvian bolicheras still lacked the most powerful types of power blocks (deck-mounted) and rigging (purse winch). This made maneuvers more challenging for the crew, especially when they attempted to extract the extraordinarily large schools of anchoveta characteristic of the northern Humboldt Current System.[53] "To a European fisherman," he told the attendees at a conference in Reykjavik in 1970, "these vessels look rather unseaworthy and it would be difficult to convince them that they carry as much fish as they do." But he also conceded that they were in fact "extremely serviceable" for the specific conditions of the waters off Peru, which were calmer and less windy than those of the North Sea and North Atlantic.[54]

Certain attributes of the anchoveta's behavior differentiated this fish from the North Sea herring, a frequent comparison made by European fisheries experts, and shaped the adaptations that Peruvians made to their methods and equipment. Their tiny size, fast speed, and tendency to remain near the sea surface required nets with small mesh that were long, but not deep, in order to encircle the large schools. Most Peruvian fishermen visually located anchoveta schools by observing feeding seabirds from a distance and pulling up next to the fish—a reliance on traditional methods that annoyed foreign technicians who insisted on the superiority of new technologies. "Absurdly enough," FAO scientist Hermann Einarsson wrote in 1965, "the primary task here is to get the skippers to use the equipment they already have and teach them to interprete [sic] the echograms in a rough way."[55] Once they had located the fish schools by sight, however, the crew used echosounders (*ecosondas,* installed on 98.5% of the fleet) to measure the size, speed, and direction of their movement.[56] The bolichera then moved ahead of the school and released a small motorboat (*panga*) from its back deck, which held the net in place while the main vessel set it by encircling the school and cinching the line. In cases of large schools, whose weight was further increased by water trapped inside the small mesh, the crew typically separated the catch into two concentrated "bags," then used the hydraulic pump and hose to move the anchoveta into the boat's hold.[57] Notwithstanding the wide disparity among vessel size, age, and type, the overall fishing effort continued to rise throughout the decade, contributing to an astronomical rise in harvests from 1956 to 1968–69 (a more than eighty-three-fold increase by some estimates).[58]

LIVING THE INDUSTRIAL DREAM IN A "PROBLEM CITY"

Boomtown Chimbote did indeed attract thousands seeking better opportunities than those available in rural and highland Peru. The steel mill (Siderperú, opened in 1956) had attracted the first waves of immigrants, but nearly a dozen tuna canneries also provided employment. By 1959, Chimbote had the country's highest concentration of canneries along the coast, nearly a third of the national total.[59] A graphic history of Chimbote's labor movement depicted the typical story of many who migrated to the town during this period, constituting a new phase in the city's historical narrative and collective identity. Aimed at a working-class audience, the story described how migrants—called *enganchados* (literally, the "hooked ones")—were lured to work in the tuna canneries with false promises by company representatives. Upon arrival, they had little choice but to accept the poor conditions of the jobs offered them, indebted to the recruiters for the expenses of the trip.[60] While men worked on fishing boats or in other industrial jobs, the canneries employed a predominantly female labor force that was displaced with the emergence of fishmeal. Because the pay was abysmally low and the conditions dangerous, the cannery workers organized to appeal for improvements, forming connections with other local unions and thereby integrating into the well-organized labor movement in their adopted city.[61]

The golden years of the boom were an especially prosperous time for the fishermen who labored aboard the bolicheras, which could scoop up an entire school of anchoveta in a single set. These workers were the most important element of the extractive process, since without them the plants would have no fish to grind. While cannery and plant workers earned low pay, fishermen working at sea were said to earn in a single trip as much as a professor or bank employee in a month—and during the boom, a boat could often make as many as three trips in a single day.[62] Those who lived in Chimbote during that era related tales of ostentatious displays of wealth: newly rich fishermen with abundant gold jewelry, multiple mistresses, lighting their cigarettes with 500-*sol* bills (about US$20 at that time).[63] Their notoriety was symbolic of the economic success and conspicuous consumption associated with the boom. But their heyday was short lived; this image of wealth and success belied the conditions of poverty and political struggle in which most chimbotanos lived.

While Peruvian exports grew at a cumulative annual rate of 8 percent from 1950 to 1965, the exports of the fishery sector grew 26 percent annually to account for a quarter of all exports, followed closely by copper. At its height in the 1960s, fisheries and the fish processing industries not only contributed significantly to the Peruvian national balance of payments but employed thirty-nine thousand, without counting those in ancillary activities such as shipyards.[64] While small-scale artisanal fishing for local consumption employed seven thousand, the fifteen hundred vessels in the industrial fleet employed nearly twenty thousand in January 1969, including fifteen hundred skippers, fifteen hundred engineers, and more than sixteen thousand as crew (*tripulantes*).[65]

Labor on board was contracted through verbal agreements between outfitters, launch skipper, and engineers. Crews were hired by the skipper with everyone paid a "proportional share of catches." This practice tended to ensure smaller crews, since one less crew member meant higher payments to all those hired.[66] Crewmembers' pay, typically about a third of the earnings that captains (*patrones*) received and slightly less than engineers, was also directly related to the fish caught and supplied to the plants.[67]

A study of twenty thousand members of the Caja de Beneficios del Pescador revealed that those who worked on the boats were mostly young, literate men, largely from the coastal provinces.[68] Twenty-two percent were from mountain provinces, while another important group was composed of immigrants who had left Spain and Italy under fascism, and their descendants, bringing their experience with the Mediterranean sardine and anchovy fisheries to the Southeast Pacific.[69] US scientists had complained about the resistance among Italian fishermen to adapt the latest fishing technologies, but local entrepreneurs in Peru and Chile seemed to value their specialized knowledge of fish-capture methods.[70]

A typical day on a Peruvian bolichera during this time began before dawn, when the crew waited at the pier for a small motorboat (*lancha*) to transport them to the bolichera anchored in the harbor. Although observers had often reported masses of anchoveta close to the shore, by the mid-1960s, fishing vessels typically needed to travel four to five hours from the coast (approximately one hundred nautical miles) in order to fill their holds.[71] Crew members often faced treacherous working conditions aboard the bolicheras, since safety regulations were irregularly enforced: not only did men occasionally suffocate from the toxic ammonia released from decomposing anchoveta in the holds; many complained about the lack of adequate safety and communications equipment, and feared the threat of immediate dismissal if they called attention to these deficiencies.[72] Unofficial estimates placed the rate of death or severe injury among Peruvian fishermen at 12 percent.[73]

On-shore fishmeal production employed 11,838 of the total 13,645 workers in fish processing (including canning, freezing, drying, and whaling).[74] About 62 percent of those in fishmeal plants were entirely unskilled—an FAO employment specialist noted in his 1971 report that almost no fishmeal processing workers had any "serious training" given the "relative simplicity and uniformity of the processes."[75] It was this work that was most likely to draw impoverished migrants from the Peruvian *sierra*.

Chimbote's growing chaos and disorder captured the interest of a new generation of international civil servants and technocrats during the 1960s. The troubles the city faced were partly representative of broader transformations taking place across Peru, as thousands of families migrated from rural areas—particularly the Andes and the northern provinces—to coastal cities in search of opportunities for socioeconomic advancement. Despite the interventions of the Inter-American Cooperative Health Program and other

NGOs during the previous decades, the rapidly growing settlements on the periphery of town continued to lack basic services and sanitation.

At the peak of the fishmeal boom during the 1960s, Chimbote pulsed with the energies of workers, capitalists, activists, and intellectuals. As the epicenter of the fishmeal revolution, the port city of Chimbote had been transformed demographically, environmentally, and culturally by the rise of industrialized fishmeal production. The explosive human and environmental terrain of boomtown Chimbote saw the clash between the conflicting agendas among fishmeal magnates and their "mafias," local fishermen and union leaders, student activists from Lima and abroad, Peace Corps volunteers, and even renowned Peruvian novelist José María Arguedas who left a memorable portrait of Andean migration to the city.

Boomtown Chimbote was intensely inspiring for many radical students, activists, and intellectuals, who saw great political potential in its socioeconomic conflicts. French-born labor sociologist Denis Sulmont wrote his doctoral thesis about Chimbote under the direction of Alain Touraine, later becoming a professor at the Pontificia Católica Universidad del Perú.[76] "Chimbote was the door through which I introduced myself in 1967 to the popular world of Peru," he later wrote.[77] Sulmont's extensive personal collection of photographs from 1967, the year he began his fieldwork, provide ethnographic evidence of Chimbote at the height of the fishmeal boom.[78] In the *barriadas* Sulmont photographed, there was no pavement, electricity, or running water, and most homes were made of reeds bundled or woven together. Children played in the street in the hillside communities while smoke hovered around the factories near the bay below.[79] Another sociologist drawn to the coastal "melting pot" was the *limeño* F. Hernán Peralta Bouroncle, who graduated from the National Agrarian University of La Molina in the late-1960s. Peralta worked in Chimbote as an organizer for the left-wing political party Revolutionary Vanguard (*Vanguardia Revolucionaria*) from 1971 to 1983.[80] "I found in Chimbote the laboratory of my life," he later recalled.[81] On the tumultuous, stinky industrial frontier, these two men encountered fast urban growth, a clash of cultures, and a vibrant political scene that were deeply transformative for their own lives, which were further shaped by the arrival of General Juan Velasco Alvarado's reformist military regime in 1968.

Industrial expansion in boomtown Chimbote produced an aesthetic of urban development whose notoriety was infused with the stench of fish and the hastily constructed dwellings that surrounded the factories and city center. Day and night during the boom, millions of tons of anchoveta fed dozens of fishmeal plants, pumping smoke throughout the urban industrial core. The growing *barriadas* (slums) sandwiched between them shared sticky, squalid air, while the bay received an endless supply of oily effluents as well as heavy metals from the steel mill. Discourses of progress gave way to cultures of excess: rotting fish awaited processing by overburdened plants; extraction and air and water emissions lacked governmental control; and fishermen and executives, who saw no end to the bonanza, engaged in conspicuous consumption of alcohol and sex.

The quick profits in the booming fishmeal factories subsidized what some observers portrayed as a culture of excess. Looking back, Peralta recalled his frustration at the debauchery he observed among the fishermen. "Everything was cash, everything was sex," he said: "I never belonged to that world. What a fisherman earned in a week could have lasted him for two months. What did they do? They wasted it and lived in shacks ... instead of building a house.... A boat captain who didn't spend his money and didn't have four or five women [and a ton of kids], all of whom he supported, you know? ... An austere man would save his money and within three years he could buy himself a boat."[82] In Peralta's view, unconstrained spending on alcohol and women perpetuated rather than combatted the systemic poverty of the barriadas. Deeply committed to the intellectual and political project of worker mobilization, Peralta lamented that fishermen who had the economic means to improve their situation during the anchoveta boom seemed to squander their wealth on fleeting luxuries.

Chimbote's metamorphosing cultural world also became a key site of intellectual and creative inspiration for the acclaimed Peruvian writer and scholar José María Arguedas (1911–1969). Arguedas "proposed an alternative politics of knowledge" that held "Andean ways of being" alongside "western reason"—a plurality of coexisting perspectives that seemed incompatible to the academic establishment but that was fertile terrain for fiction-writing.[83] A native Quechua-speaker and professor of anthropology, Arguedas undertook an ethnographic study of Chimbote at the peak of the fishmeal boom in the 1960s, which provided the inspiration for his last novel, *The Fox from Up Above and the Fox from Down Below* (published posthumously in 1971).[84] Arguedas reported to his colleague John Murra that he had interviewed five men who had migrated from the Andes, in addition to collecting data on 3,645 fishermen and 3,840 workers during his ethnographic research.[85] Framed around characters in Andean mythology, the novel is comprised largely of an imagined dialogue in which the fox from above (representing the culture of the Andes) meets the fox from below (representing the culture of the coast).[86]

Even as a work of fiction, *The Fox from Up Above and the Fox from Down Below* provides a kind of socioeconomic and ecological register of boomtown Chimbote. Throughout the text, Arguedas drew clear parallels between the setting, characters, and events in the novel and real-life Chimbote of the 1960s.[87] He also described the harvest of anchovetas and the processing of fishmeal with a notable degree of technological detail. Arguedas conveyed a dystopian seascape, stained with bloody water and dead fish, whose atmosphere was choked by the rancid haze spewing out of smokestacks built too low in the sky:

> The stench of the sea displaced the reek of the smoke from the boilers in which millions of anchovies were coming apart, melting, exhaling that rather foodlike odor as they were boiling and sweating oil. The dense odor of the waste matter, of blood, of the tiny entrails trampled in the trawlers and hosed out over the sea, and the smell of the water that gushed out of the factories onto the beach made jellylike worms rise up out of the sand; that stench kept drifting along at ground level and rising.[88]

This was a wrenching critique of fishmeal's environmental and aesthetic impact on the Chimbote shoreline, the site of one of the most rapidly industrializing fisheries of the twentieth century. Chimbote was at the core of profound sociocultural changes taking place across Peru at the time.[89]

Living conditions worsened further following a major earthquake on May 31, 1970, drawing even more international attention to the locale. Researching for the Ford Foundation between 1970 and 1972, John Robin and Frederick Terzo were appalled after visiting the city, citing a report that had described Chimbote as "a mere collection of shacks." It was "almost a 'non-place,'" the original report noted: "[N]othing exists there apart from a large collection of nondescript buildings. Indeed, the only buildings which might be said to characterize Chimbote are the SOGESA Steel Mill and the fish meal factories from whose bowels belches the dreadful and all-prevading [sic] smell of fish meal, and whose waste products have fouled the waters of the bay."[90] If before the earthquake Chimbote was a "problem city," as Peláez claimed in the early years of the boom, it was now proclaimed by international experts to be "the worst urban environment we have seen since leaving India."[91]

In the aftermath of this event, the revolutionary military commander General Juan Velasco Alvarado (1968–1975) launched a grandiose—but

FIGURE 10. People on the beach in front of fishmeal plants, Chimbote, Peru (2008). Photo by the author.

ultimately only partially realized—plan to reclaim Chimbote's place as a major center of economic and political power. The Velasco regime pledged to counteract the negative impacts of rapid industrialization and uncontrolled population growth through the creation of a new ministry, the Rehabilitation and Reconstruction Committee for the Affected Zone (CRYRZA), whose agents set out to register residents of the barriadas, improve local roads and sewerage, and designate new industrial and commercial zones. Following the advice of a team of French geologists who visited Chimbote after the earthquake and determined that its soils were unstable, the government attempted to persuade residents to move to an area with more solid ground on the south side of the city—but to no avail. Many residents still preferred the homes and communities they had built and their closer proximity to centers of employment, despite the smelly smoke and sticky effluents that poured from the dozens of fishmeal plants operating in the urban core and surrounding areas.[92]

The catastrophic collapse of the anchoveta fishery in 1972 soon brought these plans, and Chimbote's incredible fishing bonanza, to an abrupt halt. The sudden and unexplained disappearance of the golden anchoveta, prized symbol of Peru's fourth region and "westward march," delivered a tremendous blow to both the local and national economy. A confluence of human and natural setbacks left chimbotanos with the persistent challenge of rebuilding their hopes and dreams amid the rubble of decaying fishmeal factories and eroding beaches—a rusty urban zone of sacrifice from which a new generation of civic and environmental leaders later emerged.

Chimbote's transformation had depended on the vast supplies of energy and nutrients in local and peripheral ecosystems. Andean water and mineral resources provided the coal and hydroelectric power that sustained the new factories; the coastal waters provided a seemingly endless source of fish, and thousands of humans migrated in the hopes of cashing in on the prosperity by laboring on boats, in processing plants, and in the auxiliary industries that supported the fishing economy. It was a wrenching trajectory in which the fates of local, national, and international actors intertwined in a city and seascape sacrificed for the promise of prosperity.

Boomtown Chimbote was an "evil and magic place," wrote Peruvian geographer César Caviedes, "in which the two worlds of Peru [had] converged."[93] The city was not only a site where the rugged Andes met the dry, desert coast, creating the "unfathomable human hotbed" that so fascinated Arguedas and other intellectuals and activists of the boom era.[94] It was also a site where foreign and local capital clashed, a forum for the conflicting agendas of various international and national organizations, and a stage for the ongoing battles between organized labor and state control. It was a crucible for twentieth-century social, political, economic, and ecological experiments in which leaders and locals alike projected their visions of progress, as they sought to forge a modern, autonomous, and prosperous nation.

FIVE

States of Uncertainty

SCIENCE, POLICY, AND THE BIO-ECONOMICS
OF PERU'S 1972 FISHMEAL COLLAPSE

I am not ... one of those who think Peru is the "end." On the contrary, I've always felt that there must be two or three other "Perus" around the world.

MAX COHEN
International Proteins Corporation, 1969

NEWS OF THE PERUVIAN BOOM spread among members of the transnational business elite throughout the 1960s, a time of momentous change in the global food industry. Consumers in the urbanizing postwar United States were entering into a "golden age" of processed foods.[1] While food scientists experimented with chemical compounds that imitated the flavors, smells, colors, and textures of specific foods, pharmaceutical researchers worked to extract and isolate the elements that were linked to their nutritional qualities (fats, proteins, sugars, salt). By manipulating the properties of fruits, vegetables, and meats in order to preserve and market them to consumers, food processors created new products to fill the shelves of the growing number of supermarkets in the industrializing world.[2] Peruvian fishmeal and oil provided a much-needed input to this emerging industrial ecosystem.

Corporations consolidated ownership and expanded their operations both horizontally and vertically across many sectors of the global economy in the decades following World War Two. Equipped with larger refrigerated holds, more powerful engines, and the latest fish-finding tools, modernized fleets traveled farther and reached deeper than ever before. At the same time, new technologies transformed the production, processing, distribution, and consumption of agricultural commodities, greatly increasing the scale and scope of their market access. In 1963, Ralston Purina purchased Van Camp Sea Foods, which had expanded from tuna canning and fishmeal in California to new operations in Peru and all along the Latin American Pacific Coast. The same year, H.J. Heinz Co. acquired the tuna packing company Star-Kist, which supplied 20 percent of the US canned tuna market and also operated fishmeal plants and canneries in Peru.[3] In the vast and varied marine ecosystem off the Peru-Chile coast, fish processors in the United States and Northern Europe—whose growth was limited by dwindling supplies of tuna, sardines, menhaden, and herring between the 1940s and 1960s—found opportunities to expand their extractive geographies into the Southeast Pacific.

The complex dynamics of the Humboldt Current system presented a powerful challenge to emerging models of fishery management, both in the postwar international political economy and in the "new oceanography" that began to emerge from Cold War–era trans-Pacific collaborations.[4] In Peru, neither numerous warnings by fisheries scientists that unrestricted fishing of the anchoveta could lead to an ecological catastrophe nor the regulations enacted by the Ministry of Fisheries prevented the fishery's collapse in 1972. Chaos ensued in global commodity markets, as a sudden drop in fishmeal supplies drove up the prices not only of fishmeal but also of other protein-feed commodities such as soy, and in turn also impacted everyday staples at the grocery stores. Waves of panic affected everyone from small farmers to the executives of agri-business giants in the United States, Germany, and elsewhere.[5] The collapse clearly illustrated the interdependence of global commodity webs and the distant ecosystems that had supported them: it forced policy makers to consider the ecological and institutional limits to growth in the industrial fisheries, particularly when faced with the uncertainty of El Niño cycles.

Large quantities of Peruvian fishmeal entered international commodity markets in 1959, bringing new geopolitical prominence to producers from the Global South. As the dominant suppliers of a commodity that was highly valuable to the emerging international political economy, Peru embraced fishmeal as a new global currency. Although scientists, businessmen, and government officials extensively debated the question of how best to regulate the fishery, their measures ultimately proved incapable of averting its collapse—a catastrophe from which it would take more than two decades to recover.

THE IMPACT OF PERU IN INTERNATIONAL COMMODITY MARKETS AFTER 1959

The sudden increase in the production and export of anchoveta fishmeal at the end of the 1950s shifted market power from the traditional fishmeal-producing nations of the North Atlantic toward the Southeast Pacific.[6] Reminiscent of the international reputation that Peruvian guano had earned a century before for its unparalleled efficacy as a nitrogenous fertilizer, this new source in the world's nutrient cycle quickly became essential to the growing food and agricultural enterprises in various parts of the Global North. In 1959–1960, Peru's momentous entry into the fishmeal export business, combined with market speculation in the trading of fishmeal contracts, precipitated a drop in world prices for fishmeal to as little as 50 percent of its previous market value.[7]

Dismayed by the instability this created in international price structures, European and US experts were intrigued by the apparent "capitalist success story" that was suddenly underway in a country they tended to regard as technologically backward and culturally un-modern.[8] German scientist Gerhard Meseck noted that most of Peru's fishmeal production utilized older technology, which at the time consisted of "simple, largely home-made drying plants of the open-fire type," and that only about 20 percent of the total output came from "modern steam-plants" such as those used in Germany.[9] To an international audience of fishmeal industrialists in Rome, he downplayed Peru's industrial growth while highlighting what he assumed had been an unforeseen macroeconomic mistake: "The drop in prices that occurred in mid-1959 is attributed not so much to the rapid increase in Peruvian production as to the lack of discipline and market knowledge on the part of the Peruvian exporters."[10] Meseck's explanation for this market shift casually dismissed the Peruvians' entrepreneurial success in generating huge profits in the newly established fishing sector, the growth of which aligned squarely with Peruvian state interests in developing national industries. His oblique reference to the speculation that had occurred in fishmeal contracts drew on well-worn stereotypes about undisciplined and uneducated Latin Americans in order to explain the unfamiliar disadvantage in which European fishmeal producers suddenly found themselves.

But leaders of Peru's fishing sector were well aware of their newfound power. At the October 1960 meeting of the Fishmeal Exporters Organization (FEO) in Paris, the Peruvian delegation successfully negotiated 60 percent (six hundred thousand tons) of the total global fishmeal export quota—an agreement that the Peruvian government quickly ratified.[11] Within Peru, the outcome of this meeting and the country's new membership in the FEO generated proud declarations hailing the "triumph" of the Peruvian anchoveta.[12] Responding to criticisms of the country's outsized role in the international market, Vicente Cerro Cebrián, president of the Peruvian delegation, reminded the world's fishmeal producers that their position in the quota system had a larger political and economic justification, rooted in international inequalities:

> We must say frankly that as a producer of raw materials our country is determined to combat honestly and tenaciously the restrictive import policies of industrial countries. We firmly believe in free trade and are opposed to anything that hampers commercial exchange. Our country maintains low tariffs at great sacrifice since we, too, have nascent industries.... All American and European statesmen now agree that the modernizing of underdeveloped countries is of capital importance to the free world. Peru, no less, needs world help in eliminating restrictive policies that operate to impede progress at the production sources in countries that are going through this stage of economic development.[13]

The aggrieved tone in Cerro Cebrián's comments doubtless recalled the restrictive tariffs set by the United States against canned bonito imports a decade earlier, which crippled the Peruvian industry while allowing for the reestablishment of California fishing firms' dominance in US consumer markets, based in large part on increasing harvests from the waters of the Latin American Pacific.

The rise of Peru also pressed the traditional North Atlantic fishing sector's bottom line, depressing the value of their lower-quality and less abundant fishmeal, even as the fisheries on which they depended showed signs of crisis. With the ready availability of anchoveta fishmeal, superior in protein value to that made from fleshy white fish or fish scrap, it became unprofitable for European fishers to sell surplus or bycatch directly to fishmeal plants—except in the case of "mass-scale catches, as in the Norwegian winter herring fishery."[14] Furthermore, with North Sea herring (*Clupea harengus*) stocks in decline from the 1940s until their ultimate collapse in the 1970s, German agriculturalists and other European consumers of herring fishmeal were forced to look elsewhere for protein-feed supplies.[15] Similarly, in the United States, where the West Coast sardine industry lay in ruins, the Atlantic and Gulf menhaden fisheries (*Brevoortia tyrannus* and *Brevoortia patronus*) that had typically supplied fishmeal producers in the Southeast were also evincing signs of overfishing by the mid-1960s. Amid a "serious decline" in the "great menhaden resources adjacent to our shores," the director of the US National Fish Meal and Oil Association requested that fisheries scientist Wilbert

Chapman speak at an upcoming symposium in order to "tell the dramatic story of the great fish potential of the worlds [sic] oceans and the contribution to foods through feeds that is potentially possible from this source.... It seems to me that it would be quite assuring to this audience, which is particularly interested in fish meals for use in poultry feeds."[16] Other Latin American nations, inspired by Peru's boom, including Chile and Mexico, also began to attract foreign investment and build up their fishmeal production and export capacity.[17]

Wilbert Chapman held a PhD in fisheries biology from the University of Washington, and built his career working for various state, national, and international agencies, later becoming an outspoken representative of private California fishery interests from 1951 to 1969.[18] Well known for his sense of wit and a mastery of language that he employed in many forums, Chapman spoke widely about the potential contributions of industrial fishing around the world. He also believed that the rightful role of science and government was to serve the needs of US fishing companies.[19] He sought to build strategic collaborations during his time as an industry executive: "Probably the thing that is of the most long range importance to the Ralston-Purina fish business on a global basis that I am involved with is gently crowding the U.S. Navy and the U.S. Bureau of Commercial Fisheries into a working relationship which will make the results of the enormous environmental research program of the Navy in the world ocean practically available to the fish business."[20] Having served in the Bureau of Economic Warfare in the Central and South Pacific theaters during 1943–44, Chapman had a keen understanding of the range and scope of oceanographic data these US agencies had collected. Japan's World War Two defeat created new opportunities for California firms to expand into the Central and Western Pacific.[21] But as a fishing company executive during the latter years of his career, Chapman's claims about the potential for virtually limitless growth in global fisheries were decidedly optimistic, offering rhetorical justification for the continued expansion of these firms into new fishing grounds around the world.

At a 1964 conference of California industry representatives, Chapman proclaimed that during the 1950s, the state's fishing industry had responded to the challenges of foreign competition by expanding "sharply as to production but even more broadly and basically in a geographical and political sense." He emphasized that the industry was already "operating on substantially a global basis," and cited large contributions that local firms made to the total US fishery landings. Highlighting their vested role in Peru's rapid expansion, he further suggested that the landings in Peru that year might exceed those of the traditional long-distance fishing nation of Norway.[22] Wherever California industry had expanded, Chapman proudly noted, researchers from top institutions such as the Scripps Institution of Oceanography (SIO, affiliated with the University of California at San Diego) had preceded. At the same time, he made a plea for Californian authorities to lift the restriction on utilizing North Pacific anchovies (*Engraulis mordax*) for fishmeal—a regulation that had been put into place in 1949 in order to prevent a repetition of the sardine scenario—urging that it was the only way to make the industry profitable against Peruvian producers.[23]

Peruvian fishmeal producers had made it clear in the 1960 Paris meeting that they recognized—and intended to fully exercise—the power they held in controlling the production, commercialization, and global market supply of their irreplaceable product. Domestically, too, ownership and market control of the sector remained in the hands of a few industrialists. Most of them were Peruvian nationals who did not come from the country's "traditional" landed elites. Many of the fishmeal enterprises were ventures that included some amount of foreign capital.[24] In 1968, the top twenty firms in Peru operated 54 of the 120 active plants and produced 67 percent of the fishmeal. Luis Banchero Rossi, a Peruvian entrepreneur whose other holdings also included ownership of major newspapers, operated eight fishmeal plants at the height of the boom years, accounting for 13.2 percent of the country's total production.[25]

Both the National Fishing Society (Sociedad Nacional de Pesquería, SNP, a trade association) and the Fishing Consortium of Peru (Consorcio Pesquero del Perú, CPP, a cooperative marketing group) represented the interests of the large industrialists and effectively monopolized the production and sale of fishmeal, to the distinct disadvantage of smaller firms.[26] Peruvian critics complained that government policy makers "only listen to the industrialist Banchero, who doesn't represent all of the sector."[27] They claimed that foreign intermediaries earned windfall profits from the country's most valuable resource by brokering imports and exports elsewhere. Furthermore, representatives of government and industry openly clashed with Banchero on the question of foreign capital investment in Peru's fisheries—one deputy stated in 1967 that up to 60 percent of all foreign capital was linked to the sector.[28] "Hamburg passes through Peru in order to concentrate all of its marketing power in Paris," decried one editorial in the Lima periodical *Oiga*.[29] Hamburg, Germany, was (and remains today) one of the world's primary export-import markets for fishmeal and oil, and a major port of entry for shipments to other parts of the country and the rest of continental Europe. During the 1960s, ongoing tensions over the role of foreign capital and the concentration of ownership in the sector overshadowed scientific, policy, and macroeconomic debates in Peru.

THE LIMITS TO GROWTH: SCIENCE, POLICY, AND THE BUSINESS OF PERUVIAN ANCHOVETA MANAGEMENT, 1960–1976

The feeding habits and interrelationships among species in the Humboldt Current ecosystem were active areas of research among international teams of scientists well before the 1960s. "The best of the fisheries management scientists in 1947–48 were already keenly aware of what they needed to learn in areas where they had little or no data—on problems such as interspecies competition," relationship of populations to upwelling, nutrients, and other oceanic conditions.[30] Yet the complexity of this region's food webs posed an ongoing challenge to scientists: more than twenty years later, in a 1969 letter, the California-based marine scientist Milner B. Schaefer noted his continued desire to examine the relative proportion of phytoplankton to zooplankton in the anchoveta's diet as one of the keys to "understanding the trophodynamics of the Peru Current, since the anchoveta is so dominant."[31]

While business groups sought to stabilize the supply, demand, and price of fishmeal and other commodities, the entire global system had become increasingly vulnerable to large-scale shifts in climate, influenced by intricate oceanographic systems on multiple scales. Researchers since the 1950s have systematically recorded sea surface temperatures (SST) in specific zones of the Pacific in order to identify and monitor El Niño conditions as they unfold.[32] However, the phenomenon is fundamentally unpredictable because of its slow development over a period of months, and the variations of temperatures across a wide area of the Eastern Tropical Pacific.

Certain voices in Peru appealed loudly for state protection of anchoveta stocks, even before the fishmeal boom began. Their arguments often emphasized the long-term potential of the species as a renewable resource. In September 1954, members of the Peruvian National Committee for Environmental Protection printed an open letter to the Peruvian minister of agriculture in the Lima newspaper *La Nación*, calling on the government to fulfill its "fundamental duty" to protect the stability of Peru's marine ecosystem. They noted that the interdependence among species hinged upon a "natural dynamic equilibrium" within the "biome" of which humans were an integral part.[33] In their use of such terminology, the committee demonstrated its recognition of the complex processes and linked prior interactions operating within the marine ecosystem to the formal application of management practices that took such interactions into account. The committee's letter also insisted on humans' ability to dramatically disrupt natural processes with unforeseen secondary and tertiary effects.[34] Failure to protect the *Engraulis ringens* could lead to a "true disaster," it argued, as had already happened in California; on the other hand, if the fishery were properly regulated by the state, this "renewable resource" could nourish the Peruvian people while also sustaining numerous profitable enterprises for the benefit of the country.[35]

The writer Francisco Pulgar Vidal made a similar appeal in a 1959 editorial, in which he advocated state control of the fishery in order to protect the "wealth" (*riqueza*) of resources offshore, which, he claimed, "if utilized intelligently, will yield ongoing benefits, without danger of extinction or impoverishment."[36] Both articles pleaded for state intervention in the anchoveta fishery, echoing scientists' decades-long concerns about overfishing. But Pulgar Vidal's comments also revealed a flawed but common assumption about fisheries management, namely that scientists and policy makers were capable of successfully designing and implementing regulatory mechanisms that avoided disrupting the equilibrium of the marine ecosystem while still allowing fishers to commercially exploit the fisheries. In fact, regulations have proven an ineffective means of influencing the behavior of governments and fishermen. In any case, the demands for regulatory controls went largely unanswered during the first phase of the exponential growth of Peru's fishmeal industry.

By the mid-1960s, however, it was clear that fish populations along the coast fluctuated dramatically, but unpredictably, every few years. Even the largest producers recognized the enormous risk posed to their vertically integrated operations (and the value of their futures contracts) if the anchoveta fishery were to fail, or even to fall short in any one strategic coastal zone. Max Cohen, an executive at the International Proteins Corporation, recalled the anxiety he felt concerning the uncertain dynamics of the Peruvian marine ecosystem after spending a year and a half in Huacho during the mid-1960s: "When the subject of a completely new fishery with so many unknowns comes up, I get cold chills thinking about the ways in Peru right in the middle of the season when a thousand boats with the best equipment and crews came back empty for a week." Recognizing the devastating impact of these events, together with the uncertainty created by shifting government policies during times of regime change, the International Proteins Corporation shifted much of its capital to other fisheries frontiers outside Peru prior to the 1972 collapse, confident that there "must be two or three other 'Perus' around the world."[37]

Other industrialists spread their risk against this variability by making considered calculations about how best to distribute their fleets along the coast, particularly in relation to the location of each processing plant, the time of year, and the capacity of each vessel. An executive at the Peruvian subsidiaries of Van Camp reported to his colleagues after collecting several months of data that the optimal way to build their fleet was to have a "mixture of capacities," particularly on the central coast of Peru. "The problem is that when the bases are loaded everybody hits home runs. The home runs with bases empty are few and far between which is the time we need them."[38] In other words, even though some boats would remain idle at certain times due to local conditions, the differentiated size and location of the vessels would allow the greatest flexibility of the fleet in the case of recurring and unpredictable fluctuations in fish stocks.

Even without state regulations in place, then, fishing firms took steps to adjust their behavior according to the uncertain conditions. Biologists affiliated with US and international institutions (SIO, CalCOFI, FAO), along with their Peruvian counterparts at the Marine Resources Research Institute (Instituto del Mar del Peru, IMARPE), held numerous international conferences to discuss their latest research. Comparing data they had collected across fishing seasons between 1962 and 1964, these scientists processed and interpreted their results using the latest tagging methods and mathematical models. They struggled to ascertain the precise relationship between fishing pressure and the rate of recruitment of juvenile anchoveta into adult populations (necessary since sexually immature juveniles cannot reproduce), and to predict the impact of low recruitment on the anchoveta's ability to recover in subsequent years. They were also perplexed by the relatively different rates of abundance off Chimbote (Peru's most important fishing port), Callao, and Ilo.[39]

These localized variations in the productivity of the Humboldt Current marine ecosystem were related to the dynamics of its three upwelling subsystems: the first located off Chimbote, the second in the area near the Peru-Chile border between Ilo and Arica, and thirdly, farther south off the Chilean coast. Yet among the specialists studying the population dynamics of the anchoveta, there was no consensus on exactly what steps should be taken to avert the ecological catastrophe that many observers had warned could be imminent. To be sure, fishmeal industrialists (both Peruvian and foreign) had a proven reputation for resisting the imposition of any measures that would cut into their profits. Banchero frequently criticized the government for excessive taxation of the fishing sector and its failure to support industry's growth through credits and loans, which they knew the private sector enjoyed in Chile.[40] Others (Banchero excluded) resisted the imposition of an additional tax specifically to help fund IMARPE's research, which was especially needed as the FAO prepared to transfer administration of the institute to Peruvian staff in 1963–64.[41]

Reflecting on his prior experiences with Icelandic herring, FAO fisheries scientist Hermann Einarsson believed firmly in the need for thorough research into the relationship between fish populations and oceanic conditions. Einarsson, who was then stationed at IMARPE in Callao, felt that the 1963–64 catch had portended a "pretty gloomy" forecast for the 1965 anchoveta fishery. The high number of juveniles (*peladilla*) being harvested, he feared, would prevent the fish from reproducing in sufficient numbers to sustain ongoing fishing pressure.[42] At the same time, Einarsson and other scientists at IMARPE were aware of their relative lack of influence on Peruvian government officials—already skeptical of international interventions in local affairs—who hoped to protect an important source of state revenue.[43] "The Institute is without any power and the best we can hope is that our basic work may serve as a guide for those who can influence the industry," he lamented. "Only the big companies and their advicers [*sic*] may be able to negotiate some sort of regulation."[44]

The year 1965 nonetheless became a turning point in the Peruvian state's management of the anchoveta, after which it enacted a number of measures to limit the fishery.[45] During the early months of the 1965 fishing season, SNP representatives (including Banchero, Elguera, and others) met with IMARPE scientists to discuss their concerns over the lack of effective controls on the fishery and the continued predominance of *peladilla* among the landings.[46] The government soon implemented the first *veda* (seasonal closure) of the fishery during the winter months of June–August.[47] To the south, in the waters off Chile, oceanographic conditions associated with the 1965 El Niño dramatically impacted the fishmeal industry. Although these conditions had little immediate effect on total Peruvian anchoveta landings because of the highly productive zone off Chimbote, there was a major decline in Humboldt Current guano bird populations (cormorants, gannets, and pelicans).[48]

On the other hand, an *economic* crisis occurred in the Peruvian fishmeal sector over the next two years, as production costs exceeded the global market price of fishmeal. This was due not to an ecological shift but to the industry's own limited commitment to upgrading factories. In a context of windfall profits during the early part of the decade, the average output of fishmeal in Peru was limited by outdated processing equipment, despite the availability of more efficient technology. This reduced the profit margins of many firms and made them unable to withstand the drop in world market prices that occurred in 1967.

The ensuing economic crisis in turn increased pressure on fish stocks to supply even more quantities of fishmeal for export—an economic-ecological feedback loop that tends to occur even when policy measures are in place, as governments are pressured by the threat of unrest to relieve the socioeconomic impacts not only on the industrialists but also on the workers, who are the most affected by such downturns.[49] Peruvian authorities limited fishing activities to five days per week in 1967 in attempts to protect the reproductive capacity of anchoveta stocks.[50] The ecological impact of these measures was unclear, since anchoveta landings continued to fluctuate. By 1968, the proportion of young anchoveta (less than 12 cm in length) to the total catch had risen to 62 percent, from the 14 percent observed six years prior.[51]

Nonetheless, the Peruvian anchoveta fishery had not yet reached its peak landings. In the 1969–70 season, the catch climbed to eleven million tons, despite the fishery's early closure in May 1970. In a mid-year report to the Peruvian government, a panel of FAO fisheries scientists warned that "there are grounds for fearing that there will be little of the stock left [in the September–December 1970 season] and, if this is followed by a poor year-class entering the fishery, some very bitter fruits of excess capacity will be harvested in 1971."[52] The report emphasized the overcapacity of both fishmeal processing (at forty-eight million tons per year and over eight thousand tons per hour) and the anchoveta fleet (78% larger than needed for the estimated "maximum sustainable yield" of 9.5 million tons). It also discussed the potential impact of a variety of measures: a 20 percent reduction in fishing effort using quotas for both plants and vessels; an increase in the efficiency of fishmeal processing through newer technology (a strategy that Chilean producers successfully implemented); and a redistribution and relocation of plants along the coast.[53] "The status quo will not maintain itself," the panel cautioned, urging action in order to avert disaster for the industry.[54]

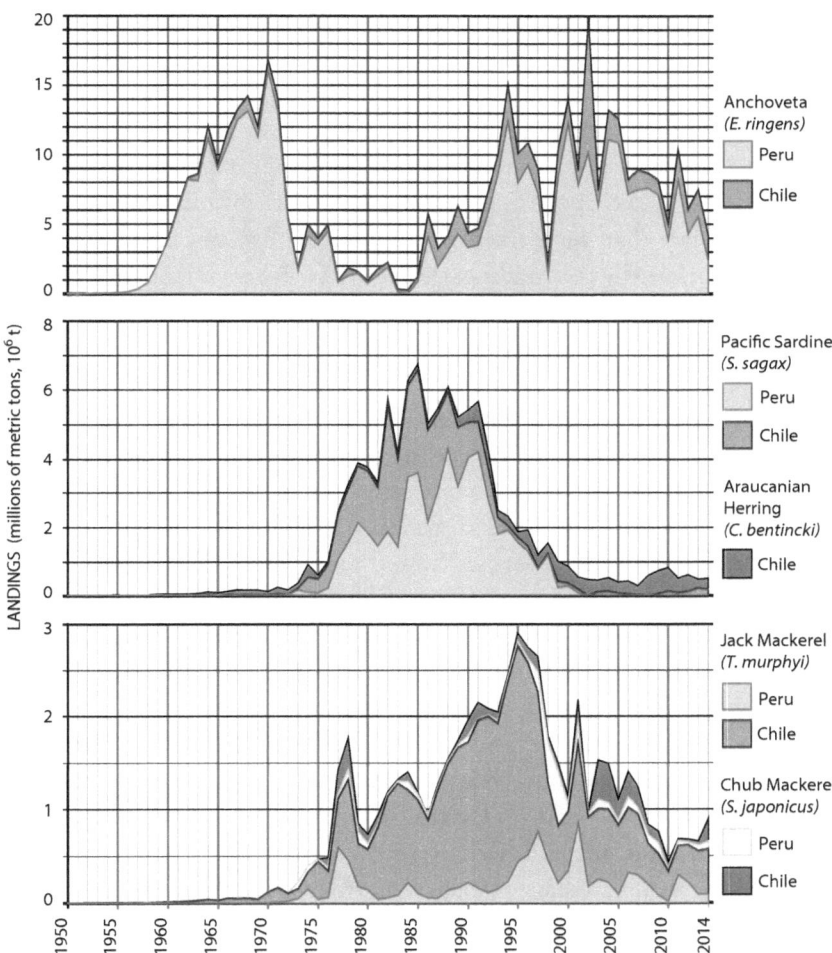

FIGURE 11. Principal reduction fisheries of the Humboldt Current ecosytem, 1950–2014. Graph by the author. *Sources:* Reconstructed catch data from *Sea Around Us*, ed. D. Pauly and D. Zeller (www.seaaroundus.org, 2017). For Chile, see also L. Van der Meer, et al., "Reconstruction of Total Marine Fisheries Catches for Mainland Chile (1950–2010)," University of British Columbia Fisheries Centre, Working Paper #2015-91 (2015): 1–15. For Peru, see also J. Mendo and C. Wosnitza-Mendo, "Reconstruction of Total Marine Fisheries Catches for Peru: 1950–2010," University of British Columbia Fisheries Centre, Working Paper #2014-21 (2014): 1–23.

For the revolutionary government of General Juan Velasco Alvarado, which took power in 1968, the fishing industry was of less concern to the new anti-imperialist agenda than the foreign-dominated oil sector, which the regime nationalized immediately. When the new minister of fisheries, General Javier Tantaleán Vanini, was sworn into office in February 1970, he declared that year that the fishing industry would not meet the same fate, despite the fact that the marketing of both fresh fish and fishmeal/oil had been expropriated by the middle of that year.[55] He reiterated the government's intent to continue expanding the industry, with greater attention to the socioeconomic goals of a more equitable distribution of its profits among fishermen and workers, as well as the promotion of the food-fish industry. "Our fisheries policy is clear, since it is based on the maximum exploitation of [our] hydrobiological resources, but with an adequate scientific control ... in such a way that its extraction, processing, and marketing favors this country that so needs it, and [also] the world in general."[56] However, since all available resources and scholarly expertise had previously focused exclusively on the anchoveta, there was a general lack of information concerning other marketable species in Peruvian waters. This limited experts' ability to make recommendations about reorienting the industry toward food production.[57]

In a marked departure from the previous era, when the Peruvian government had played a relatively limited centralized role in fisheries policy making apart from taxation, the Velasco government's comprehensive five-year Fisheries Plan (*Plan Pesquero*) for 1971–1975 included fifty policy objectives spanning all areas of the fisheries sector: research, extraction, processing, marketing, taxation, credit, management, training, and social programs.[58] The 1971 General Fisheries Law was the Peruvian government's first significant attempt to control the industry, but many of its measures conflicted with the goal of resource conservation.[59] The law established cooperatives (*comunidades pesqueras*) for worker co-participation in all private and state-owned enterprises, stipulating that 20 percent of profits be distributed among the employees, and a 1972 decree guaranteed job security for workers in the food-fish industry.[60] The Ministry of Fisheries (*Ministerio de Pesquería*, MIPE) built fish market complexes (*terminales pesqueros*) in various towns order to improve local fish distribution.[61] Additionally, Peru contracted with foreign governments, including the Soviet Union, Cuba, and Poland, to allow factory trawlers to operate off the Peruvian coast in exchange for supplying fish to the local population. Japanese trading firms Mitsui and Mitsubishi also invested in boatbuilding and fish processing in Peru.[62] These measures, based primarily on socioeconomic considerations, contributed to General Tantaleán's poor legacy in the stewardship of Peruvian marine resources.

Between 1970 and the end of 1971, industrialists were permitted to continue fishing at record rates even after surpassing the quota that had been established. MIPE officials perhaps hoped that high catches would indicate their competence and success amid criticism of the agency's bloated bureaucracy and questionable management practices.[63] However, in the first few months of 1972, it became apparent that the arrival of El Niño coincided with the start of the fishing season. Anchoveta landings declined precipitously throughout April and May—the much-feared ecological catastrophe had finally arrived. Nonetheless, the Peruvian government allowed the bolicheras to continue operating six days per week until June 30, against scientists' recommendations.[64] The ensuing collapse of the fishery was ruinous for both the industry and the marine ecosystem. As fishmeal firms and factories failed, displacing thousands of workers, the Velasco government kept them on the payroll and made loans to individual fishermen, aiming to alleviate the most extreme economic consequences. *Los Angeles Times* reporter David Belnap likened the event to the collapse of the California sardine industry in the 1940s.[65] Although the government partially lifted the fishing ban in March 1973, anchoveta remained scarce for more than a decade: populations did not recover enough to sustain significant industrial activity until the 1990s.

Finally, on May 7, 1973, the Velasco government nationalized the fishing industry, creating the enormous state enterprise PescaPerú.[66] In addition to Argentine, French, Norwegian, British, and Japanese companies, five US firms were expropriated in this measure: General Mills, Cargill, Heinz, Gold Kist, and International Proteins Corporation (IPC). The *New York Times* reported their combined total value (approximately one-third of the total fishing industry operating in Peru at the time), at US$40 million, even after IPC had withdrawn over $1 million from its subsidiary there amid rising political tensions.[67] PescaPerú remained nearly bankrupt for over a decade after its creation, maintaining an estimated twenty-seven thousand permanent workers, as boats and plants remained idle.[68] It also absorbed the sizeable debt that fishmeal producers incurred following the anchoveta collapse, 58 percent of which was owed to the Peruvian National Bank (Banco Nacional).[69] It was a controversial decision, though not altogether disagreeable to the industrial debtors. "The Peruvian people were obligated to absolve the deficits and privileges of these business elites," complained one newspaper

FIGURE 12. Industrial purse seiners in El Ferrol Bay, Chimbote, Peru (2009). Photo by the author.

editorial.[70] Citing the 1970 FAO report, whose authors had placed heavy emphasis on socioeconomic considerations in their evaluation of the various regulatory measures on fishermen and small producers, government leaders insisted that this step was necessary in order to protect the non-elites from the devastating impact of the industry's collapse.[71] "There was no other way," said a solemn Minister Tantaleán, appearing on the cover of the Lima weekly *Oiga*.[72] In 1976, the government announced the re-privatization of the bolichera fleet, causing outrage among the fishermen and establishing the first step in a protracted process that eventually displaced thousands of workers and smaller producers.[73]

While the crisis-ridden industry languished with aging equipment and excess capacity, the Peruvian government continued to focus its efforts on promoting fish for human consumption throughout the 1970s and 1980s by improving local infrastructure.[74] Public health programs and marketing campaigns promoted the consumption of sardines, anchoveta, and other species.[75] However, in the late 1970s, many canned products were exported to South Africa, suggesting that domestic markets did not provide the hoped-for returns.

Peruvian authorities were also wary of Chile's rising prominence as a fishmeal producer. Fishermen complained that Chilean fleets were harvesting anchoveta populations that straddled the maritime frontier, while in Peru the fishery was officially closed to industrial fleets in order to allow for the stocks' recovery.[76] At the same time, observers in 1980 noted the increased presence of sardine, jack mackerel, and chub mackerel in Peruvian waters, which became the new targets of industrial fleets, ostensibly for human consumption. But Peruvian technology in both harvesting and processing continued to lag behind its competitors. The state therefore developed partnerships with other fishing nations in order to increase production: in the early 1980s, Germany funded 60 percent of the cost for a new research vessel, the *Humboldt*, to explore deep-water fisheries; agreements with the USSR allowed Soviet factory trawlers to operate in Peruvian waters while supplying a small percentage of their landings (up to 15%) to domestic markets.[77] In 1987, a new General Fisheries Law reiterated the government's attention to social welfare.[78] Although this law also stressed the "rational" exploitation of fisheries resources, by the end of the decade, the impact of the factory fleets on the seafloor off Peru's northern coast was devastating.[79]

During the 1980s, another major industry emerged as a significant source of demand for "reduced" fish proteins, especially fish oil: salmon aquaculture. Peruvian producers took notice of this trend, and by 1989, Peru was the second-largest fish oil producer after Japan.[80] However, without the recovery of its anchoveta stocks, Peru did not return to its prime position in world fishmeal markets until the 1990s. At the same time, the election of Alberto Fujimori to the presidency (1990–1998) began an era of neoliberal reforms, including the re-privatization of the plants that had been taken over by the state enterprise PescaPerú, which opened new possibilities for international capital. In 1992, Peru's third General Fisheries Law promoted foreign investment and further institutionalized a free-market approach.[81] Industrialists finally began upgrading old equipment with international capital from Germany, Denmark, and China, among others, as well as investing in a renovated fishing fleet, as anchoveta stocks began to rebound during the 1990s.[82] By the end of the decade, private capital had reconsolidated within the sector, and Peru reclaimed its status as the leader of anchoveta-based fishmeal production.

SIX

The Translocal History of Industrial Fisheries in Iquique and Talcahuano, Chile

IN THE EARLY 1970S, researchers were perplexed by the "abrupt discontinuities" and "flip flops" they observed in several of the world's fish populations.[1] They debated the causality of dynamic interspecies interrelationships while they were unfolding: In the Humboldt Current region, Pacific sardines (*Sardinops sagax*) became more abundant following the 1972 anchoveta (*Engraulis ringens*) fishery collapse. In the Northwest Pacific, Japanese sardines (*Sardinops melanostictus*) also rapidly increased during the 1970s while anchovies declined.[2] Observers also noticed sardine-anchovy correlations off the coasts of California and West Africa.[3] Were these species competitors within their respective ecosystems, or were their population fluctuations linked more fundamentally to large-scale environmental dynamics? Scientists eventually confirmed a global pattern of synchronicity among sardines and anchovies, in which the species alternate in abundance every few decades.[4]

Peruvian and Chilean responses to local oceanographic conditions led to distinctive historical outcomes for fishmeal producers in these two nations. The Chilean fishmeal industry was severely impacted by the 1965 El Niño, but relatively less affected by the 1972 event that so devastated the Peruvian anchoveta fishery to the north. While Peru's single-species industry struggled for nearly two decades to recover from the anchoveta collapse, a multispecies industry supplied Chilean fishmeal factories, facilitating continued flows to protein-hungry global markets. By the end of 1980, Chile had surpassed Peru as the world's leading fishmeal producer, exporting 40 percent of its supplies that year to Germany.[5]

After the 1972 fishery collapse, the once-massive anchoveta schools were absent from Peruvian waters, but new populations of anchoveta and jack mackerel soon concentrated in two regions easily accessible to Chilean industrialists:

in the "upwelling shadow" along the Peru-Chile border, near the city of Iquique; and off the central-south coast, near Talcahuano.[6] As labor, capital, and technology moved between these and other fishing ports, Iquique and Talcahuano became two of Chile's premier industrial cities, their trajectories linked partly to the ebbs and flows of the Humboldt Current.

The intertwined yet divergent histories of these two cities illuminates the translocal connections among fishmeal industry hubs along the coast of Chile between the 1960s and late 1990s as fleets relocated to follow shifting fish populations. While Iquique transitioned from nineteenth-century nitrate mining to fishmeal production after 1960 and eventually to tourism, Talcahuano ultimately became the most important industrial and fish processing center on the Chilean coast. Fishing fleets based in Iquique were well-positioned to exploit stocks near the Peru-Chile border region as well as the central-south zone of the Humboldt Current (18–30°S). Scientists later identified a distinctive, sardine-dominated phase in the marine ecosystem between 1970 and 1985; their southward migration led to peak landings off Chile and southern Peru during the early 1980s, while catches off north and central Peru remained low.[7] After 1974, abundant jack mackerel populations drew more industrialists toward Talcahuano, further solidifying its position as Chile's primary fishmeal port. Talcahuano thus became a steel- and fishmeal-producing hub—the Chimbote of Chile—while Iquique restyled itself as a tourist destination, boasting sandy shores, oceanside restaurants, and a duty-free shopping zone.

On the whole, Chilean fishmeal producers were able to thrive because of the industry's ability to exploit distinct fish populations as they shifted in density, quantity, and spatial distribution along the coast. The state also shaped the economic and political geographies of the fisheries by taking over private debts in times of crisis (as the Corporación para el Fomento, CORFO, did following the 1965 El Niño), and later by facilitating the consolidation of industry ownership among wealthy elites (as General Augusto Pinochet did with neoliberal policies during the 1970s and '80s). However, in this transnational "race for fish," the unpredictable and irremediable consequences of El Niño posed a persistent challenge, leading to catastrophe once again in 1997–98. The decisive yet differentiated role of climatological variations in the process of industrialization along the Peru-Chile coast sheds light on the complex relationships among human societies and their environments— relationships whose historical intricacies are easily lost in studies limited to an exclusively local, national, or global frame.

TRANSLOCAL ECOLOGIES IN IQUIQUE AND TALCAHUANO BEFORE 1960

Near the twenty-first-century maritime frontier between Peru and Chile, the course of the northward-flowing cold current curves slightly to the west, echoing the continent's elbow-shaped western edge. Along with the guano-covered islets offshore, the vast coastal plains and inland *altiplano* (high plain) of the Atacama had supplied enormous quantities of nitrogen for the emerging agricultural and warfare industries of North America and Europe throughout the nineteenth century. The desert's "caliche ore" provided cheap supplies of sodium nitrate for the production of fertilizer, gunpowder (potassium nitrate), sulfuric acid, and other chemicals ranging from powerful new explosives (nitroglycerine) to "superphosphates," thus helping to fuel the "fertilizer revolution of the mid-nineteenth century."[8] William Bollaert and George Smith, who surveyed the region under commission from the Peruvian government in 1827–28, described the details of the ecological impacts of colonial-era mining: the small areas of living woodlands were extinct by 1852, and up to eight thousand draft animals annually traversed the Pampas between northern Argentina and the Atacama, consuming desert grasses as well as imported feedstocks, their skeletons accumulating across wide areas of the rocky earthen terrain.[9] After visiting the region in the early twentieth century, US ornithologist Frank Chapman wrote that "the excessive aridity which prevails in this region renders it almost lifeless."[10] By the end of the 1920s, the Haber-Bosch process for synthesizing ammonia had finally displaced Chilean nitrates in global markets. The industry that had helped to transform the Atacama "into a dead desert waste" left once-booming towns across the *pampa* abandoned to nostalgic memorials.[11]

Following the War of the Pacific (1879–83), the governments of Chile, Peru, and Bolivia bitterly disputed their terrestrial borders for decades. In 1929, Chile and Peru signed the Treaty of Lima, returning Tacna and land to its north to Peruvian control, and ceding the territory south of Arica, including the mineral-rich provinces of Tarapacá and Antofagasta, to Chile.[12] In this hyper-arid landscape, thick marine fog (*la camanchaca*) blanketed the rainless coast almost daily for six to eight months of the year, and the coastal waters teemed with fish.[13] Robert Cushman Murphy noted that Alacrán, an islet off Arica, was in some seasons "black with Guanays." The islet was also their southernmost known colony, although by Murphy's estimation (writing in 1936), they had been spotted as far south as the Gulf of Arauco (c. 37°S), near the port of Talcahuano.[14]

FIGURE 13. Boats in Iquique, Chile, harbor (1907). From the American Geographical Society Library, University of Wisconsin–Milwaukee Libraries.

The Bío Bío River empties into the Gulf of Arauco just south of Talcahuano. The river had marked the boundary of the indigenous territory of Araucanía during the long Arauco War (1536–1883), as the Mapuche peoples fought against encroaching Spanish and Chilean forces for control of the land and southern archipelago.[15] In the south of Chile, moisture along the windward slope of the Andes formed dense temperate forests, and coastal estuaries supported ecosystems rich with shellfish—a terrain that contrasted starkly with the bleak desert-scape of Tarapacá and the Atacama region. Situated on a peninsula between Concepción Bay and the smaller San Vicente Bay just north of the Bío Bío, Talcahuano had been a nineteenth-century port of call for merchant ships, explorers seeking adventure in the South Pole, Forty-Niners seeking fortunes in California, and whalers—including both local and long-distance fleets, traversing the South Pacific—the latter until well after World War Two.[16] In the nineteenth century, coal mines in the adjacent towns of Coronel and Lota supplied fuel to steamships and to the sodium nitrate refineries in Tarapacá.[17] Travelers entering the port encountered "green mountainsides, broken here and there by a patch of corn or wheat, or possibly by a few rows of fruit trees clinging to the slopes—slopes so steep that all on them seemed about to tumble into the bay and cover the thousands of waterfowl that crowded its waters." With arable land and abundant marine resources offshore, by 1849, in the words of historian John J. Johnson: "Talcahuano was a boom town; money flowed freely; it looked good to many, some stayed."[18] While Iquique was a center of mining, this southern coastal town became a regional hub for fishing and trade.

Talcahuano was by the early twentieth century one of the country's most important seaports, surrounded by smaller *caletas* (fishing wharves) and operating as a commercial gateway along the route between the far south and the more populated central regions of Chile. Fish processors there supplied markets as far away as Santiago, a nine-hour journey by truck. As a business and industry hub, Talcahuano, like Chimbote and Iquique, was also a regional center for organizing among fishermen. In 1911, lacking a pier, Talcahuano fishermen requested that the state concede a dedicated zone along the beach for unloading their catch.[19] But problems of infrastructure persisted, even as the state sought to increase industrial activity; in 1928, at the invitation of the Chilean government, Hamburg-based researchers arrived in the area to experiment with new trawling technologies offshore.[20]

The first National Convention of Fishermen met in Talcahuano in 1936. Reporting on the event, US Consul General Edward Dow noted that community members were dissatisfied with the lack of infrastructure and aspired to increase their commercial production. They were prepared to present a set of demands to the Chilean president, seeking government funds for housing construction, credits for building ports, and improvement of infrastructure to better provide freezing and cold storage for fish products. They even proposed the establishment of no-liquor zones around landing areas, and "the founding of colonies composed of fishermen who give part of their time to farming and gardening," attesting to the importance of local subsistence practices and quality of life among the imagined goals of development prior to industrialization.[21]

Talcahuano-based fishermen harvested modest quantities of small pelagic fish, primarily Araucanian herring (*Clupea bentincki*) and anchoveta (*Engraulis ringens*) within sixty miles of the coast, although the most important species for artisanal fishers at the time were *sierra* (*Thyrsites atun*) and hake (*Merluccius gayi gayi,* or "*merluza*").[22] In 1941, the Arauco Fishing Company (*Compañía Pesquera Arauco*), with assistance from CORFO, also began landing hake with deep-water trawlers.[23] Despite government- and

FIGURE 14. Fish drying in Talcahuano, Chile (1930). From the American Geographical Society Library, University of Wisconsin–Milwaukee Libraries.

FAO-sponsored campaigns designed to increase human consumption of these fish during the 1940s and '50s, the trawlers' yield far exceeded local market demand—especially given the lack of infrastructure for preservation and distribution—leaving the surplus to be "reduced" to fishmeal.[24]

Along Chile's northern maritime frontier with Peru, where the Italian-born businessman Anacleto Angelini established his first fishmeal venture in 1956, relations were increasingly strained by the transgressions of fleets that strayed too far north in pursuit of the densest schools.[25] US fisheries scientist and industry executive Wilbert Chapman highlighted the abundance of fish species in the angle between Iquique and Ilo, in southern Peru, between fifteen and eighty miles off the coast—but he concluded that the schools of tuna, as well as the species on which they foraged, were generally more numerous to the north of the Peruvian border.[26] FAO scientist Ivan Popovich similarly observed that the "best fishing area for Arica . . . would be north in Peruvian waters," noting a concentration of fish in an eddy off the coast of Ilo.[27] A 1954 tripartite agreement between Peru, Chile, and Ecuador established a "tolerance zone" of ten miles on each side of the maritime border in order to minimize fishing conflicts.[28] Chile's Ministry of Agriculture and Fisheries warned its nationals not to "violate Peruvian waters," but these interventions did not appear to deter them, as Chilean officials continued to receive complaints of infringements by Angelini-owned fleets thereafter.[29] These scuffles underscored the strategic importance of the resources in this offshore zone, a source of persistent diplomatic tensions until a formal resolution was reached in 2014.[30] One Lima-based newspaper repeated the oft-cited anxiety surrounding foreign competition for species in a fluid ecosystem: "Effectively, the hydrobiological masses are migratory. They do not wait for the fisherman. They follow their course and if they are not taken by the Peruvian [bolichera], they go on to become fishmeal, oil, dividends, and development in Chile or in Ecuador."[31]

From 1951 to 1959, Chile's fishmeal production tripled, by which time there were thirty "reduction" factories operating along the coast.[32] In 1959, Iquique surpassed Talcahuano as the country's primary fishing port.[33] The domestic market for fishmeal also expanded tenfold in the same period, owing almost entirely to its use in poultry feeds.[34] Still, a 1960 report from the US Embassy in Santiago on Chilean fisheries noted the fishmeal industry's lack of raw material, despite well-equipped factories.[35] CORFO general manager Humberto Díaz remarked that in the waters near Arica, "important fishing enterprises … have an abundance of raw material during eight months of the year," leading him to conclude "without fear of error" that an equally successful fishing industry could be established by exploiting the "great potential fishery riches" near Iquique and Pisagua. He wrote of the tuna, "that move in great schools in search of food. If these species are not captured when they pass by our littoral, they go elsewhere without benefit to anyone."[36] His five-page memo went on to note the frequent presence of foreign tuna fleets just 100–150 miles off the Chilean coast.[37] On both sides of the Peru-Chile border, industrialists competed for access to resources that migrated without regard for legal or regulatory norms.

On March 25, 1960, CORFO announced its plan to "transform Iquique into the most important fishery port of Chile."[38] The Plan Pesquero subsidized new infrastructure, research, and loans for the construction of new plants, boats, and equipment.[39] Construction of at least nine new plants was also planned for the region.[40] When the international price of fishmeal plummeted due to the rapid increase in Peruvian exports by the end of the decade, this state support helped to avert bankruptcy for producers in northern Chile.[41] The balance of national industrial fisheries had shifted dramatically: while Talcahuano supplied 30–45 percent of Chile's industrial catch between 1950 and 1960, its share dropped suddenly to 11 percent in 1961 and 9 percent in 1962.[42] Iquique soon became the new center of Chile's fishmeal industry.

As fishmeal cargoes increased, new life came to the town with the flourishing export trade. City officials expanded Iquique's industrial sector (Barrio Industrial), including the construction of a warehouse to store fishmeal in transit, as well as space for new refrigeration facilities.[43] In 1963, *New York Times* columnist Edward C. Burks proclaimed that "Iquique has found new wealth in the sea," with ten plants in Iquique and fifty-six total across the three northern provinces (Tarapacá, Antofagasta, and Atacama).[44] The local newspaper *El Tarapacá* cheerily reported: "The port has presented in recent days a characteristic that is truly exciting, as never, in recent years, had there been more activity in shipments and landings."[45] The reporter reveled in the spectacle of various ships arriving in the port of Iquique to load their cargoes, predominantly of fishmeal and oil. Local institutions celebrated the economic boost this new industry brought to the languishing city. A resident of Iquique at the time, sociologist Bernardo Guerrero Jiménez, recalled that fishmeal was the fragrance that defined his city's identity during the 1960s—a "perfume of progress and riches"—in a time of newfound prosperity when fishermen and other workers from the sector flooded the city and enlivened its nightlife.[46] Burks, on the other hand, described a shantytown with makeshift residences: "Iquique's fishermen and fish meal workers live in wood shacks that can only be described as hovels."[47]

Ignoring the policy initiative that helped precipitate the economic resurgence, as well as the particular abundance of the marine ecosystem offshore, the *New York Times* attributed Chile's newfound industrial success to the arrival of imported technology, scientists, and international capital. The first American-style steel seiners were imported from Peru during the 1960s; others arrived from shipyards on the US West Coast and Europe, replacing the older, wooden fleet of *goletas* that operated through the end of the 1950s.[48] This new influx, the paper suggested, would update fishing practices with tools and knowledge that un-modern locals were implicitly ill-equipped to implement on their own. One article declared disparagingly that small-scale Chilean fishers, "who have carried out the tradition of their forefathers for centuries by sailing in their tiny boats, are no match for the modern fish-catchers."[49]

The fate of the nascent industry hinged on the continued presence of the pelagic schooling fishes that had until then flourished in coastal waters. "'Chile's maritime wealth is incalculable,'" remarked one German scientist in an interview with the *New York Times*, but he also warned against "'too great an increase'" in the region's anchoveta fishery.[50] Chilean authorities

FIGURE 15. Fishmeal plant in Arica, Chile (1965). From the American Geographical Society Library, University of Wisconsin–Milwaukee Libraries.

introduced Decree Law 524 in 1964, which established fishing permits and assigned annual harvest quotas, but the measure was not effectively implemented or enforced.[51] Harvesting and processing capacity was clearly overdeveloped following the frenzied period of investment, with the northern fleet reaching its maximum number of vessels in 1965 (251 in all), mostly dedicated to the harvest of anchoveta and sardine for fishmeal production.[52]

News of the abundant anchoveta schools also attracted investors from all over the world, eager to cash in on the boom: "Norwegian, South African, Canadian, Japanese, German, and other firms rushed to obtain concessions to install small plants," while Danish, Swedish, German, and US equipment filled Iquique's fishmeal factories.[53] In 1963 the "fishmeal king" of the US Gulf Coast, Harvey Smith, brought four *goletas*—as Chileans called US-style purse seiners used locally—for use in his majority-owned Chilean Fishing Company (Compañía Pesquera Chilena).[54] The US pharmaceutical concern Pfizer also expanded into Chilean anchoveta fishmeal production: the firm operated six fishing boats of its own by 1966, utilizing state-of-the-art echo-sounding technology, huge nets, and spotter planes to supply its Iquique

FIGURE 16. Men hauling sacks in a fishmeal plant, Coquimbo, Chile (1964). Unknown photographer. Archivo Zig-Zag/Quimantú, Colección Museo Histórico Nacional, Santiago, Chile.

plant with abundant raw materials.[55] The lure of a new resource frontier in the Southeast Pacific proved irresistible to this international mélange of capital, expertise, and technology during the period of rapid growth, though this romance would ultimately be short-lived.

In 1965, the arrival of El Niño's warmer waters led to the disappearance of the anchoveta from the northern coast of Chile. The 1965 event was not as catastrophic for Chilean fisheries as the 1972 El Niño would be for the single-species Peruvian fishmeal industry, but it thwarted the economic recovery efforts in the north, leaving bewildered local authorities with little recourse than to hope for their return. At least one firm responded to the crisis by switching to a new target species: Pesquera Eperva reached an agreement with its workers to fish for sardines in order to continue operating. But other companies' processing plants remained shuttered while workers went on strike.[56] With industrialists unable to pay their debts to the state, CORFO resolved to take over the ailing enterprises.

The ecological rupture of the 1965 crisis resonated throughout global commodity markets, leading speculators to engage in fishmeal futures trading in an effort to cash in on supply swings.[57] With that, distant capitalists incorporated the natural volatility of Humboldt Current fishmeal production into the profit-generating financial machinations of global commodity markets. But even while scientists and local officials knew that the anchoveta's disappearance was linked to the anomalous "warm current" off the coast, they lacked an understanding of the cyclical fluctuations within the ecosystem. Some observers speculated freely: a 1967 *Washington Post* article mistakenly suggested that the current's temperature changes stemmed from "earthquake tremors in the ocean bed."[58] The industry that had seven years prior seemed to "[hold] the promise of prosperity" instead brought yet another wave of economic ruin to the region. The collapse of the anchoveta fishery left local officials to seek other, more creative (if improbable) means of remedying their economic woes, such as remaking the city into a "divorce resort" that would ostensibly allow Chileans to circumvent the legal impossibility of divorce via a three-month residency in the northern city.[59]

Yet when the 1965 El Niño sent the northern industry into peril, firms and much of the fleet relocated to the central-south, where the industry continued its steady growth through the end of the decade.[60] The itinerant fishermen, some now captains of their own boats, also returned, seasoned by their experience working aboard the large northern seiners. During this initial period of industrial expansion, local shifts in fish populations shaped the development of the industry in Talcahuano, as industrialists adapted their gear to the shifting trophodynamics of the southern Humboldt Current ecosystem. By 1969 some vessels had replaced their fine-meshed anchoveta nets with others designed for jack mackerel, a larger and deeper-swimming migratory schooling species.[61] These and other technological adjustments allowed industrialists to capitalize steadily on multiple, fluctuating populations in a dynamic marine environment.

The state's role in fisheries management changed profoundly throughout the 1970s. During his brief tenure, Socialist president Salvador Allende Gossens (1970–1973) sought to increase the domestic supply of food fish by establishing a partnership between Chile's state-run Arauco Fishing Company and the USSR. A 1972 agreement allowed the Chilean government to lease four deep-sea trawlers in order to supply hake to local markets.[62] This program aimed to supplement the limited quantities of animal proteins available to consumers amid meat shortages, which had led authorities to restrict sales to only three days per week by March of that year.[63] However, these factory ships processed their catch into large blocks of frozen fish, which were ill-suited to both consumer preferences and the local infrastructure. Warehouses reportedly sat full of unsold fish blocks, eliciting ridicule in the international press.

After the September 1973 coup d'état removed Allende from power, the fishing industry underwent a process of consolidation. The neoliberal regime of General Augusto Pinochet reprivatized the firms that CORFO had taken over during the crisis of the late-1960s, selling fishmeal either as complete operations or as separate components of used machinery. Requests for the newly available equipment revealed the increasing environmental burden that fishmeal production brought upon local communities. Talcahuano's governor, Captain Fernando Carrasco Herrera wrote to CORFO executives expressing his urgent support for the request by a new local firm, Exportmar S.A., to purchase used equipment from a CORFO-owned northern plant that was being auctioned. Citing a "very old, grave, and progressive sanitation problem" of "bad smells that invade the city" and the "constant epidemics" that residents endured, Carrasco emphasized the need for pollution control mechanisms for the liquid effluents (*agua de cola,* or stickwater) that flowed from the city's fourteen fishmeal plants.[64] The requested machinery would divert untreated organic effluents away from the bay, while also allowing industrialists to recover the oil for further processing.

In 1976, El Niño again spurred a dramatic reduction in local fish stocks off Talcahuano, prompting a wave of migration of fishermen to the north.[65] "There was not a single fish here," one experienced fisherman from *caleta* San Vicente recalled in an interview, "[not] sardine, not anchoveta, not jack mackerel." He resolved to take his family north to Arica, traveling by boat along with others from San Vicente, only to discover upon arrival that their nets were unsuitable to the conditions there.[66] Worse, the schooling fishes they came to harvest disappeared from the northern seas.[67] "It went badly, badly for us. We didn't even have anything to eat, we had to go to the boats of the other companies, so they would give us something to eat, and we slept usually on the boat." After three months in Arica, the San Vicente fisherman recalled hearing a rumor that sardines (*Sardinops sagax*) and bonito (*Sarda chiliensis chiliensis*) were abundant off the coast of Coquimbo, a town in Chile's Norte Chico, and so he went there and eventually sent for his family. Although he did well in the fisheries after that, by 1977 a new, more intensive expansion was beginning to take hold of the Talcahuano fishing industry—so when a local firm bought a new boat a few months later and set off for the south, he hitched a ride.[68]

Toward the end of the 1970s, schools of jack mackerel (*Trachurus murphyi*) congregated unusually close to south-central Chilean shores.[69] These fish typically swim off the Chilean and Peruvian coast (2°N–51°S, 106°E–79°W) between ten and seventy meters of depth, migrating across a broad swath of the Pacific Ocean from the Humboldt Current upwelling, where they feed, to well beyond two hundred nautical miles from the coast.[70] Chilean scientists later concluded that after the mid-1970s, shifts in ocean currents and wind patterns affected the water temperature and upwelling system, which likely caused jack mackerel stocks to move toward the shore.[71] In closer proximity to the coast they were more accessible—and more visible to fishermen. These newly available schools, along with the increase in sardines that followed shortly thereafter, thus supported yet another phase of rapid growth, allowing Talcahuano to reclaim its position as the primary fishing port of Chile.

Large-scale regime shifts also affected the northern region of Chile's marine ecosystem. After 1973, whereas anchoveta populations had collapsed in northern Chile and Peru, Pacific sardines (*Sardinops sagax*) increased in abundance, while Araucanian herring (*Clupea bentincki*) populations declined. By 1979 jack mackerel and, secondarily, sardines became the two most exploited species in the central-south region. The same two species also dominated the (now reduced) northern fishery, but in reverse proportion—with sardine harvests greater than those of jack mackerel.[72] Overall, however, the high catch volumes of the latter, and its migrations between national and international waters, made it the most important fish—both commercially and politically—for Chilean industrialists beginning in this period.

The new importance of this species also increased the competition between Chilean producers and foreign vessels operating near the margins of territorial waters. In 1979 the Chilean government outlawed fishing by non-Chilean-flagged factory ships within the two-hundred-nautical-mile coastal zone.[73] Nonetheless, from 1978 to 1992, Soviet factory fleets fished heavily for jack mackerel outside the two hundred miles, while marine scientists investigated the possibility of a "mackerel belt" circling the Pacific or perhaps even "the entire Earth," collecting data from more than 150 oceanographic cruises.[74] In Chile, only a small portion of the catch typically went to the canneries—as one executive explained, "about a quarter of the jack mackerel is good for food. The rest will be sent to our fish meal factory."[75] Whether due to market demand or poor quality of the fish landed, the reduction and export of jack mackerel remained a primary engine of the Chilean fishmeal industry for nearly two decades.

In 1980 Chile surpassed Peru—where anchoveta stocks had not yet recovered—as the world's top producer of fishmeal, exporting 40 percent of its supplies that year to Germany.[76] Although Chile's industrial success was owed in large part to the increasing exploitation of jack mackerel off Talcahuano, the Peruvian press was quick to blame this development on fishery closures in the region near the Peru-Chile maritime boundary. "Chile has put itself at the head of world production of fishmeal," complained an article in the Lima newspaper *El Comercio*, "thanks to the advantage given by our *vedas* [fishery closures] along the southern coast."[77] Peruvian minister of fisheries Rene Deustua articulated the collective desire to harvest the straddling stocks before the Chileans could: "[T]he fish is migratory," he told an audience in Ilo, "and if we abstain from [fishing it] during the *veda*, it will simply fill the Chilean nets."[78] By 1981, the Peruvian government had lifted the *veda* for anchoveta along a 150-mile stretch of the southern coast near the Chilean border, in order to prevent their escape into the nets of the competition.[79] However, at the same time, Deustua also advocated a shift toward fisheries for human consumption. In the early 1980s the Peruvian government prohibited the processing of sardines into fishmeal—much like the regulations enacted in California following the anchovy collapse decades earlier—in order to reserve them for human consumption.[80] The explicitly socially oriented aims of the Peruvian regime clashed with the interests of industrialists, who generated higher profits by selling those proteins as feed commodities on global markets.

Under Pinochet's neoliberal regime (1973–89), by contrast, no such usage restrictions existed for sardines.[81] Chilean entrepreneurs such as Anacleto Angelini, Sergio and Roberto Sarquis, and Fernández y Cifuentes consolidated their fisheries interests into large business empires with enormous political influence during this era.[82] In the mid–1980s, 90 percent of the northern Chilean catch were sardines harvested within forty miles of the coast, from just south of Iquique to the northern limit at Arica—the same stocks that straddled the maritime border with Peru.[83] The frequent wanderings of Chilean fishing vessels across the maritime boundary compounded the tensions generated by Chile's rising status as a fishmeal producer, while Peruvian producers faced regulations that limited their own activities in the region.[84] Out-fished by its southern neighbor, where industrialists utilized a greater variety of species and were thus better able to adapt to the fluctuating fisheries regimes, the state-owned enterprise PescaPerú languished while waiting for the anchoveta to recover.[85]

Whereas PescaPerú was dismantled and reprivatized in a protracted process that began after 1976, leading to the sale of used boats and plants to Chile, Ecuador, and even California, Chilean fishmeal producers upgraded their harvesting and processing capacity, investing heavily in boats, machinery, nets, and other gear.[86] By 1979, fleets incorporated spotter planes and began to operate at night.[87] Chilean firms also began investing in new, Norwegian-style vessels, better suited to the long distances, deeper fishing, and rougher conditions in the southern waters.[88] In the central-south zone, eighteen Norwegian-style vessels operated as of 1985.[89] These "combination" models were equipped to fish with either purse nets for sardines, anchovies, and jack mackerel or mid-water trawl nets used mainly for jack mackerel—thereby increasing the adaptability of the fleet to shifting local ecologies.[90] In 1987 a new method for drying the fishmeal by using steam instead of direct heat increased the nutritional yield of the final product, which then increased its value and price on global commodity markets.[91] Chilean fishmeal producers thereby elevated their profile as producers of "prime" or "special-grade" fishmeal, while Peruvian technology remained largely outdated, forcing plants still working with greatly diminished supplies of fish to produce greater quantities of lower-value product in order to turn a profit.[92]

The booming fishing industry in Talcahuano supported a parallel, informal economy: the small-scale appropriation of fish from the industrial harvest. Talcahuano lacked adequate port facilities, which required most fishmeal producers to transport their catch from the docks to the plants in open-top trucks. Both at the docks and as the loaded trucks drove through the city center, industrialists lost up to eighty kilograms per load to "*los gatos*" (the cats)—young men in groups of ten to twenty who climbed quickly aboard and filled their own nets with the catch.[93] This occurred regularly and in open view in the overlapping residential and industrial zones of Talcahuano.

Fishmeal production left its imprint on the land, atmosphere, and sea in the surrounding areas. As they did in Chimbote, residents in both Iquique and Talcahuano complained of "living in a fetid environment, created exclusively by the fishing industries."[94] In 1993, residents of San Vicente (Talcahuano) witnessed a catastrophic fire, ignited by a welding spark that fell onto water that was reportedly (and routinely) covered by a "layer of grease."[95] The fire took four hundred volunteers seven hours to extinguish, killing one person and destroying nine industrial fishing boats, along with dozens of artisanal boats.[96] As a site where multiple types of heavy industry comingled, the floating grease likely came from a combination of sources—but there is no doubt that the notorious incident helped to solidify Talcahuano's enduring image as the primary zone of sacrifice along the Chilean coast.

CHILE'S RETURN TO DEMOCRACY AND THE NEED FOR COMPREHENSIVE FISHERIES LEGISLATION

By the mid-1980s, as social and political discontent with Pinochet mounted, activism among fishermen's unions constituted a powerful force in resisting the regime. The onslaught of El Niño in 1982 again squeezed the fishing industry and constituted one of the strongest and longest-lasting events of the twentieth century. Across the Chilean economy, the economic crisis of the "Lost Decade" intensified the impoverishment of non-elites.[97] In 1983, Chilean fishermen participated in a national strike against poor pay and inadequate provisions at sea.[98] Such actions were part of the nationwide unrest that unraveled Pinochet's power by the end of the decade. They also helped to formalize the organizational structure that later became fundamental to the legislation and implementation of fisheries regulations.

Small-scale fishermen formed the National Artisanal Fishermen's Confederation (CONAPACH) in 1988, just as industrialists and policy makers began to debate a new general fisheries law. The need for comprehensive national fisheries legislation had by then become increasingly clear. Although myriad ad hoc regulations had been implemented in the fishing sector since at least 1956, none had effectively prevented overfishing of the most commercially important species. Since the 1930s, fishery access had been based in part on "historic rights," but a 1978 decree (D.L. 2442) weakened this principle in order to bolster the growth of firms during the process of re-privatization. Finally, in 1989 the Ley Merino (Merino Law) proposed the creation of a regulatory mechanism based on a ranking of the level of overexploitation (*"plena explotación"* and *"productividad excedente"*). Meant to enter into effect with the transition to the newly elected democratic government in March 1990, it also laid the groundwork for a system of individual transferable quotas (ITQs), which was ultimately embodied in the 1991 General Law of Fisheries and Aquaculture (D.L. 18892, Ley General de Pesca y Acuicultura).

The quota system elicited opposition from northern industrialists because it required the establishment of regional fishing zones, thus restricting their ability to freely relocate their fleets to the southern fishing grounds in Talcahuano and elsewhere. Industrialists from the south, on the other hand, supported the law as a way of limiting their competition.[99] Artisanal fishers denounced it as a form of "privatization of the sea," noting the conflicts of interest among policy makers and industrialists that visibly influenced the assignment of quotas.[100] And some economists pointed out that the assignation of licenses based on historic participation contradicted the free market by restricting the entry of new enterprises.[101]

By the end of the twentieth century, Chilean industrialists had solidified their position as producers of high-grade "special" fishmeal based on a multi-species fishery that was more capable of adapting to ecosystem fluctuations than the single-species Peruvian anchoveta fishery. Fisheries in Chile's northern zone (off Arica, Iquique, Antofagasta) nonetheless suffered from general depletion during the 1990s, facilitating the transition to tourism as one of Iquique's main economic activities. "In [this] port perched on the edge of the towering mountains of the Atacama Desert, the stench of fishmeal plants has disappeared," announced a 1991 article in the *Financial Times*. "The plants are silent, facing an idle fishing fleet moored in the bay. Even the vultures and pelicans circling overhead look hungry."[102] In Talcahuano, meanwhile, the jack mackerel fishery remained highly profitable, as industrialists expanded the fleet and their fishing grounds farther west and south into the Pacific.[103] The fishery as a whole yielded even greater landings in the 1990s than it had during the previous decade of voracious industrial growth. However, since jack mackerel is a species whose habitat range "straddles" the boundaries of multiple fishing nations as well as the high seas, landings figures likely disguised a "spatial reorganization" of the fishing effort as stocks waned or shifted.[104]

With Chile's industrialists and artisanal fishermen embroiled in a decades-long political battle over the quotas and access rights assigned by the 1991 fisheries law, long-distance industrial fleets looked toward their next oceanic frontier on the high seas, where factory vessels from across the Pacific trawled for the migrating jack mackerel. Although fisheries scientists were still working to determine the precise reproductive and migration habits of this species in the Southeast Pacific, the voracious extraction on display in Talcahuano during the early 1990s elicited concern and critique from local experts.[105]

At the same time, rapid growth in aquaculture (farmed fish) production, particularly in East Asia, Scandinavia, and Chile itself, created a new source of demand for fishmeal and oil. By 1995, salmon farmed in freshwater lakes in the far south of Chile transformed the country into the world's second largest salmon producer, after Norway.[106] Chile also became the leading exporter of salmon to the United States. The booming salmon industry created a domestic market for fishmeal and oil produced by Chilean firms, transforming the country from an exporter to a net importer of concentrated fish proteins (much of which came from Peru).[107] As part of a larger program of natural resource–based exports, salmon aquaculture also generated new social costs for workers (a predominantly female labor force in the processing sector), as well as ecological costs, as antibiotics and other contaminants crept into the lakes of the Chilean south.[108]

But once again, in 1997–98, a strong El Niño created a crisis in the Humboldt Current region's fisheries, forcing fishermen and policy makers in both countries to contend with environmental variability and its differential impacts at a regional level. Off the south-central Chilean coast, this event caused a significant shift in jack mackerel migrations—an effect that lasted for several years as it rippled through the species' reproductive biogeography.[109] During the last two decades, Chile's legislative attempts to regulate its fisheries have led to mixed results: while the legal regime has slowed the "race for fish" and increased profits for the producers of higher-value products, it has also led to a consolidation of ownership and capital in the sector.[110] Further study of specific outcomes for communities and marine ecosystems will enable future historians and social scientists to better understand the translocal socioeconomic and environmental impacts of these important regulatory interventions.

Conclusion

MILLIONS OF TONS OF FISH have passed through the maze-like machinery of "reduction" factories in Peru and Chile, becoming valuable commodities that remain virtually invisible in the modern industrial ecosystem. *The Fishmeal Revolution* has demonstrated the central importance of Humboldt Current marine fisheries in the global circulation of nutrients that supported the increasingly large-scale production of chickens, hogs, and farmed fish during the past century. Although supplies were inconsistent in quantity and quality until after World War Two, the meteoric expansion of the Peruvian and Chilean fishmeal industries after the late 1950s transformed the global landscape of food and agricultural commodity production.

Concomitantly, the Pacific Ocean's climatological oscillations became increasingly visible as they rippled through international commodity markets. These shifts created different impacts at the local level: the 1965 El Niño precipitated a major crisis for industrialists in Northern Chile, but the same event had a much lesser impact in Peru, where the industry depended almost exclusively on the massive anchoveta schools that typically swam farther north. Seven years later, however, the 1972 El Niño arrived after more than a decade of uncontrolled growth in the single-species Peruvian anchoveta fishery. The collapse was an ecological and socioeconomic catastrophe for Peru, whose recovery, particularly in the fishmeal producing hub of Chimbote, would take decades.

The international profiles of Peru and Chile as fishmeal-producing nations diverged after the 1972 collapse. In Chile, a multispecies fishery exploited sardines, mackerel, and other species for fishmeal. Chilean industrialists also focused on producing higher-grade ("special") products, which received greater returns on global markets.[1] As fishing fleets incorporated more technology, Peruvian and Chilean industrialists continued to produce fishmeal amid distinctive national contexts. Both countries reprivatized their state-owned enterprises beginning in the mid-1970s, but in Peru, where the industry had been exponentially larger than in Chile, the process was much more protracted. Throughout the 1970s and '80s, both countries continued to develop their food fisheries through trawling for mid- and deep-water species, while authorities maintained some restrictions on the reduction to fishmeal of the fish they considered "food-grade."

After 1980, as Chilean fishmeal production surpassed Peru's, a fisheries "regime shift" facilitated a renewed focus on the sardine populations that were more abundant following the anchoveta collapse.[2] Chilean industrialists were better able to withstand the impact of the 1982–83 El Niño: that year, when all other sectors were in recession, Chile's industrial fisheries in fact grew.[3] Peruvian industrialists slowly recovered fishmeal production during the 1980s and increased the production of fish oil, with the result that by 1989 they became the second-largest producers, after Japan. Although the state of technology in Peruvian fishmeal plants continued to lag behind that of the Chilean industry, as reprivatization brought about greater consolidation in the sector and new investments in fishing and processing technology during the 1990s, Peru eventually reclaimed its status as the world's top fishmeal producer.[4] The two neighbors have continued to compete for resources and market share, particularly in the Peru-Chile maritime border region, in a shifting global landscape.

Over the last several decades, the use of fishmeal and oil in poultry and swine feeds has declined substantially, while new sources of demand have grown.[5] Since at least the 1980s, fish oil has been used in the hydrogenation of margarine, and its inclusion in aquaculture feeds and "nutraceuticals" (nutritional supplements for humans and pets) have continued to increase the markets for these products.[6] Although demand has remained strong, the availability of Humboldt Current marine proteins has continued to fluctuate: during the 1990s, Peru's sardine fishery declined by 99 percent, and catches of anchoveta and jack mackerel fell off in both Peru and Chile after the middle of that decade.[7] In 1997–98, the onset of another El Niño once again greatly disrupted the industry and global commodity markets. The ENSO events of 1982–83 and 1997–98 registered as the most severe during the twentieth century, forcing industrialists to contend once again with dramatic, but familiar, ecological fluctuations and the inevitable limits to the fishmeal revolution.[8]

UNCERTAINTY AND FISHERIES POLICY: LESSONS FROM THE HUMBOLDT CURRENT

The questions posed by the logic of fishmeal production hold crucial lessons for policy making at the local, national, and international levels. The study of history can contribute to the policy making process in at least three principal ways: by offering insights into institutional culture; by evaluating conceptual models; and by assessing program and policy outcomes.[9] *The Fishmeal Revolution* has further shown how ecological and spatial contingencies—translocal variations, and humans' reactions to those variations within a larger dynamic system—have shaped important aspects of the historical development of cities, national industries, and the global circulation of nutrients.

The spatial and temporal scale of ecological variations are particularly relevant to debates over the sustainability of the oceans given the worldwide synchronicity of forage fishery population dynamics—from the multimillennial history of sardine-anchovy "regime shifts" to the human-led forage fishery catastrophes of the industrial era. Worldwide, collapses of anchovy fisheries followed collapses of sardine fisheries in at least four cases during the mid-twentieth century.[10] Beginning with the case of the California sardine industry in the 1940s, these fisheries served as laboratories for some of the first large-scale scientific investigations into population dynamics—studies that became both feasible and necessary as commercial exploitation increased.[11] Yet even today, these species still hold many secrets, not least in their complex linkages to climate dynamics.

Seasoned experts recognize that cause and effect in fisheries management is far from straightforward. At the time of its collapse, and still today, Peru's anchoveta fishery was "among the most carefully supervised and rigorously regulated the world had ever seen."[12] Renowned fisheries scientists meticulously studied the feeding and reproduction habits of the anchoveta throughout the 1960s—but a few years of data were not sufficient to arrive at a deep understanding of the complicated interrelationships that characterized the Humboldt Current marine ecosystem, and the extreme nature of the climatological fluctuations further intensified the challenge of understanding its dynamics.[13] As one FAO scientist stated bluntly in 1973, "[O]ne is entirely fooled if one takes these short intervals of a decade or so and decides there is some sort of simple probability associated with it."[14] Even in the early twenty-first century, scientists still had trouble discerning "clear trophic links on decadal timescales," signaling that much mystery remains in the nature of interspecies relationships.[15]

Because of its ecological and commercial importance, the Peruvian fishmeal industry's infamous "boom-and-bust" cycle received worldwide media attention in 1972–73, and it has since endured as a case study in fisheries policy debates. But the precise lessons of the crisis have often been obscured by explanations that primarily blame Peruvian authorities' mismanagement or the greed of the fishermen for the anchoveta's disappearance.[16] On the other hand, industrialists have tended to emphasize the role of El Niño in the collapse, an expedient explanation since it limits the culpability of individual actors.[17] Studies in historical ecology describe a complex interaction among human and natural factors "working in concert."[18] In Peru, scientists, industry executives (both foreign and national), and government officials were all deeply concerned about the state of the anchoveta fishery in the context of its rapid growth during the 1960s, and they sought to implement formal measures to curtail overfishing after 1965. Although the Peruvian government restricted the anchoveta fishery early in the 1972 season, heavy fishing continued well beyond the officially established limits. The regulations had ultimately been insufficient to govern human behavior or prevent overfishing.

Not only are fish populations' productivity dependent on the complex interactions of climate and ocean, but their variance under anomalous (ENSO) conditions has repeatedly demonstrated humans' flawed ability to predict or fully anticipate the impacts of their actions on natural ecosystems.[19] Even today, the persistent "el Niño definition problem . . . can cause uncertainty and affect perception of risk, depending on which region of the equatorial Pacific one uses to identify an event."[20] In other words, El Niño's uneven impact in terms of localization and intensity complicates the forecasting that is necessary for making policy recommendations, although new "deep learning" tools have recently allowed climatologists to more accurately predict its occurrence with greater spatial and temporal detail.[21]

In 2017, scientists noticed a distinctive pattern in the onset of El Niño conditions, describing an "El Niño costero" (coastal)—distinctive from the more familiar Pacific basin–wide phenomenon—"which came as a surprise to the scientific community, governments, and populations in northwest South America in terms of its rapid development and localized impacts."[22] They believe that the 2017 event was similar to the one that Murphy observed in 1925, rather than a new phenomenon, and that its ecological and socioeconomic impacts were similar to those associated with other "extraordinary"

ENSO events of the twentieth century, such as those in 1982–83 and 1997–98.[23] Even if fishermen and industrialists believe that the key to profitability depends on their ability to withstand episodic climate shifts, no one can fully predict fisheries' reproductive dynamics, their population density, or their spatial distribution. Scientists confront an additional challenge in modeling the trophic webs in the Humboldt Current marine ecosystem, as in other Eastern Boundary Current Upwelling systems, since the oceanographic conditions that shape these ecosystems are themselves highly variable.[24] This makes both the calculation and the implementation of ecologically and socially sustainable catch limits even more difficult.

The limitations of scientific knowledge concerning these interconnected processes and their impacts on marine and terrestrial ecosystems introduces yet another degree of uncertainty into the policy making process. As environmental historians Frank Uekötter and Uwe Lübken have warned, "the information problem underlying the quest for sustainable paths of resource use is more complicated, and more troubling, than scholars have assumed so far."[25] For one thing, in making their policy recommendations, fisheries scientists rely heavily upon reported catch data, which provide only a partial view of the total biomass of a given species under the sea surface. Furthermore, around the world as in the Humboldt Current ecosystem, local contexts vary in terms of the relative strength of the government institutions that are charged with monitoring and regulating industry, thus creating margins of error that require specialized knowledge to recognize. In some cases, political incentives to alter the reported numbers—as in the case of China, whose catch data scientists believe to be grossly inflated—can further compromise the accuracy of modeled projections.[26] FAO's global marine capture datasets are comprised of annual totals of landings per species, self-reported by individual fishing nations.

These conditions make a multidisciplinary approach to the study of fisheries, whether local or global, all the more relevant. Indeed, it is not only ecological conditions that shift unpredictably; human behavior is also subject to a number of intersecting factors that shape choices and actions. Social scientists began to debate the bio-economics of fisheries management following H. Scott Gordon's 1954 article, which theorized the problem of resource depletion in relation to the nature of common-property regimes, wherein resources (such as fish) are not privately owned but are "exploited under conditions of individualistic competition."[27] Gordon defined the "optimum degree of utilization" in terms of a fishery's "net economic yield" (subtracting the value of fish caught from the total cost, including fishing effort)—a concept that assumed that any fish not extracted from the sea had no value (since it was not a measurable commodity in relation to a market economy).[28] Ecologist Garrett Hardin articulated the better-known "tragedy of the commons" thesis in 1968 in relation to the problem of population growth and the increasing pressure on finite supplies of natural resources.[29] Applied to the context of fisheries, Hardin's thesis held that the "tragedy" of resource exhaustion would occur inevitably, since as a fisher pursued his individual self-interest in a closed system (i.e., by maximizing his catch in a given fishery), this would diminish the quantity available to others.

These deterministic explanations resonate powerfully with capitalist modes of private ownership, but leave little room for individual agency, collective forms of governance, or historical contingency.[30] Historian Joaquim Radkau has noted various examples of historical commons among premodern European farming-herding societies that upheld some elements of ecological self-regulation.[31] Scholarly debates surrounding Hardin's thesis have themselves often failed to account for "the complexity, uncertainty, and dynamic qualities that underlie ecological processes and environmental change."[32] When applied to environmental policy problems such as fisheries management, the question of how to achieve sustainability (whether social or ecological) has often been reduced to the role of government regulations versus private property rights. But this theoretical formulation is ill-fitted to the complexity and interconnectedness of oceans and social systems: "[P]rivate property regimes and markets rarely, if ever, provide real-world solutions to the tragedy of the commons in the absence of government regulation."[33] Impractical in its inability to project complex and dynamic human-ecological relationships over time, the "rational-choice" model—which assumes that human behavior is consistently and predictably driven by the goal of optimizing utility, or maximizing individual gains—can scarcely account for the ways in which uncertainty limits humans' ability to respond to shifting local landscapes and climatological patterns.[34]

John A. Gulland, a British fisheries scientist who helped to assess Peru's fishing industry with other FAO experts in 1970, noted that fishing regulations must inherently incorporate economic calculations. He recognized that in a context of rapid ecological change, management decisions sometimes need to be made before scientific interpretations of fish population dynamics are conclusive.[35] Gulland observed that, in Peruvian fisheries as elsewhere, state-imposed harvest restrictions limit the profits and income of fishers, who in turn are then likely to pressure government officials to increase the quotas. Some might also resort to fishing illegally (or increase the frequency of this practice). Thus, the management of an overcapitalized fishery produces a sociopolitical-economic-ecological "feedback loop" that limits the effectiveness of any regulatory measures imposed.[36] The actual challenges of determining, assigning, and enforcing sustainable catch limits require critical reflection as well as ongoing dialogues between fishers, scientists, and policy makers in order to devise creative institutional approaches and enforcement mechanisms.[37]

Fishmeal and oil from the Southeast Pacific region contributed significantly to post–World War Two flows of capital, goods, and people worldwide.[38] Throughout the twentieth century, industrialists moved capital and technology in pursuit of more abundant forage fisheries: from California, the North Sea, the US Gulf and Atlantic Coasts to the waters off Peru and Chile, and later, in search of "other Perus," to new resource frontiers in the Middle East and Africa. The transnational search for more profitable conditions of production contends with distinct challenges at the margins of national territorial waters and on the high seas: "The fugitive nature of the resource, its propensity to straddle territorial waters, and the potential for irreversible overexploitation make [fish] stocks extremely vulnerable to unregulated market forces."[39] Conservation and resource management interventions must contend with the transboundary movements of the marine species as well as fishing fleets themselves.

Both small- and large-scale spatial shifts by fish schools influence the methods and movements fishing fleets employ in their pursuit. Some of the world's major fishery collapses, including that of the Peruvian anchoveta, followed "a dramatic spatial reorganization of the stock . . . and fishing activity," where fish and fishers concentrated in smaller geographical areas. These movements are imperceptible in the commonly reported statistics, making it difficult to assess the overall abundance and total biomass of the fish stocks.[40] A 2017 study found that under El Niño conditions, the Chilean fleet has tended to fish farther away from the coast than under normal (non-ENSO) conditions, indicating a corresponding spatial shift of the species in the sea.[41]

Nevertheless, most regulatory approaches to fisheries management whether at the national or international level, involve the establishment and/or recognition of geopolitical boundaries. (Appendix D shows overlapping governance regimes in global fisheries.) Such boundaries work in tandem with quota systems that place limits on fish landings—whether per vessel or in total—for a given season. The fundamental contradiction that emerges in applying fixed institutional and legal mechanisms to the "fluid biophysical" realm of the seas, along with the historic tendency to envision the maritime world as an "unpeopled" space, gives rise to a particular "politics of scale in oceans governance."[42] "Unable to accommodate alternative ways of knowing," such as indigenous and informal or small-scale subsistence practices, the resulting institutions and policies constitute ill-fitting solutions to the dynamic and multidimensional challenges of fisheries management.[43]

One of the earliest efforts to manage trans-Pacific fisheries was the establishment of the Inter-American Tropical Tuna Commission (IATTC) in 1949, which sought to manage the harvest of migratory tuna species among the signatory nations, first Costa Rica, followed by other states in the Americas with a Pacific coastline.[44] This multinational coalition was initially dominated by US scientists with close connections to California-based tuna fishing concerns—an uneven balance of power that diminished some Latin American leaders' confidence in the collaboration. Cold War tensions further strained diplomatic relations and permeated debates over how best to regulate the oceanic realm.

The most comprehensive approach to ocean resource management at the global level was created through the United Nations Convention on the Law of the Sea (UNCLOS). Drafted during the third international convention (UNCLOS III), which took place between 1976 and 1982, the new Law of the Sea finally entered into force in 1994 with the required sixtieth nation's ratification.[45] This legislation created the "Exclusive Economic Zone" (EEZ), assigning coastal nations control over resources in the sea and beneath the ocean floor up to two hundred nautical miles from shore.[46] The EEZ codified elements of maritime claims, made by Chile, Peru, Ecuador, and other coastal nations since the late 1940s, to a two-hundred-nautical-mile coastal region as part of their maritime domains.[47] These nations have occasionally made defiant assertions of sovereignty over their coastal resources—particularly in cases of US tuna fleets that ventured frequently into the waters off Peru and Ecuador.[48]

Although the UN Law of the Sea discouraged the unchecked extraction of fish within EEZs, those species that traverse the high seas but were not classified in the convention as "highly migratory" remained vulnerable to overexploitation when outside territorial waters. At the margins of their territorial waters, whether at the Peru-Chile maritime frontier or the boundaries of the high seas, fishing fleets jealously competed for fish that threatened to migrate into the nets of their neighbors. In Peru, responding to local anxieties over southward-migrating sardine and anchoveta stocks, authorities have at times lessened restrictions on the Peruvian vessels operating south of Ilo in order to prevent the transborder loss of revenue. After 1989, Chilean and Peruvian producers grew increasingly concerned about long-distance fleets targeting jack mackerel on the high seas, by then one of the most commercially important species for both countries. Although Soviet factory fleets had been fishing the species since the 1960s, pressure began to increase during the last decade of the twentieth century, reportedly after a Japanese scientist found a single jack mackerel specimen in a trawler-haul off New Zealand—a discovery that signaled a possible shift in the geographical range of their migrations.[49] Coastal nations of the South and Southeast Pacific formed a Regional Fisheries Management Organization (SPRFMO) in order to collectively manage the fisheries in this zone through an international quota system.[50]

In 1991, Chile's new General Fisheries Law (Ley General de Pesca y Acuicultura) articulated the controversial "Presential Sea" ("Mar Presencial") doctrine, a unilateral claim designed to limit foreign fishing in areas adjacent to its EEZ, which effectively established control over a nine-million-square-mile triangle of oceanic territory in the Southeast Pacific, extending from Chile's coast westward to the islands of Rapa Nui (Easter Island) and Sala y Gómez, and south to Antarctica.[51] Debates over this doctrine, its legal viability, and its potential impact on high seas fisheries figured prominently in international discussions leading up to the 1995 UN Agreement for the Conservation and Management of Straddling Fish Stocks and Highly Migratory Fish Stocks, which established guidelines for the stewardship of transboundary fisheries (those that straddled a nation's EEZ and the high seas).[52] However, tensions surrounding access to oceanic resources in the Southeast Pacific have persisted, as evinced by the years-long dispute between Peru and Chile over their maritime boundary. Although a 2014 Hague arbitration formally settled the case, this highly productive zone of the Humboldt Current ecosystem remains a contested space when it comes to fishing practices.[53]

SUSTAINABILITY AND THE PERSISTENCE OF THE "PROTEIN GAP"

Marine proteins and oils have played an integral but hidden role in shaping twentieth- and twenty-first-century diets. In Peru and Chile, industry, government, and scientific attempts to harvest and redistribute commoditized marine resources after the 1950s—part of the "second industrialization" of global fisheries—went hand in hand with the rapid and profound changes that occurred in methods of agricultural production, processing, and distribution after World War Two. The Green Revolution brought about momentous technological shifts in modern agriculture, which "raised the carrying capacity of the land through mono-cropping and the use of artificial fertilizers and mechanized equipment."[54] Increasingly powerful, multinational agribusinesses applied these new methods of biological intervention, thereby reducing production costs, decreasing time-to-market, and minimizing their financial risk. Meanwhile, technocrats in international organizations such as the FAO worked to implement top-down institutional and technological reforms in agriculture and fisheries in the industrializing nations of Latin America, Africa, and Asia. Ultimately, measuring the historical impacts of these policies and practices on socio-environmental realities at different points in their global value chains remains a challenging but essential undertaking for contemporary researchers across the academic and policy making spheres.[55]

The history of industrial fisheries and of fishmeal in particular reveals the interconnectedness among seemingly disparate localities, marine and terrestrial ecosystems, and the circulation of nutrients within the emerging industrial food system. In situating the Humboldt Current's fishmeal revolution within this larger story, this study sketches the broad contours of what British development scholar Ian Scoones has called "the 'messy middles' between the local, national, and global," connecting Peruvian and Chilean experiences with the profound environmental and political-economic changes that have shaped our contemporary life-ways.[56] Deeper, more nuanced understandings of these relationships are critical for designing more sustainable practices at any scale of governance.[57]

Unsurprisingly, the costs and benefits of these transformations have been unevenly distributed. A recent study quantifying the relative values of global nutrient production according to farm size found that the intensification of agriculture has tended to reduce the diversity of food production, particularly in North and South America, Australia and New Zealand—countries where large farms contribute 75–100 percent of the cereal, livestock, fruit, and other commodities.[58] Comparative historical data from FAOSTAT show that, between 1976 and 2013, there was a dramatic increase in poultry supplies in all major fishmeal-producing nations (Chile, China, Germany, Norway, Peru, United States), but highly unequal outcomes among those nations in terms of the availability of diverse types of animal proteins (beef, pork, chicken, seafood). In this context, the case of Peru is particularly glaring.[59] With more land and ocean resources directed toward large-scale agricultural production worldwide, there has also been a reduction in overall biodiversity, as well as encroachment into natural preserves and indigenous territories.[60]

It is crucial that we include fisheries and marine ecosystems in our studies of global food production. In these ecosystems, a historically rooted perspective is key to gaining a more nuanced understanding of how people and their technologies, institutions, and policies have interacted with dynamic natural processes.[61] As this study has shown, the scaling-up of factory farms has depended on largely invisible flows of high-protein feed ingredients, removing nutrient-rich forage fish species from Humboldt Current food webs. At the same time, our twenty-first-century food system faces a remarkably different scenario than that of the 1960s and '70s, when experts hoped that fish protein concentrate (FPC) would provide "a major boon for the undernourished world."[62] While hunger and malnutrition remain significant problems in many areas of the world, affluent consumers have continued to increase pressure on certain fish species, as policy makers wring their hands over the conflicting priorities of economic growth versus ecological conservation.

Fisheries scientist Daniel Pauly has rightly proclaimed that "it is our monstrous appetite which is one of the key reasons why we can't live sustainably on this planet."[63] Over the past decade, scholars have warned of the threats to global food security posed by the ongoing reliance on wild-capture fisheries for animal and fish feeds, as fishmeal and oil have continued to comprise a significant proportion of world fisheries landings.[64] The 2008 Peruvian fisheries law aimed to redirect some of these fish to the human diet by permitting only industrial landings for fishmeal and oil production, but observers have noted that, nonetheless, "a large share of the small-scale fleet's catch has been targeted for fishmeal production."[65] Even while the total worldwide proportion of landed fish that is reduced into these commodities has declined in recent years relative to direct human consumption, the anchoveta still accounts for almost a third of fish supplied for such purposes, and both Peru and Chile remain important fishmeal and oil producers.[66]

In recent decades there has been a movement at both the national and international levels to shape consumers' behavior in order to limit or shift humans' impact on marine fisheries. For consumers in distant markets, eco-labeling and various certification programs rate the relative level of environmental sustainability of specific products based on factors such as species, catch methods, and region of origin. However, such campaigns have generated little verifiable evidence of their success in terms of advancing conservation goals.[67] In Peru, despite the ancient traditions of anchoveta consumption among indigenous peoples, twenty-first-century surveys of consumer spending habits suggest that poultry is the preferred source of inexpensive protein among Peruvians. As researchers recently noted: "It might be surprising that, in a country where malnutrition and caloric deficit constitute major issues, only a tiny fraction of a low-priced and highly nutritious fish such as anchovy is marketed for domestic consumption."[68] Conservation biologist Patricia Majluf has begun promoting "sustainable gastronomy" as a way to develop new markets for value-added products such as gourmet restaurant fare.[69] Beginning in 2006, the Peruvian government implemented programs that aimed to increase the domestic consumption of anchoveta, including subsidies, promotions, and consumer education campaigns.[70] Peruvian producers also relabeled the *Engraulis ringens* as "Peruvian sardine" in order to increase the prestige of products exported to foreign markets.[71] However, in Peru, several factors—including limited cold-storage infrastructure, the need for a larger labor force, and the greater capital investments required for processing equipment—persist in making fishmeal and oil more profitable than cured or fresh anchoveta products, which are costlier to produce.[72]

With the turn toward aquaculture (fish farming) in Chile and Peru, industry has brought new vulnerabilities to the producing regions, their ecosystems, and the people who live there. Since the 1980s, the so-called "Blue Revolution" has created another major source of demand for fishmeal and oil in aquaculture feeds, thus sustaining pressure on wild-forage fisheries even while the worldwide use of fishmeal and oil in poultry and swine feeds has declined substantially.[73] As with land-based agriculture, single-species fish farming requires costly inputs to protect against disease (antibiotics) and to provide sufficient nutrients (high-protein pellet feeds) for profitable growth. The farms' release of organic matter into fragile marine environments has contaminated water supplies and decimated native species, while their fish stocks have become vulnerable to "commodity diseases," as Chile's own salmon industry experienced in 2008–2010, when conditions led to the rapid spread of a virus throughout the farms, leaving behind an infected landscape.[74] The long-term impacts to marine ecosystems are less well-known, but in the south of Chile, salmon producers were unable to recover once the pathogen had entered the industrial ecosystem, leading the industry to abandon the entire region and reestablish operations farther to the south. Not unlike the ruinous effect of fungal diseases on banana plantations, these ecological vulnerabilities have sometimes led to production "shocks," impacting businesses and consumers throughout the global supply chain.[75]

These unintended ecological consequences—and the concomitant socioeconomic impacts they have on the surrounding regions—are somewhat less obvious (but no less harmful) examples of zones of sacrifice created by industrial fisheries. In fishmeal cities not only along the Peru-Chile coast but around the world, the imprints of fishmeal's boom and bust can be discerned in the marine ecosystem, the coastal landscape, and the social fabric of local communities. In Siglufjördur, Iceland—once a thriving center of the herring reduction industry—the "few remote ghost factories" whose structures remained decades after the fishery's collapse have inspired reverence among a few observers who sought to memorialize the area's distinctive chapter in the global history of fishmeal.[76] One enterprising researcher created a museum there using salvaged components of various factories, "important objects beautiful in their decay."[77] In cities like Chimbote, where the fishmeal industry continues to operate but on a lesser scale than it had during the boom years, the postindustrial landscape is dotted with crumbling factories that continue to bear witness to this history.

The fishy odors emanating from vessels, wharves, and fishmeal factories create a nuisance and a public health concern for coastal residents, but the economic needs of workers hungry for the "smell of success" still take priority.[78] The 1960s-era battle to relocate Lima's fishmeal industry to Chimbote demonstrated that locals have long suspected the connection between particulate matter in the atmosphere around the plants and the respiratory maladies they and their children suffered. The hazards of working in fisheries, and fishmeal processing in particular, have been documented since at least the 1970s, with Chilean workers reporting symptoms including "eye diseases, skin eruptions, and loss of consciousness," even death.[79] Such injuries stem from the noxious fumes emitted from decomposing fish, which can become fatally toxic when a worker becomes trapped in a confined space such as the vessel's hold.

Some fishmeal factories in Chile and Peru continued to discharge their untreated effluents into the sea well into the twenty-first century.[80] Such effluents contain a high proportion of suspended organic matter—proteins that can be recovered and reincorporated into the production process, thereby reducing pollution and also increasing the value of the fishmeal produced. In the context of the fishmeal and food fish industries, engineers have studied microfiltration technologies that produce protein concentrates or "liquors" with various applications for human or animal consumption.[81] Technologies that reduce the pollutants released by fishmeal plants have existed for decades, but in Peru and Chile, industrialists incorporated them only when resource scarcity created a market incentive for doing so.[82]

Despite the increasingly inescapable reach of fishing technologies and the relentless pressures that humans have placed on marine ecosystems, forage fish stocks such as anchoveta and sardine have demonstrated remarkable resilience, particularly after fishing has been reduced or halted. But their resilience is not inexhaustible: repeated crises have shown that overfishing can also push fish populations past their capacity to reproduce in sufficient numbers. Fisheries scientists have incorporated data on the fishmeal and oil industry's carbon emissions and "marine footprint," the latter measuring how much primary production they appropriate in extracting forage fish species, into their analyses.[83]

As the ecological impact of sustained fishing has become clearer, Chile and Peru have taken measures to limit overfishing and increase transparency. By the early 1990s, both countries had implemented general fisheries laws that, though imperfect, established quota systems and institutional frameworks that were then further refined through the respective national legislative processes.[84] Chile has since taken steps to protect marine areas in response to pressure from conservation groups, including the international NGO Oceana: in 2017, Chilean authorities banned bottom trawling in 98 percent of its EEZ, following a 2016 Oceana report that showed the practice affected 3,905 square kilometers of marine surface annually.[85] In 2018, Peru became the second country to make real-time satellite data from its national Vessel Tracking System (dating back to 2012) accessible through an interactive online platform maintained by the international nonprofit Global Fishing Watch.[86] When bolstered by detailed, accurate, and accessible data, laws and regulations can better respond to changing local conditions.

Yet the existence of legal regimes "on paper" is not a guarantee of their successful application or enforcement, nor do they necessarily protect traditional and small-scale fishing communities' rights of access.[87] In some cases, socioeconomic inequalities have persisted or worsened following the introduction of the system of individual transferable quotas (ITQs), which function not as "property rights but rather dedicated access privileges" that limit entry to only those who own shares, typically based on historic participation in a given fishery.[88] In 2008, the Chilean government introduced legislation establishing exclusive access rights for indigenous (Lafkenche and Williche) use of coastal marine resources in the southern region, but community leaders have reported dissatisfaction with the law's impact on their ability to self-govern.[89] The threat of dispossession—"*desplayamiento*"—of artisanal and indigenous fishers continues to loom as coastlines are increasingly transformed by commercial tourism.[90]

A 2010 assessment of management strategies concluded that the management approaches best able to account for the social complexity of fisheries take a broad view of space (ecosystem-based management) or time (historically based restoration). "With political will and societal awareness," the authors wrote, "fishing and eating lower down in the food web may become economically viable, ecologically sustainable, and socially just, both as a right and privilege."[91] Fisheries scientists Dirk Zeller and Daniel Pauly conclude unequivocally that industrial fisheries must be scaled back and capacity-enhancing subsidies eliminated in order to reduce overfishing worldwide.[92] They argue that small-scale, locally owned and operated fisheries, which employ more people and better contribute to food security, have the capacity to maintain or even increase overall landings globally, and therefore to satisfy the projected demand for seafood in the coming decades.[93]

Critical media attention has recently shed further light on exploitative labor practices in some fisheries and the selective impacts of our (and our pets') food preferences on people and marine ecosystems around the world.[94] As the restaurant industry embraces innovative culinary techniques and ingredients, often inspired by indigenous knowledge or the desire to implement more socially and ecologically sustainable practices, chefs' experiments in "cooperative market building"—while themselves not beyond critique—are nonetheless well-positioned to shift popular attention toward issues that cut across social class and identity, ideology, and discipline.[95] Certainly, their use in haute cuisine of species once labeled as "trash" represents a more palatable alternative to 1980s-era export products such as dehydrated "marine beef."[96] Promoting the culinary possibilities and presumed ecological benefits of consuming nontraditional seafood, a *Bon Appétit* writer recently admonished: "You, individual eater with good intentions, can do the planet a teeny tiny favor and order the weird fish instead."[97]

Our contemporary, twenty-first-century existence is shaped by recurring and increasingly extreme shifts in climate and precipitation, including those created by El Niño and the Pacific Decadal Oscillation. At the same time, we continue to face many of the same uncertainties that a columnist described in 1972: "Our dilemma is that we do not have a very good idea of exactly what the limits are and how much slack remains in the system."[98] Scholars are increasingly incorporating the concepts of variability and uncertainty into their ways of understanding social systems, particularly as compared to twenty years ago; social science and policy debates have since moved beyond "a static and equilibrial view."[99] Indeed, we must contend with not only "dynamic uncertainty" but also "an unruly politics, involving diverse knowledges and multiple actors" in order to improve the ecological and social sustainability of our global food system.[100]

As humanity seeks to explore and exploit resources beyond the Earth's terrestrial margins, not only delving deeper into the sea but also traversing the interplanetary realm, it is urgent that we work to increase the capacity of our policies and institutions (and indeed, our very imaginations) to foresee multiple and divergent outcomes. By anticipating the inherent limitations of our own designs, we will be more adept at weathering our inevitably shifting ecological realities.

APPENDIX A

Glossary of Marine Species

This glossary includes the fish, bird, and whale species mentioned in this study, listed alphabetically by English common name, followed (where applicable) by the Spanish-language name(s) commonly used in Peru and/or Chile. In addition to the sources noted below, species information is synthesized from Froese and Pauly's online *FishBase* and, Robert Cushman Murphy's *Oceanic Birds of South America*.[1]

ANCHOVETA, PERUVIAN (*ENGRAULIS RINGENS*) Following the patterns of the Humboldt Current upwelling and the availability of plankton for feeding, this tiny fish forms enormous schools near the sea surface, primarily within eighty kilometers (128 miles) of the coast between Peru and northern Chile. It is "the most heavily exploited species in world history," and the basis for the largest single-species fishery on the planet in Peru.[2]

ANCHOVY, NORTH PACIFIC (*ENGRAULIS MORDAX*) This schooling species is found in coastal waters, bays, and inlets of Pacific North America, from Vancouver Island to Baja California.

BONITO, EASTERN PACIFIC (*SARDA CHILIENSIS*) A subtropical tuna-like fish that dwells in coastal waters between northern Peru and Talcahuano, Chile, the bonito has been an important species for canneries on the Peru-Chile coast since the 1940s and '50s.

BOOBY, BLUE-FOOTED (*SULA NEBOUXII*) A rival of the Peruvian booby (*Sula variegata*), this bird species prefers the warmer waters of tropical regions from Ecuador to the north, only occasionally entering the northern Humboldt Current when warmer conditions prevail.

BOOBY, PERUVIAN (*SULA VARIEGATA*) – SP. *PIQUERO* Robert Cushman Murphy observed in 1936 that piqueros were the "nosiest and most numerous" guano bird species, with frequently a "loud chorus, a medley of whistles, gabblings, and trumpet-like calls ringing out from each community."[3] This bird prefers the cold waters of the Humboldt Current.

BOOBY, WHITE (*SULA DACTYLATRAGRANTI*), SP. "PIQUERO BLANCO" A species not normally found in the Humboldt Current upwelling zone, Murphy observed in 1936 that its unusual presence "serves as an index of the advancing water of the [El Niño] countercurrent."[4]

COD, NORTH ATLANTIC (*GADUS MORHUA*), SP. *BACALAO* Found in diverse habitats from inshore areas to deeper waters above the continental shelf, with juveniles preferring complex shallow waters and adults preferring deeper, colder waters. This omnivorous fish forms schools during the day approximately thirty to eighty meters from the bottom and disperses at night to feed.[5] In the mid-twentieth century, it was the object of multiple confrontations between Britain and Iceland, dubbed the "Cod Wars."

CORMORANT, PERUVIAN (*PHALACROCORAX BOUGAINVILLII*), SP. *GUANAY* These were deemed "the most valuable birds in the world" by Robert E. Coker.[6] A long wingspan enables this species, which discovers its prey from the air, to fly for hours against the strong coastal winds of the Humboldt Current.

DOGFISH *(MUSTELUS CANIS)* A small shark that dwells throughout the northern and western Gulf of Mexico, as well as the Caribbean, and off the Atlantic coasts of both North and South America, this species swims in schools and feeds on large crustaceans.[7]

HAKE, PERUVIAN (*MERLUCCIUS GAYI PERUANUS*), SP. *MERLUZA* A cod-like fish found primarily off the coast of Peru, from Paita southward to Huarmey, along the continental shelf and upper continental slope, this subspecies is biologically and commercially similar to *Merluccius gayi gayi*.[8]

HAKE, SOUTH PACIFIC (*MERLUCCIUS GAYI GAYI*), SP. *MERLUZA* A cod-like fish found primarily off the coast of Chile between Arica and Chiloé along the continental shelf and upper continental slope, this species migrates from the ocean's depths to midwater to feed at night, and from southern coastal areas to northern deeper waters in winter and spring.[9] It was intensively harvested by factory trawlers beginning in the 1940s, often frozen into large blocks or reduced into fishmeal.

HERRING, ARAUCANIAN (*CLUPEA BENTINCKI,* ALSO KNOWN AS *STRANGOMERA BENTINCKI*),[10] SP. *SARDINA, SARDINA COMÚN* (CHILE) Small coastal species that forms schools at or near the sea surface between Coquimbo and Talcahuano, Chile. It feeds on plankton and usually breeds between June and November.

HERRING, NORTH ATLANTIC (*CLUPEA HARENGUS*) Forms large schools that move between coastal spawning grounds and open-water feeding grounds in the North Atlantic.

MACKEREL, CHUB (*SCOMBER JAPONICUS*), SP. *CABALLA* Coastal pelagic species that sometimes forms schools with bonito (*Sarda chiliensis*) or sardine (*Sardinops sagax*).

MACKEREL, JACK (*TRACHURUS MURPHYI*), SP. *JUREL* One of the most commercially important species for both Peru and Chile, this schooling species swims across the South Pacific in its migrations.

MENHADEN, GULF (*BREVOORTIA PATRONUS*) A schooling fish that migrates seasonally within the Gulf of Mexico.

MENHADEN, NORTH ATLANTIC (*BREVOORTIA TYRANNUS*) This migratory schooling fish is especially abundant near estuaries along the North American Atlantic Coast.

PELICAN, PERUVIAN (*PELECANUS OCCIDENTALIS THAGUS*), SP. *ALCATRÁZ* A large, brown bird frequently encountered in large flocks along the littoral of the Humboldt Current zone.

PETREL, HORNBY'S (*OCEANODROMA HORNBYI*) A sea bird of the Humboldt Current, found between the Gulf of Guayaquil and northern Chile, which in 1913 alerted the Brewster-Sanford Expedition to the singular oceanic conditions within this marine ecosystem off the western coast of South America.

PILCHARD *see* **sardine, Pacific**

SARDINE, JAPANESE (*SARDINOPS MELANOSTICTUS*) One of three "lineages" of sardines in the Pacific, this schooling species dwells off the coast of Japan.

SARDINE, PACIFIC (*SARDINOPS SAGAX*), ALSO PILCHARD, SP. *SARDINA COMÚN* (PERU), *SARDINA ESPAÑOLA* (CHILE) Coastal schooling species, one of three "lineages" of Pacific sardines, found primarily off western South America, and sometimes off the North American coast.

SIERRA (*THYRSITES ATUN*), SP. *SIERRA COMÚN* (CHILE) A subtropical, mid-water-to-bottom-dwelling fish whose diet includes anchovy and pilchard, this species inhabits continental shelves and island areas along the South American Pacific coast.

TUNA, ATLANTIC BLUEFIN (*THUNNUS THYNNUS*), SP. *ATÚN* This highly migratory, endangered fish sometimes schools together with other species of tuna, but it is typically much larger, weighing up to nine hundred kilograms, and can live up to forty years. Especially prized for sashimi, this species is also cultured in Japan.

TUNA, PACIFIC BLUEFIN (*THUNNUS ORIENTALIS*), SP. *ATÚN* Living mainly in the North Pacific, this highly migratory, endangered species is able to tolerate wide temperature intervals, traveling close to the shore on a seasonal basis, and has also been documented in the Southern Hemisphere.

TUNA, SKIPJACK (*KATSUWONUS PELAMIS*), SP. *ATÚN* A highly migratory, warm-water species, this fish tends to form schools near the surface with birds, sharks, whales, or even drifting objects.[11] Females spawn almost daily, year-round in the tropics; they are prey for large pelagic species and target species for commercial fishers.

TUNA, YELLOWTAIL (*THUNNUS ALBACARES*), SP. *ATÚN, ATÚN ALETA AMARILLA* This highly migratory schooling species is found throughout tropical and equatorial oceanic waters. It is the most commercially important tuna species in the Pacific.

WHALE, BLUE (*BALAENOPTERA MUSCULUS*) The "largest mammal that has ever existed on this earth," measuring up to 106 feet and weighing up to 150 tons, this species feeds primarily on krill. It was one of the most commercially important whales until a 1965 moratorium slowed the rapid decline of its populations. On at least one occasion, in 1910, this species proved capable of sinking a whale-catching vessel by repeatedly ramming its head into the side of the boat in an apparently deliberate act.[12]

WHALE, SPERM (*PHYSETER MACROCEPHALUS*) The iconic species made famous by Captain Ahab's obsession in the 1851 novel *Moby Dick*, its distinctive square head, which comprises more than a third of its body, contains "the largest brain on earth," along with the spermaceti organ for which it is named.[13] Sperm whales feed mainly on deep-water cephalopods. Globally, sperm whale oil was a key source of fuel from 1712 until the International Whaling Commission's moratorium on whaling in 1985. The industry spread from the Atlantic to the Pacific and Indian Oceans in the nineteenth century, peaking in the 1960s.[14]

APPENDIX B

Diagram of Humboldt Current Trophic Web

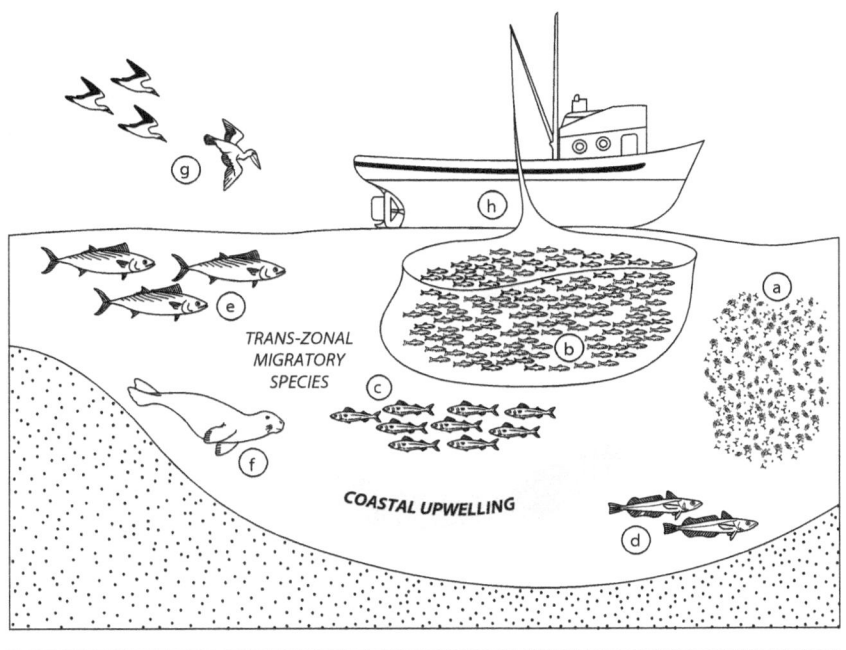

FIGURE 17. The Humboldt Current marine ecosystem: key species in the trophic web. Illustration by the author and Katherine Wintersteen. *Source:* D. Pauly et al., *The Peruvian Upwelling Ecosystem: Dynamics and Interactions* (Manila: ICLARM, 1989).

APPENDIX C

Map of Major Current Systems of Eastern and Central Pacific Ocean

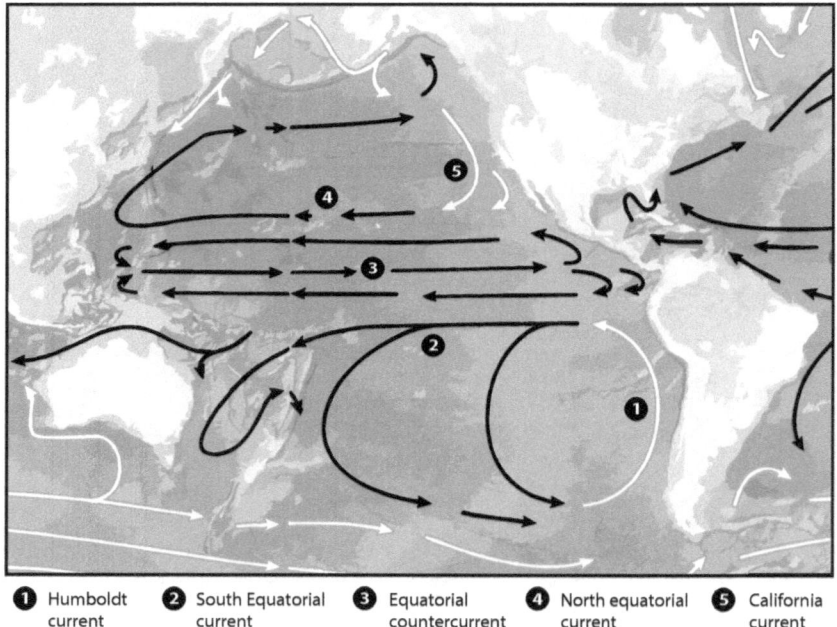

① Humboldt current ② South Equatorial current ③ Equatorial countercurrent ④ North equatorial current ⑤ California current

MAP 2. Major surface current systems of the central and eastern Pacific Ocean. Map by the author. *Sources:* ESRI, GRID Arendal, NOAA, NWS, US Army, Maps.com.

APPENDIX D

Map of World Fisheries Management Zones

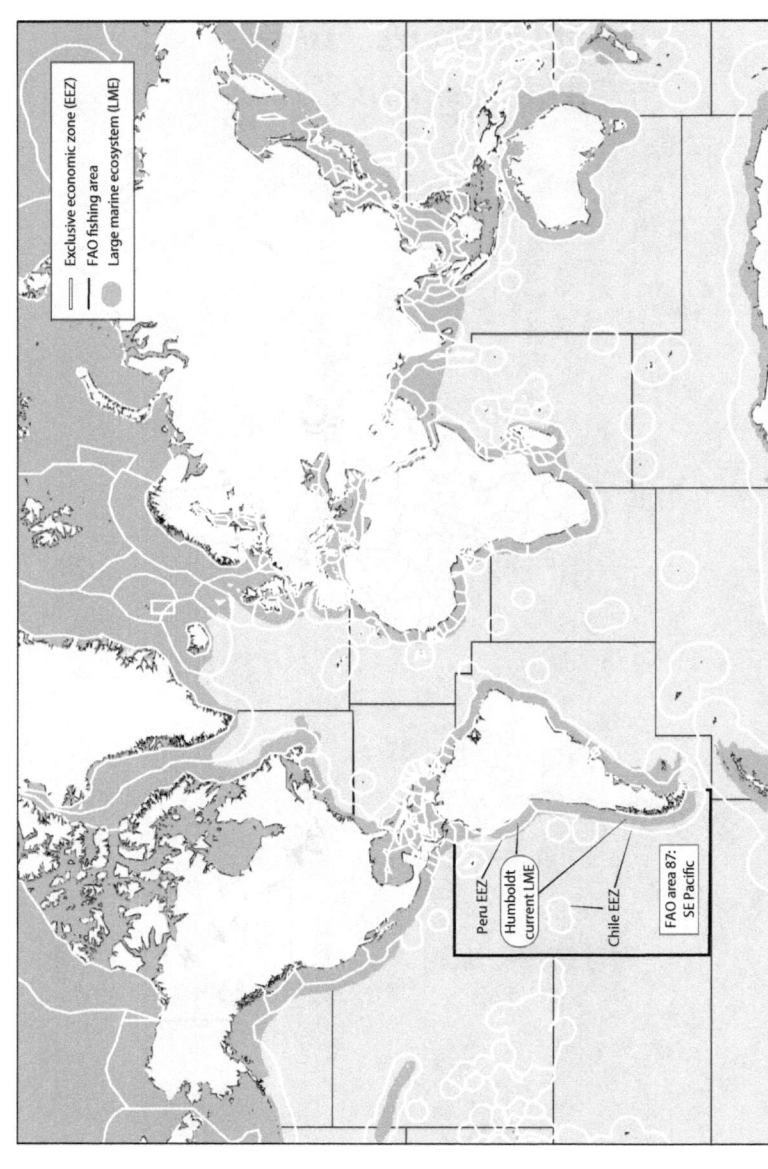

MAP 3. World fisheries management zones. Map by the author. *Sources*: ESRI, VLIZ, NOAA, FAO.

APPENDIX E

Graph of World Fisheries Landings and ENSO Events, 1950–2014

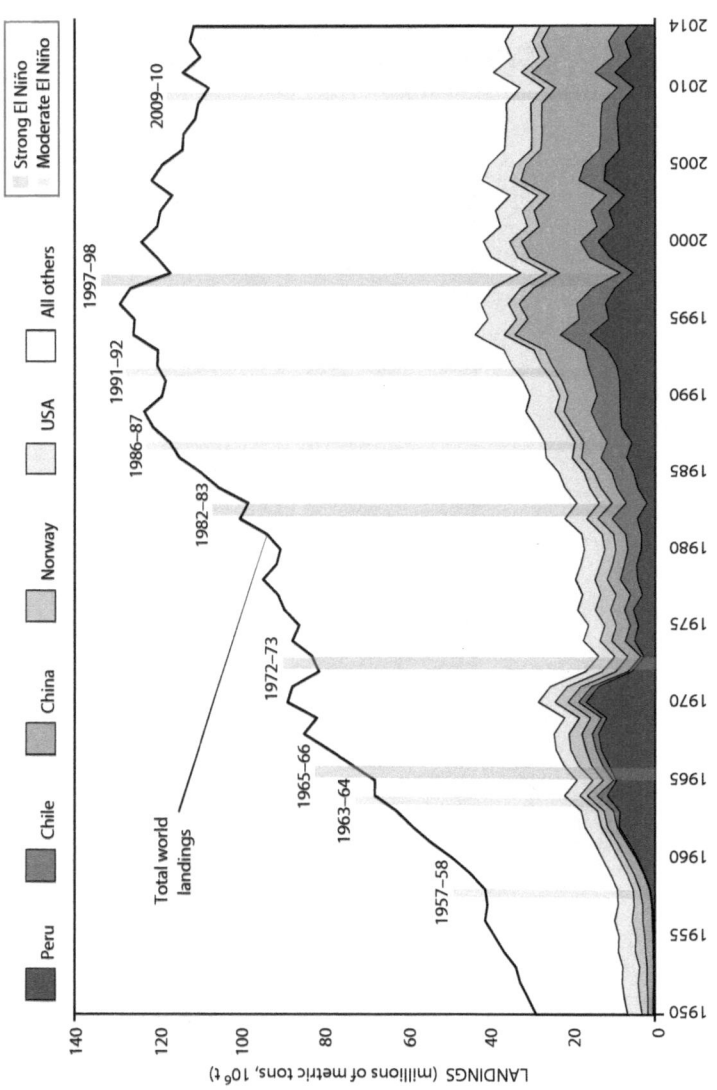

FIGURE 18. World fisheries production and the El Niño Southern Oscillation (ENSO) 1950–2014. Graph by the author. *Sources*: Reconstructed catch data from D. Pauly and D. Zeller, eds., *Sea Around Us* (www.seaaroundus.org, 2017). "Moderate" (ONI=1.0–1.4°C SST anomaly) and "Strong" (ONI>1.5°C SST anomaly) warming events from Oceanic Niño Index Data Series, NOAA and U.S. National Weather Service.

NOTES

INTRODUCTION

1. Robert Cushman Murphy, "Fisheries Resources in Peru," *The Scientific Monthly*, 16, no. 6 (1923): 600, 601.
2. Murphy, "Fisheries Resources."
3. Writing in 1941, Rachel Carson narrated a similar scene where seagulls hovered above a school of herring while a swordfish—"a great dark shadow that whirled and darted and lunged in a frenzy of attack in the midst of the closely packed ranks"—ate his fill; they then swooped in for the leftovers. In "Under the Sea-Wind," in *The Sea* (London: Readers Union, 1965 [1941]), 302.
4. Carson, on the other hand, offered a more fish-centered version of events, describing the predator-prey relationships of the sea partially through the life-journey of a mackerel named Scomber. Carson, "Under the Sea-Wind."
5. On the global ecological history of guano, see Gregory T. Cushman, *Guano and the Opening of the Pacific World* (Cambridge: Cambridge University Press, 2013).
6. Robert E. Coker, "The Fisheries and the Guano Industry of Peru," *Bulletin of the U.S. Bureau of Fisheries* 28 (1908): 338.
7. Robert Cushman Murphy, *Oceanic Birds of South America, 2 vols.* (New York: Macmillan, 1936); see especially vol. 2, 819–820, 838–840, 899–902.
8. Murphy, *Oceanic Birds*, 1:2.
9. Daniel H. Sandweiss et al., "Environmental Change and Economic Development in Coastal Peru between 5,800 and 3,600 Years Ago," *Proceedings of the National Academy of Sciences* 106, no. 5 (2009): 1359–63; Daniel H. Sandweiss et al., "Geoarchaeological Evidence for Multidecadal Natural Climatic Variability and Ancient Peruvian Fisheries," *Quaternary Research* 61 (2004): 330–34; E. R. Gunther, "Variations in Behavior of the Peru Coastal Current," *The Geographical Journal* 88, no. 1 (1936): 37–61; Robert Cushman Murphy, "Notes on the Findings of the 'William Scoresby' in the Peru Coastal Current," *Geographical Review* 27, no. 2 (1937): 295–300.

10. The origin of the name is in fact unsubstantiated, O. H. K. Spate noted, as scholars' repeated association of the name "Pacific" with Magellan was unverified in the historical record. See "From 'South Sea' to the 'Pacific': A Note on Nomenclature," The Journal of Pacific History 12, no. 4 (1977): 205–11; and Spate, The Spanish Lake (Cambridge: Cambridge University Press, 1977).

11. Margaret Deacon, *Scientists and the Sea, 1650–1900: A Study of Marine Science* (London: Academic Press, 1971), 53–56; see also Eric L. Mills, *The Fluid Envelope of Our Planet: How the Study of Ocean Currents Became a Science* (Toronto, 2009), 22–26.

12. See Gunther, "Variations in Behaviour of the Peru Coastal Current"; E. Schweigger, *El litoral peruano*, 2nd ed. (Lima: Universidad Nacional Federico Villareal, 1964), 33–54.

13. Murphy, *Oceanic Birds*, 1:95.

14. Coker, "The Fisheries," 338.

15. Murphy, *Oceanic Birds*, 1:27; 2:845.

16. Coker, "The Fisheries," 339.

17. Murphy, "Fisheries Resources," 595.

18. On the post–World War Two expansion of poultry, hog, and fish farming, see (among others): William Boyd and Michael Watts, "Agro-Industrial Just-in-Time: The Chicken Industry and Postwar American Capitalism," in *Globalising Food: Agrarian Questions and Global Restructuring*, ed. D. Goodman and M. Watts (New York: Routledge, 1997), 192–225; Roger Horowitz, *Putting Meat on the American Table: Taste, Technology, Transformation* (Baltimore: Johns Hopkins University Press, 2006); Henning Steinfeld et al., *Livestock's Long Shadow* (Rome: FAO, 2006).

19. Boyd and Watts, "Agro-Industrial Just-in-Time."

20. These findings challenge the assumption that species destined for industrial purposes are inedible or commercially unviable, as the misnomer "trash fish" implies. So-called directed industrial fisheries target small schooling species such as anchoveta, herring, or menhaden, and send their catch directly to fishmeal and oil plants, but researchers also found that an unknown but significant quantity of bycatch (non-target species), such as those landed in shrimp trawl nets, were fed directly to the animals. Tim Cashion et al., "Most Fish Destined for Fishmeal Production Are Food-Grade Fish," *Fish and Fisheries* 18 (2017): 837–44, see especially fig. 1 and table 1; see also fig. 7 in: Jacqueline Alder et al., "Forage Fish: From Ecosystems to Markets," *Annual Review of Environment and Resources* 33 (2008): 153–66. For a colloquial example of the "trash fish" label, see Earl Arnett, "A Plan for Trash Fish Use," *The Sun* (March 7, 1975): B1.

21. Cashion et al, "Most Fish Destined," table 1.

22. David H. Cushing, *The Provident Sea* (Cambridge: Cambridge University Press, 1988).

23. Cushing, *The Provident Sea*, 129, 256.

24. A purse seine (called *bolichera* in Peru and *goleta* in Chile) is a fishing vessel that employs a large net, which is sometimes set by a smaller motorized skiff, in order to encircle an entire school of fish or portion thereof; one side of the net sinks and encloses the fish from below when cinched.

25. Cushing, *The Provident Sea*, 234–36; see also Paul Josephson, "The Ocean's Hot Dog: The Development of the Fish Stick," *Technology and Culture* 49, no. 1 (2008): 41–61.

26. Anna Tsing, "Natural Resources and Capitalist Frontiers," *Economic and Political Weekly* (November 28, 2003): 5101.

27. FAO, "*Engraulis ringens*: Species Fact Sheet," http://www.fao.org/fishery/species/2917/en.

28. Cashion et al., "Most Fish Destined," table 1.

29. Francisco P. Chavez et al., "The Northern Humboldt Current System: Brief History, Present Status and a View towards the Future," *Progress in Oceanography: The Northern Humboldt Current System: Ocean Dynamics, Ecosystem Processes, and Fisheries*, 79, nos. 2–4 (October 2008): 95–105.

30. R.W. Hardy and Albert G.J. Tacon, "Fish Meal: Historical Uses, Production Trends and Future Outlook for Sustainable Supplies," in *Responsible Marine Aquaculture*, edited by R. R. Stickney and J. P. McVey (New York: CABI, 2002), 315.

31. Brian G. Henning, "The Ethics of Food, Fuel, and Feed," *Daedalus* 144, no. 4 (2015): 90–98; Henning, "'Standing in Livestock's Long Shadow': The Ethics of Eating Meat on a Small Planet," *Ethics & the Environment* 16, no. 2 (2011): 63–93; Steinfeld et al., *Livestock's Long Shadow*.

32. Sandweiss et al., "Environmental Change," 1359.

33. Vivian Montecino and Carina B. Lange, "The Humboldt Current System: Ecosystem Components and Processes, Fisheries, and Sediment Studies," *Progress in Oceanography: Eastern Boundary Upwelling Ecosystems Symposium*, 83, nos. 1–4 (December 2009): 65–79; Coker, "Ocean Temperatures," 132.

34. The three subregions of the HCS have "distinct seasonal patterns in the oceanographic and meteorological settings": Peru (5–18°S), northern Chile (18–30°S), and central-southern Chile (30–42°S). Ruben Escribano and Carmen E. Morales, "Spatial and Temporal Scales of Variability in the Coastal Upwelling and Coastal Transition Zones off Central-Southern Chile (35–40°S)," *Progress in Oceanography: Variability of the Coastal Upwelling and Coastal Transition Zones off Central-Southern Chile*, 92–95 (January 2012): 1–7; Montecino and Lange, "The Humboldt Current System."

35. Trophodynamics refers to the fluctuating interspecies relationships within an ecosystem, in which prey transfer nutrients and energy to predators through feeding. Scientists use the Marine Trophic Index (MTI) to classify these relationships on a quantitative scale. See K. Kleisner, H. Mansour, and D. Pauly, "The MTI and RMTI as tools for unmasking the fishing down phenomenon," University of British Columbia Fisheries Centre: Sea Around Us, 2015. http://www.seaaroundus.org/mti-fib-rmti/

36. Montecino and Lange, "The Humboldt Current System," 65, 68; Arnaud Bertrand et al., "From Small-Scale Habitat Loopholes to Decadal Cycles: A Habitat-Based Hypothesis Explaining Fluctuation in Pelagic Fish Populations Off Peru," *Fish and Fisheries* 5 (2004): 296–316.

37. Ruth Calienes, "Producción primaria, ambiente marino, Pacífico sudeste, Perú, 1960–2000," *Boletín IMARPE*, 29, nos. 1–2 (2014): 231.

38. The anomalous temperatures along the South American coast usually peak in April–June, and for the next six months these warmer waters extend toward the northwest, eventually joining together with the warmer waters of the central Pacific to cover up to one-quarter of the globe. Calienes, "Producción primaria," 233.

39. Coker, "Ocean Temperatures," 132.

40. For example, the white booby (*Sula dactylatra*), a species usually absent during normal upwelling, signaled an advance of warm waters associated with the coastal countercurrent from the north (Murphy, *Oceanic Birds*, 2:848).

41. Murphy, *Oceanic Birds*, 1:102.

42. Murphy, *Oceanic Birds*, 2:840.

43. "Las Corrientes Marinas," *Chile Pesquero* 7 (1979): 36.

44. Sandweiss et al., "Environmental Change"; Sandweiss et al., "Geoarchaeological Evidence."

45. *Sea Around Us* lists sixty-six LMEs, although there are sixty-four that are officially recognized, in order to account for two additional LMEs under consideration due to the splitting of existing arctic areas (see D. Pauly and D. Zeller, "Large Marine Ecosystems [definition]," http://www.seaaroundus.org/sea-around-us-area-parameters-and-definitions/#_Toc421807917). See also M. Spalding et al., "Marine Ecoregions of the World: A Bioregionalization of Coastal and Shelf Areas," *BioScience* 57, no. 7 (2007): 573–83; K. Sherman et al., "Policy Brief: Large Marine Ecosystems," *Global Forum on Oceans, Coasts and Islands* (March 30, 2008), https://globaloceanforumdotcom.files.wordpress.com/2013/03/lme-pb-june18.pdf.

46. Jürgen Alheit and Miguel Niquen, "Regime Shifts in the Humboldt Current Ecosystem," *Progress in Oceanography* 60 (2004): 201. See also Alec D. MacCall, "The Sardine-Anchovy Puzzle," in *Shifting Baselines: The Past and the Future of Ocean Fisheries*, ed. Jeremy B. Jackson, Karen E. Alexander, and Enric Sala (New York: Island Press, 2011), 47–58; Francisco P. Chavez and Monique Messié, "A Comparison of Eastern Boundary Upwelling Ecosystems," *Progress in Oceanography: Eastern Boundary Upwelling Ecosystems Symposium*, 83, nos. 1–4 (December 2009): 80–96.

47. Greater precision is possible in the post–World War Two era with the availability of detailed recordkeeping in fisheries landings; cooler temperature phases correlate to anchovy regimes from 1950 to 1975, and 1985 to 2005, and warmer phases corresponding to a sardine regime from 1970 to 1985. Alheit and Niquen, "Regime Shifts," 201.

48. Sandweiss et al., "Geoarchaeological Evidence."

49. Chavez et al., "The Northern Humboldt Current System," 97.

50. Matt K. Matsuda, *Pacific Worlds: A History of Seas, Peoples, and Cultures* (Cambridge: Cambridge University Press, 2012), 5–6; Sebastian Conrad, *What Is Global History?* (Princeton, NJ: 2016), 11–12, 6.

51. For a thorough accounting of El Niño and La Niña events, and their durations and strengths, between 1871 and 2008, see table 1 in Benjamin S. Giese and Sulagna Ray, "El Niño variability in Simple Ocean Data Assimilation (SODA), 1871–2008," *Journal of Geophysical Research: Oceans* 116, no. C2 (2011).

52. Mary C. Stiner and Gillian Feeley-Harnik, "Energy and Ecosystems," in *Deep History: The Architecture of Past and Present*, ed. Andrew Shryock and Daniel Lord Smail (Berkeley: University of California, 2011), 98.
53. Elspeth Probyn, *Eating the Ocean* (Durham, NC: Duke, 2016), 131.
54. "All descriptive spatial categories need to be situated historically." Jürgen Osterhammel, *The Transformation of the World: A Global History of the Nineteenth Century* (Princeton, NJ: Princeton University Press, 2014), 91.
55. MacCall, "The Sardine-Anchovy Puzzle," 48.
56. Cushing, *The Provident Sea*, 253.
57. MacCall, "The Sardine-Anchovy Puzzle," 48.
58. Arthur F. McEvoy, *The Fisherman's Problem: Ecology and Law in the California Fisheries, 1850–1980* (Cambridge: Cambridge University Press, 1986), 155.
59. Gregory Cushman, "Enclave Vision: Foreign Networks in Peru and the Internationalization of El Niño Research During the 1920s," *History of Meteorology* 1, no. 1 (2004): 71.
60. Reginald H. Fiedler, Norman D. Jarvis, and Milton J. Lobell, "La pesca y las industrias pesqueras en el Peru," Informe de la Misión Pesquera Norteamericana (Lima: CAG, 1943); Milton J. Lobell et al., *Misión pesquera norteamericana en Chile: Un informe preliminar sobre la situación pesquera en Chile* (Santiago, Chile: CORFO and USFW, 1945).
61. Lisa M. Campbell et al., "Global Oceans Governance: New and Emerging Issues," *Annual Review of Environment and Resources* 41 (2016): 524.
62. For an overview of this dataset, see Dirk Zeller et al., "Still Catching Attention: *Sea Around Us* Reconstructed Global Catch Data, Their Spatial Expression and Public Accessibility," *Marine Policy* 70 (2016): 145–52. For a discussion of the data for Chile and Peru, respectively, see Lisbeth van der Meer et al., "Reconstruction of Total Marine Fisheries Catches for Mainland Chile (1950–2010)," University of British Columbia Fisheries Centre, Working Paper #2015-91 (2015): 1–15; Jaime Mendo and Claudia Wosnitza-Mendo, "Reconstruction of Total Marine Fisheries Catches for Peru: 1950–2010," University of British Columbia Fisheries Centre, Working Paper #2014-21 (2014): 1–23.
63. Gregory T. Cushman, "Humboldtian Science, Creole Meteorology, and the Discovery of Human-Caused Climate Change in South America," *Osiris* 26, no. 1 (2011): 16–44.
64. Michael J. McPhaden, Stephen E. Zebiak, and Michael H. Glantz, "ENSO as an Integrating Concept in Earth Science," *Science* 314, no. 5806 (2006): 1740–45.

CHAPTER ONE. A DEEP HISTORY OF THE HUMBOLDT CURRENT ECOSYSTEM

1. Eliot G. Mears, "The Callao Painter," *Scientific Monthly* 57, no. 4 (1943): 331–36; see also Horace Loftin, "Nature Ramblings: The Callao Painter," *Science News Letter* (September 22, 1956): 192; E. R. Gunther, "Variations in Behaviour of the

Peru Coastal Current: With an Historical Introduction," *Geographical Journal* 88, no. 1 (1936): 51.

2. Burt Franklin Jenness, "The 'Callao Painter,'" *Sea Lanes and Other Poems* (Boston: Cornhill Publishing Company, 1921), 27–28.

3. "Las Corrientes Marinas," *Chile Pesquero* 7 (1979): 36.

4. Joel W. Hedgpeth and Harry S. Ladd, eds., *Treatise on Marine Ecology and Paleoecology*, Memoir 67, 2 vols. (Boulder, CO: Geological Society of America, 1957): 1:981. The authors make the particular distinction between the two phenomena, noting that others had conflated the two.

5. This refers to calibrated samples from the Monte Verde site in Patagonia, Chile; Karen Moreno et al., "A Late Pleistocene Human Footprint from the Pilauco Archaeological Site, Northern Patagonia, Chile," *PLoS ONE* 14, no. 4 (2019): e0213572. This chapter uses the dating system favored by archaeologists and other scientists who rely upon radiocarbon dating techniques to calibrate their samples by comparing them to radiocarbon measurements of tree rings or other samples whose ages have already been determined. Dates are expressed in thousands of years "before present" (BP), where "present" refers to the year 1950. Since it is assumed that the proportion of radiocarbon in the atmosphere has been consistent since 1950, calibrated radiocarbon dates can be compared directly to calendar years in the Western system (see OxCal, "Radiocarbon Calibration," University of Oxford (updated July 26, 2019), https://c14.arch.ox.ac.uk/calibration.html).

6. Daniel H. Sandweiss et al., "Environmental Change and Economic Development in Coastal Peru between 5,800 and 3,600 Years Ago," *Proceedings of the National Academy of Sciences* 106, no. 5 (2009): 1359–63.

7. On piracy in the Pacific during this period, see Kris E. Lane, *Pillaging the Empire: Piracy in the Americas, 1500–1750* (London: M.E. Sharpe, 1998), chap. 3 and 5.

8. Alexander Von Humboldt, *Alexander Von Humboldt en el Perú: Diário de viaje y otros escritos*, ed. Estuardo Núñez and Georg Petersen (Lima: Banco Central de la Reserva, 2002), 232, 257.

9. E.R. Gunther reviews this debate at length in "Variations," and in the original "A Report on Oceanographical Investigations in the Peru Coastal Current," in *Discovery Reports, Vol. 13* (Cambridge: Cambridge University Press, 1936), 109–276.

10. Michael Dettelbach, "Global Physics and Aesthetic Empire: Humboldt's Physical Portrait of the Tropics," in *Visions of Empire: Voyages, Botany, and Representations of Nature*, ed. David Philip Miller and Peter Hanns Reill (Cambridge: Cambridge University Press, 1996), 264; see also Jürgen Osterhammel, *The Transformation of the World: A Global History of the Nineteenth Century* (Princeton, NJ: Princeton, 2014), 91–92.

11. Andrew Shryock and Daniel Lord Smail, *Deep History: The Architecture of Past and Present* (Berkeley: University of California Press, 2011), ix.

12. South of the Atacama, the landscape transitions to semiarid (the "Norte Chico" of Chile), then Mediterranean (called the Matorral), before finally reaching the temperate rainforests that begin near the present-day city of Valdivia (37°S).

13. María Rostworowski de Diez Canseco, *Costa peruana prehispánica: Obras completas, tomo 3* (Lima: Instituto de Estudios Peruanos, 2004), 311.

14. The Peru-Chile Trench measures approximately 5,000 km. Roland Von Huene, Erwin Suess, and Kay-Christian Emeis, "Convergent Tectonics and Coastal Upwelling: A History of the Peru Continental Margin," *Episode* 10, no. 2 (1987): 87; Carlos Galli-Olivier, "Climate: A Primary Control of Sedimentation in the Peru-Chile Trench," *Geological Society of America Bulletin* 80, no. 9 (1969): 1849. doi:10.1130/0016-7606(1969)80[1849:CAPCOS]2.0.CO;2

15. A. Udías, R. Madariaga, E. Buforn, D. Muñoz, and M. Ros, "The Large Chilean Historical Earthquakes of 1647, 1657, 1730, and 1751 from Contemporary Documents," *Bulletin of the Seismological Society of America* 102, no. 4 (2012): 1639. Historian Charles Walker used a single earthquake to frame his social history of colonial-era Lima, *Shaky Colonialism: The 1746 Earthquake-Tsunami in Lima, Peru, and Its Long Aftermath* (Durham, NC: Duke University Press, 2008).

16. National Geophysical Data Center/World Data Service (NGDC/WDS), *Global Historical Tsunami Database*, National Geophysical Data Center, NOAA (accessed September 16, 2019); see also S. L. Soloviev and Ch. N. Go, "A Catalogue of Tsunamis on the Eastern Shore of the Pacific Ocean [dates include 1513–1968]," Academy of Sciences of the USSR (Moscow: Nauka Publishing House), translation no. 5078 of the Canadian Translation of Fisheries and Aquatic Sciences series (Ottawa: Canada Institute for Scientific and Technical Information), 1984; cited in NGDC/WDS, *Global Historical Tsunami Database*.

17. K. Abe, "Size of Great Earthquakes of 1837–1974 Inferred from Tsunami Data," *Journal of Geophysical Research* 84, no. B4 (1979): 1561–68; Von Huene, Suess, and Emeis, "Convergent Tectonics and Coastal Upwelling."

18. Von Huene, Suess, and Emeis, "Convergent Tectonics and Coastal Upwelling," 90–91; Laurent Dezileau et al., "Iron Control of Past Productivity in the Coastal Upwelling System off the Atacama Desert, Chile," *Paleoceanography* 19, no. 3 (2004).

19. Paul A. Mayewski et al., "Holocene Climate Variability," *Quaternary Research* 62 (2004): 243–55.

20. Moreno et al., "A Late Pleistocene Human Footprint"; see also W. R. Dickinson, "Geological Perspectives on the Monte Verde Archaeological Site in Chile and Pre-Clovis Coastal Migration in the Americas," *Quaternary Research* 76 (2011): 201–10.

21. Lautaro Núñez, Martin Grosjean, and Isabel Cartajena, "Human Occupations and Climate Change in Puna de Atacama, Chile," *Science 298, no. 5594 (2002): 821–24.*

22. Ruth Shady Solís, "Caral-Supe y su entorno natural y social en los origines de la civilizacion," *Investigaciones Sociales* 9 (2014): 91; Sandweiss et al., "Environmental Change," 1359.

23. Sandweiss et al., "Environmental Change," 1359. Maize, on the other hand, played a relatively minor role in the economy and diet alongside other food sources; see Ruth Shady Solís, "Caral-Supe and the North-Central Area of Peru: The History

of Maize in the Land Where Civilization Came into Being," in *Histories of Maize: Multidisciplinary Approaches to the Prehistory, Linguistics, Biogeography, Domestication and Evolution of Maize*, ed. John E. Staller, Robert H. Tykot, and Bruce F. Benz (Cambridge, MA: Elsevier, 2006), 381–402.

24. "Mural from 3800 Years Ago Unveiled by Peru Archaeologists," *BBC News* (8/20/19).

25. The author further describes these two major phases as (1) The Stage of Maritime Gatherers and (2) The Stage of Archaic Fishermen. Agostín Llagostera, "Early Occupations and the Emergence of Fishermen on the Pacific Coast of South America," *Andean Past* 3, no. 1 (1992): 87.

26. Llagostera, "Early Occupations," 87.

27. D. Carabias, N. Lira, and L. Adán, "Reflexiones en torno al uso de embarcaciones monóxilas en ambientes boscoso lacustres precordilleranos andinos, zona centro-sur de Chile," *Magallania (Chile)* 38, no. 1: 87–108, cited in Elena Saccone, "Seafaring as a Key Element in the First Peopling of the Americas: A Perspective from the Southern Cone," *Journal of Maritime Archaeology* (2019): 8.

28. Direct evidence of maritime technology and linguistic interconnections is relatively thin for the South American Pacific coast and this has long been a subject of debate among archaeologists; for a brief review of this question, see Roger Blench, "Two Vanished African Maritime Traditions and a Parallel from South America," *African Archaeological Review* 29 (2012): 284–87.

29. Translation by the author. Ruth Shady Solís, "Caral-Supe y su entorno natural," 91–92.

30. Lisa Esquivel Wells and Jay Stratton Noller, "Holocene Coevolution of the Physical Landscape and Human Settlement in Northern Coastal Peru," *Geoarchaeology: An International Journal* 14, no. 8 (1999): 776. Nonetheless, Sandweiss et al. suggest that maritime resources held relatively less importance for coastal societies in this region after the demise of Caral-Supe.

31. César Méndez, Amalio Nuevo Delaunay, and Ramiro Barberena, "New Perspectives in Archaeological Research of Marginal Deserts in South America," in *Futuro sostenible de la vida en el desierto*, ed. Nuria Sanz (Mexico City: UNESCO, 2017): 89–101; David Beresford-Jones et al., "Refining the Maritime Foundations of Andean Civilization: How Plant Fiber Technology Drove Social Complexity during the Preceramic Period," *Journal of Archaeological Method & Theory* 25, no. 2 (2018): 393–425.

32. María Rostworowski de Diez Canseco, *Recursos naturales renovables y pesca, siglos XVI y XVII: Curacas y sucesiones, costa norte: Obras completas, tomo 4* (Lima: Instituto de Estudios Peruanos, 2005), 43; Jorge Hidalgo, "Los pescadores de la costa norte de Chile y su relación con los agricultores, siglos XVI y XVII," in *La arqueología y la etnohistoria: Un encuentro andino*, ed. John R. Topic (Lima: Instituto de Estudios Peruanos, 2009), 149.

33. Shady, "Caral-Supe;" see also Joyce Marcus, Jeffrey D. Sommer, and Christopher P. Glew, "Fish and Mammals in the Economy of an Ancient Peruvian Kingdom," *PNAS* 96 (1999): 6564–70.

34. Thomas Pozorski and Shelia Pozorski, "The Impact of the El Niño Phenomenon on Prehistoric Chimú Irrigation Systems of the Peruvian Coast," in *El Niño in Peru: Biology and Culture Over 10,000 Years*, ed. Jonathan Haas and Michael O. Dillon (Chicago: Field Museum of Natural History, 2003), 71.

35. Jorge Gamboa Velásquez and Jason Nesbitt, "La ocupación Moche en la margen norte del valle bajo de Moche, costa norte del Perú," *Arqueología y Sociedad* 25 (2012): 115–42.

36. See William Y. Adams, "On the Argument from Ceramics to History: A Challenge Based on Evidence from Medieval Nubia," *Current Anthropology* 20, no. 4 (1979): 727–44; George Kubler, "Period, Style, and Meaning in Ancient American Art," *New Literary History* 1, no. 2 (1970): 127–44; both cited in Edward Swenson and Andrew Roddick, "Rethinking Temporality and Historicity from the Perspective of Andean Archaeology," in *Constructions of Time and History in the Pre-Columbian Andes*, by Swenson and Roddick (Boulder: University Press of Colorado, 2018), 7.

37. Pozorski and Pozorski, "The Impact," 82–83.

38. See Beresford-Jones et al., "Refining the *Maritime Foundations;*" M. E. Moseley, *The Maritime Foundations of Andean Civilization* (Menlo Park, CA: Cummings, 1975); Shady, "Caral-Supe and the North-Central Area of Peru." For archaeo-botanical perspectives on the domestication of cotton, see Barbara Pickersgill, "Domestication of Plants in the Americas: Insights from Mendelian and Molecular Genetics," *Annals of Botany* 100, no. 5 (2007): 925–40; O. T. Westengen, Z. Huamán, and M. Heun, "Genetic Diversity and Geographic Pattern in Early South American Cotton Domestication," *Theoretical and Applied Genetics* 110 (2005): 392–402.

39. Donald A. Proulx, *A Sourcebook of Nasca Ceramic Iconography: Reading a Culture through Its Art* (Iowa City: University of Iowa, 2006), 13, 149–55; Rebecca Stone, *Art of the Andes: From Chavín to Inca,* 3rd ed. (New York: Thames and Hudson, 2012).

40. José Antonio del Busto Duthurburu, *Túpac Yupanqui: Descubridor de Oceanía* (Lima: Fondo Editorial del Congreso del Perú, 2006), 35–36, 67; Enrique Amayo Zevallos, "Proyecciones andinas en el Pacífico: Del pasado al presente," in *Geopolítica latinoamericana y del caribe*, ed. Leopoldo Zea y Mario Magallón (México, D.F.: Fondo de Cultura Económica, 1999), 17–18. The Norwegian explorer and ethnographer Thor Heyerdahl (1914–2002) re-created the route in 1947, sailing across the Pacific on the *Kon-Tiki,* a replica of a fifteenth-century raft, in order to demonstrate the feasibility of such an expedition; see Thor Heyerdahl, *American Indians in the Pacific: The Theory behind the Kon-Tiki Expedition* (London: George Allen and Unwin, 1952); and "Voyaging Distance and Voyaging Time in Pacific Migration," *The Geographical Journal* 117, no. 1 (1951): 69–77.

41. Marcus, Sommer, and Glew, "Fish and Mammals."

42. Daniel H. Sandweiss et al., "Geoarchaeological Evidence for Multidecadal Natural Climatic Variability and Ancient Peruvian Fisheries," *Quaternary Research* 61 (2004): 330–34.

43. The classic thesis of vertical complementarity was proposed by John V. Murra in, *El 'control vertical' de un máximo de pisos ecológicos en la economía de las*

sociedades andinas (Huánuco, Peru: Universidad Hermilio Valdizán, 1972). The concept originated in Murra's dissertation research: Murra, "The Economic Organization of the Inca State," PhD dissertation, University of Chicago (1956), cited in Mary van Buren, "Rethinking the Vertical Archipelago: Ethnicity, Exchange, and History in the South Central Andes," *American Anthropologist* 98, no. 2 (1996): 338–51.

44. Pedro de Cieza de León, *The Discovery and Conquest of Peru, Part Three,* ed. Alexandra Parma Cook and Noble David Cook (Durham, NC: Duke University Press, 1999), 117.

45. Paul Trawick, *The Struggle for Water in Peru: Comedy and Tragedy in the Andean Commons* (Stanford, CA: Stanford University Press, 2003).

46. Hipólito Ruiz, *Relación histórica del viage, que hizo a los reynos del Perú y Chile el botánico D. Hipolito Ruiz en el año de 1777 hasta el de 1788, en cuya época regresó a Madrid, Tomo 1,* 2nd. ed (Madrid: Talleres Gráficos Bermejo, 1952), 40, quoted in María Rostworowski, *Recursos naturales*, 39.

47. Pedro de Cieza de León, *Crónica del Perú: El señorío de los Incas, primera parte,* ed. Franklin Pease (Ayacucho: Fundación Biblioteca Ayacucho, 2005 [1553]), 203; see also *The Discovery*, 118–19n14.

48. Rostworowski, *Recursos naturales*, 38; see also Philip W. Rundel, "Ecological Relationships of Desert Fog Zone Lichens," *The Bryologist* 81, no. 2 (1978): 277–93.

49. Rostworowski, *Recursos naturales*, 52, 55.

50. Cieza de León, *Crónica, primera parte,* 203.

51. See Rostworowski, *Recursos naturales*, 80.

52. Rostworowski, *Recursos naturales*, 42.

53. Rostworowski, *Costa peruana*, 316.

54. Cieza de León, *Crónica, primera parte*, 18.

55. Zárate, cited in E. R. Gunther, "Variations," 38. In 1522, P. de Andagoya also mentioned the "many currents" and resulting navigational delays in the South Sea. Conversely, in 1604 the Jesuit priest José de Acosta noted the menacing northerly winds, a possible reference to the El Niño counter-current; José de Acosta, *The Naturall and Morall Historie of the East and West Indies, No. 60* (London, 1880 [1604]), cited in Gunther, "Variations," 38–39.

56. Rostworowski, *Costa peruana*, 108.

57. Eric L. Mills, *The Fluid Envelope of Our Planet: How the Study of Ocean Currents Became a Science* (Toronto: University of Toronto Press, 2009); see especially Mills's discussion of seventeenth-century scientific advances, 16–26.

58. A. F. Frezier, *Relation du voyage de la Mer du Sud aux côtes du Chily et du Perou, fait pendant les années 1712, 1713, 1714* (Paris/London, 1717 [1716]), cited in Gunther, "Variations," 42.

59. J. Juan y Santacilla and A. de Ulloa, *Relacion historica del viage a la America meridional hecho de orden de S. Mag. para medir algunos grados de Meridiano Terrestre, y venir por ellos en conocimiento de la verdadera Figura, y Magnitud de la*

Tierra, con otras varias Observaciones Astronomicas y Phisicas (Madrid/London, 1807 [1748]), cited in Gunther, "Variations," 42.

60. Richard Walter, *A Voyage Round the World in the Years 1740–1744 by George Anson Esq.* (London: Knapton, 1748), cited in Gunther, "Variations," 40.

61. Cieza de León, *Crónica, primera parte,* Cap. 74, 205–6.

62. Cieza de León, *Discovery, Part Three,* Fol. 24, 116.

63. Cited in Rostworowski, *Recursos naturales,* 80.

64. Hipólito Ruiz, *The Journals of Hipólito Ruiz, Spanish Botanist in Peru and Chile, 1777–88,* trans. Richard Evans Schultes and Maria Jose Nemry von Thenen de Jaramillo-Arango (Portland, OR: Timber Press, 1998), 195.

65. This phenomenon typically occurs in the open ocean, so probably indicated that the ship was near the frontier of the Humboldt Current system; thanks to Gregory Cushman for this insight.

66. Ruiz, *Journals,* 195.

67. W. Funnel, *A Voyage Round the World: Being an Account of Capt. William Dampier's Expedition into the South Seas in the Ship* St George (London: James Knapton, 1729), cited in Gunther, "Variations," 39.

68. John J. Johnson, "Early Relations of the United States with Chile," *Pacific Historical Review* 13, no. 3 (1944): 260.

69. Johnson, "Early Relations," 262n13.

70. John Soluri, "On Edge: Fur Seals and Hunters along the Patagonian Littoral, 1860–1930," in *Centering Animals in Latin American History,* ed. Martha Few and Zeb Tortorici (Durham, NC: Duke University Press, 2013), 250.

71. Johnson, "Early Relations," 263.

72. Rostworowski, *Recursos naturales,* 41–42.

73. Dettelbach, "Global Physics," 261.

74. Alexander von Humboldt, "Ueber Meeresströmungen im allgemeinen; und über die [kalte] peruanische Strömung der Südsee, im Gegenfasse zu dem warmen Golf- oder Florida-Strome," Sissung der Akademie der Wissenschaften zu Berlin, 27 Juni 1833, Deutsches Literaturarchiv Marbach (DLA), Cotta T/S, Kleinere Prosa, Bd. 2, fragm.

75. Humboldt's isotherm theory is depicted in the map, *System Der Isotherm-Kurven,* published by Heinrich Berghaus in *Physikalischer Atlas* (Justus Perthes, 1845 [1838]), Geography and Map Division, U.S. Library of Congress; see Mike Klein, "The First Isothermic World Maps," Geography and Maps, Library of Congress, https://blogs.loc.gov/maps/2018/04/the-first-isothermic-world-maps/ (retrieved September 26, 2019).

76. Alexander von Humboldt, *Recuil d'observations astronomiques, d'opérations trigonométriques et de mesures barométriques, faites pendant le cours d'un voyage aux régions équinoxiales du nouveau continent, depuis 1799 jusqu'en 1803,* I (Paris, 1810), cited in Gunther, "Variations," 42.

77. Alexander von Humboldt, *Cosmos: A Sketch of a Physical Description of the Universe,* Vol. I, trans. E. C. Otté (London: H. G. Bohn, 1849), 313–14.

78. Mills, *The Fluid Envelope*, 5.
79. Humboldt, "Ueber Meeresströmungen," 1833.
80. Notable exceptions include Mills, *The Fluid Envelope,* and Gerhard Kortum, "Humboldt und das Meer: Eine Ozeanographiegeschichtliche Bestandaufnahme," *Northeastern Naturalist* 8, no. 1 (2001): 91–108.
81. Ulrike Leitner and Eberhard Knobloch, eds., *Alexander von Humboldt und Cotta, Briefwechsel* (Berlin: Aakademie Verlag, 2009). The original letters are also available in the Deutsches Literaturarchiv Marbach.
82. Gunther, "Variations," 46.
83. Laura D. Walls, *The Passage to Cosmos: Alexander Von Humboldt and the Shaping of America* (Chicago: University of Chicago Press, 2009), 85.
84. Alexander Von Humboldt, "Alexander von Humboldt en el Peru: Diario de viaje y otros escritos," ed. Estuardo Nunez and Georg Petersen (Lima: Banco Central de la Reserva del Peru, 2002), 76; also cited in Cushman, *Guano*, 24.
85. Mills, *The Fluid Envelope,* see especially 14–27.
86. Gunther, "Variations," 44, 47.
87. Urbain Dortet de Tessan, *Voyage autour du monde sur la frégate* la Vénus *pendant les années 1836–1839, vol. X* (Paris, 1844), 443, cited in Gunther, "Variations," 43.
88. Humboldt to Cotta, in Leitner and Knobloch, eds., Brief 247 (1850), 434; Brief 326, 558.
89. Among the contributors were M. Le Baron de Bougainville, Urbain Dortet de Tessan, William Ferrel, Matthew Fontaine Maury, Alexander Buchan, and E. Witte. Gunther, "Variations," 42–48, passim. Furthermore, postcolonialist scholars have critiqued Humboldt's appropriation of Creole knowledge. See, for example, Jorge Cañizares-Esguerra, "How Derivative Was Humboldt? Microcosmic Narratives in Early Modern Spanish America and the (Other) Origins of Humboldt's Ecological Sensibilities," in *Nature, Empire, and Nation* (Stanford, CA: Stanford University Press, 2007), 112–28; Gregory T. Cushman, "Humboldtian Science, Creole Meteorology, and the Discovery of Human-Caused Climate Change in South America," *Osiris* 26, no. 1 (2011): 19–44.
90. Daniel Pauly, "Charles Darwin, Ichthyology and the Species Concept," *Fish and Fisheries* 3, no 3 (2002): 148.
91. Ruiz, *Journals*, 252.
92. Francisco P. Chavez et al., "The Northern Humboldt Current System: Brief History, Present Status and a View Towards the Future," *Progress in Oceanography* 79, nos. 2–4 (2008): 97.
93. Eduard Poeppig, *Reise in Chile, Peru und auf dem Amazonenstrome, Während der Jahre 1827–1832, Erster Band* (Leipzig: Friedrich Fleischer, 1835), 296. Bundesamt für Hydrographie, Hamburg, Germany.
94. Leonard Jenyns, "*Engraulis ringens*," in *The Works of Charles Darwin, Volume 6: The Zoology of the Voyage of H.M.S.* Beagle, ed. Paul H. Barrett and R. B. Freeman (New York: New York University Press, 1987), 203.

CHAPTER TWO. THE NEW INDUSTRIAL ECOLOGY
OF ANIMAL FARMING IN THE ATLANTIC
AND PACIFIC WORLDS, 1840–1930

1. The literature on food riots is vast. For a recent review of the literature on this topic, see Raj Patel and Philip McMichael, "A Political Economy of the Food Riot," *Review: A Journal of the Fernand Braudel Center* 32, no. 1 (2009): 9–35; one of the original contributions to the debate about food riots as popular uprisings is Louise A. Tilly, "The Food Riot as a Form of Political Conflict in France," *Journal of Interdisciplinary History* 2, no. 1 (1971): 23–57; for an examination of the phenomenon in a Chilean context, see Benjamin Orlove, "Meat and Strength: The Moral Economy of a Chilean Food Riot," *Cultural Anthropology* 12, no. 2 (1997): 234–68.

2. On agricultural modernization and the chemical industry, see Frank Uekötter, "Why Panaceas Work: Recasting Science, Knowledge, and Fertilizer Interests in German Agriculture," *Agricultural History* 88, no. 1 (2014): 68–86; Frank Uekötter, "Rise, Fall, and Permanence: Issues in the Environmental History of the Global Plantation," in Uekötter, ed., *Comparing Apples, Oranges, and Cotton: Environmental Histories of the Global Plantation* (Frankfurt: Campus Verlag, 2014); Ernst Homburg, Anthony S. Travis, and Harm G. Schröter, eds., *The Chemical Industry in Europe, 1850–1914: Industrial Growth, Pollution, and Professionalization* (Dordrecht, Netherlands: Kluwer, 1998).

3. Giovanni Federico, *An Economic History of Agriculture, 1800–2000* (Princeton, NJ: Princeton University Press, 2005), 26. Noting the paucity of data for most countries prior to 1950, the author refers to data from twenty-five countries that he does not list individually, likely including Europe, North America, and Japan. "Livestock" includes cattle, sheep, goats, and hogs; these numbers exclude poultry.

4. Federico, *An Economic History of Agriculture*, 5.

5. Gregory T. Cushman, *Guano and the Opening of the Pacific World* (Cambridge: Cambridge University Press, 2013), chap. 2; Paul Gootenberg, *Between Silver and Guano* (Princeton, NJ: Princeton University Press, 1989).

6. F. Lehmann, "Die Eignung von Fischmehl als Futtermittel," *Hannoversche Land- und Forstwirtschaftliche Zeitung* (1892–1893), cited in G. Meseck, "Erzeugung und Absatz von Fischmehl in der Welt," *Berichte über Landwirtschaft: Zeitschrift für Agrarpolitik und Landwirtschaft* 38 (1960): 667; also Frederick C. Weber, "Fish Meal: Its Use as a Stock and Poultry Food," *USDA Bulletin* 378 (1916).

7. U.S. Bureau of Commercial Fisheries, Memorandum S-293, cited in E. N. Hutchinson, "Food for Plant Life Is Food for Beast," *Better Fruit* 24, no. 8 (1930): 39.

8. See especially Cushman, *Guano and the Opening of the Pacific World*; Hugh S. Gorman, "Thinking in Cycles: Flows of Nitrogen and Sustainable Uses of the Environment," in *Managing the Unknown: Essays on Environmental Ignorance*, ed. Frank Uekötter and Utte Lübken (New York: Berghahn, 2014), 32–52; and Gorman, *The Story of N: A Social History of the Nitrogen Cycle and the Challenge of Sustainability* (New Brunswick, NJ: Rutgers, 2013).

9. LaDon J. Johnson, William E. Dinusson, and Duane O. Erickson, "Nitrogen in Animal Production," *Farm Research* 37, no. 3 (1979): 30.

10. Johnson et al., "Nitrogen in Animal Production"; see also A. Sundrum, K. Schneider, and U. Richter, "Report: Possibilities and Limitations of Poultry Supply in Organic Poultry and Pig Production," *Research to Support Revision of the EU Regulation on Organic Agriculture* (2005), 13, http://www.organic-revision.org/pub/Final_Report_EC_Revision.pdf.

11. Cited in H. Bruce Franklin, *The Most Important Fish in the Sea: Menhaden and America* (Washington, DC: Island Press, 2007), 52.

12. Charles H. Stevenson, "Aquatic Products in Arts and Industries," in *Report by the Commissioner of Fish and Fisheries,* US Fisheries Commission (1902): 179–180.

13. John Richards, "Whales and Walruses in the Northern Oceans," in *The Unending Frontier: An Environmental History of the Early Modern World* (Berkeley: University of California Press, 2003), 588.

14. Johan Nicolay Tønnessen and Arne Johnsen, *The History of Modern Whaling*, trans. R. I. Christophersen (Berkeley: University of California Press, 1982), 5–6; Richards, "Whales and Walruses," 588.

15. The blue whale is the largest mammal species known to humankind. Tønnessen and Johnsen, *The History of Modern Whaling*, 4–5.

16. Dictionary of the Scots Language, http://www.dsl.ac.uk/entry/snd/smear.

17. The authors explain: "Whale oil contains genuine fats (glycerides of fatty acids), while sperm oil consists mainly of compounds of wax alcohols and fatty acids." Tønnessen and Johnsen, *The History of Modern Whaling*, 7.

18. In some high-latitude regions, seal blubber provided for similar purposes. Stevenson, "Aquatic Products.".

19. Tønnessen and Johnsen, *The History of Modern Whaling*, 6.

20. Stevenson, "Aquatic Products in Arts and Industries," 182.

21. M. E. Stansby, "Development of Fish Oil Industry in the United States," *Journal of the American Oil Chemists' Society* 55 (1978): 238.

22. Stevenson, "Aquatic Products in Arts and Industries," 235.

23. Stevenson, "Aquatic Products in Arts and Industries," 255.

24. Stevenson, "Aquatic Products in Arts and Industries," 256; Stansby, "Development of Fish Oil Industry," 238.

25. Stevenson, "Aquatic Products in Arts and Industries," 271.

26. Stansby, "Development of Fish Oil Industry," 238.

27. Stansby, "Development of Fish Oil Industry," 238; Stevenson, "Aquatic Products in Arts and Industries," 257, 263.

28. Stevenson, "Aquatic Products in Arts and Industries," 257; J. W. Turrentine, "The Menhaden Industry," *The Journal of Industrial and Engineering Chemistry* 5, no. 5 (1913): 379. Turrentine notes that the logistical challenges of loading, unloading, and storage at sea made land-based processing more profitable, and thus the floating factory model was abandoned in this fishery after 1911. Stansby, "Development of Fish Oil Industry" (238), says Rhode Island producers shipped to New York earlier.

29. David H. Cushing, *The Provident Sea* (Cambridge: Cambridge University Press, 1988), 124.

30. Stevenson, "Aquatic Products in Arts and Industries," 268–69.

31. Stevenson, "Aquatic Products in Arts and Industries," 236; see also "Japanese Fishing Industry: How Oil and Fertilizer are Procured in the Island Empire—American Machinery Needed," *Los Angeles Times* (June 10, 1906): D11.

32. On the environmental history of German agriculture, see Frank Uekötter, *Die Wahrheit ist auf dem Feld: Eine Wissensgeschichte der deutschen Landwirtschaft* (Göttingen: Vandenhoeck & Ruprecht, 2010).

33. Justus von Liebig, *Die Organische Chemie in Ihrer Anwendung auf Agricultur und Physiologie* (Braunschweig, 1840); Uschi Schling-Broderssen, "Liebig's Role in the Establishment of Agricultural Chemistry," *Ambix* 39, no. 1 (1992): 21–31.

34. Schling-Broderssen, "Liebig's Role," 21, 23.

35. Mark R. Finlay, "The German Agricultural Experiment Stations and the Beginnings of American Agricultural Research," *Agricultural History* 62, no. 2 (1988): 41.

36. Finlay points out that "the practitioners were at least as influential as the theorists during the early history of the Möckern station... [and] as in America, the scientists did not win an easy victory over the farmers for control of the experiment stations" ("The German Agricultural Experiment Stations," 43).

37. Cited (in English translation) in Finlay, "The German Agricultural Experiment Stations," 47.

38. Finlay, "The German Agricultural Experiment Stations," 49.

39. Uekötter, *Die Wahrheit ist auf dem Feld*, 159, translated by the author.

40. Uekötter, *Die Wahrheit ist auf dem Feld*, 146.

41. Finlay, "The German Agricultural Experiment Stations," 49.

42. See F. Lehmann, "Tierische Mehle und Futtermittel aus niederen Tieren," in E. Mangold, ed., *Handbuch der Ernährung und des Stoffwechsels der Landwirtschaftlichen Nutztiere als Grundlagen der Fütterungslehre: Erster Band: Nährstoffe und Futtermittel* (Berlin: Springer Verlag, 1929), especially 501–12, for a discussion of the scientific findings of these early studies. Among the most important studies were those by Weiske, Kellner, and Lehmann: Weiske, *J. Landw.* (1876): 265, and O. Kellner, "Versuche über des norwegischen Fischguanos," *Landw. Versuchsstat.* 20 [1877?], 423, cited in Lehmann, "Tierische Mehle"; and F. Lehmann, "Die Eignung von Fischmehl als Futtermittel," in *Hannoversche Land- und Forstwirtschaftliche Zeitung* (1892–93), cited in Meseck, "Erzeugung und Absatz."

43. Lehmann, "Tierische Mehle," 503, 509.

44. Lehmann, "Tierische Mehle."

45. Karen Brown, "Tropical Medicine and Animal Diseases: Onderstepoort and the Development of Veterinary Science in South Africa, 1908–1950," *Journal of Southern African Studies* 31, no. 3 (2005): 519.

46. Cushman, *Guano and the Opening of the Pacific World*, 155.

47. Oswald Schreiner, Albert R. Merz, and B. E. Brown, "Fertilizer Materials," *Yearbook of Fertilizer Materials* (1938): 487–521; Cushman, *Guano and the Opening of the Pacific World*, 155; see also Gorman, *The Story of N*.

48. Turrentine, "The Menhaden Industry," 387; Weber, "Fish Meal," 2, cites a different reference from 1835.

49. Studies on the quantitative and qualitative nutrient losses in fishmeal from decomposing raw materials were numerous and lacked consensus. A 1951 study found that there was no negative effect on yield from storage time following experiments with California pilchard: Sven Lassen, E. Kyle Bacon, and H. J. Dunn, "Fish Reduction Process: Relation of Yields and Quality of Products to Freshness of Raw Material," *Journal of Industrial and Engineering Chemistry* 43, no. 9 (1951): 2082–87.

50. F. Ashbrook, "Fish Meal as a Feed for Swine," *USDA Bulletin* 610 (1917): 1.

51. Weber, "Fish Meal," 12.

52. Turrentine, "The Menhaden Industry," 388.

53. Lehmann, "Die Eignung von Fischmehl als Futtermittel" (1892), was reportedly one of the first to highlight this.

54. Ashbrook, "Fish Meal as a Feed for Swine," 13.

55. A. F. McEvoy, *The Fisherman's Problem: Ecology and Law in the California Fisheries, 1850–1980* (Cambridge: Cambridge University Press, 1986), 140; and E. Ueber and A. McCall, "The Rise and Fall of the California Sardine Empire," in *Climate Variability, Climate Change, and Fisheries,* ed. M. Glantz, (Cambridge: Cambridge University Press, 2005) 33, 41.

56. Ueber and MacCall, "The Rise and Fall," 40.

57. McEvoy, *The Fisherman's Problem.*

58. "Japanese Fishing Industry," D11.

59. J. D. Messersmith, "The Northern Anchovy (*Engraulis Mordax*) and Its Fishery, 1965–1968," State of California Department of Fish and Game, *Fisheries Bulletin* 147 (1969).

60. Correspondence from Mitsubishi Shoji Kaisha, Ltd. (MSK) San Francisco Office, to MSK Nagoya Office, January 8, 1931; RG 131, Box 9, Folder Sardine & Fish Meal (Sales Letters)—1931, NARA.

61. The country imported an estimated forty thousand tons of fishmeal and fish guano in 1912, Hutchinson, "Food for Plant Life," 7.

62. A. Thomas, "Deutsche und ausländische Fischmehle," *Die Fischwirtschaft* 1, no. 6 (1925): 93.

63. O. Sparenberg, "Perception and Use of Marine Biological Resources under National Socialist Autarky Policy," in Uekötter, ed., *Managing the Unknown*, 93.

64. MSK London to MSK Moji Branch, Subject: Fish Meal, February 16, 1931; RG 131, Box 9, Folder Sardine & Fish Meal (Sales Letters)—1931, NARA.

65. MSK London to MSK Kobe, November 31, 1931; RG 131, Box 9, Folder Sardine & Fish Meal Imports (2 of 2), NARA.

66. MSK Tokyo, Fertilizer Branch, to MSK San Francisco, "RE: Sardine Fish Meal from Korea," June 30, 1931; RG 131, Box 9, Folder Sardine & Fish Meal Imports 1931, NARA.

67. G. C. Carr, "International Trade in Fish Meal," Foodstuffs Division of the U.S. Bureau of Foreign and Domestic Commerce (1931), 16.

68. Correspondence from (MSK), San Francisco Office, to MSK Seattle Office, December 29, 1926; RG 131, Box 2, Folder 1926 California Sardine Meal, NARA.

69. MSK San Francisco Office, to MSK Seattle Office, June 25, 1926; RG 131, Box 2, 1926 California Sardine Meal, NARA.

70. Records belonging to Mitsubishi Shoji Kaisha, Ltd. (MSK), are at NARA in Record Group 131; see also George J. Carr, "International Trade in Fish Meal," *Bureau of Foreign & Domestic Commerce* (1931).

71. For example, fishmeal from California was cheaper than Norwegian fishmeal due to the conference freight tariffs on inter-European shipments, leading Mitsubishi Shoji Kaisha, Ltd., to seek ways of trans-shipping through other ports to avoid this expense. (Note that correspondence does not indicate whether they succeeded in this arrangement; it was proposing the possibility.) MSK Tokyo, Fertilizer Department, to San Francisco, "Freight for Europe Via America," February 17, 1934; RG 131, Box 10, Folder Sardine Meal 1931, NARA.

72. 1920 in United States, 1927 in Germany; Carr, "International Trade in Fish Meal," 6.

73. MSK Tokyo, Fertilizer Department, to MSK San Francisco, May 29, 1931; RG 131, Box 9, Folder Sardine & Fish Meal Imports (2 of 2), NARA.

74. MSK Seattle to MSK Osaka, "Spontaneous combustion clause in marine insurance policy on fish guano," May 28, 1926; RG 131, Box 2, Folder 1926 California Sardine Meal, NARA.

75. MSK Osaka, Fertilizer Department to MSK San Francisco, "Fish Meal and Crab Meal of Messrs. Nippon Gyoryo Kaisha, produced according to MEAKIN-Process," June 16, 1931, 5–6; RG 131 Box 8, Folder Meakin Fish Meal—Imports 1931, NARA.

76. MSK Seattle to MSK Osaka, "Alaskan Herring Meal," February 28, 1965, 3; RG 131 Box 2, Folder Alaska herring meal, NARA.

77. Hutchinson, "Food for Plant Life."

78. "*Fischmehl ist ein äußerst begehrtes Futtermittel, das aus der modernen Landwirtschaft gar nicht mehr wegzudenken ist.*" H. Papenfuss and K. Röpke, *Fischmehl, Fischöl und Andere Seetier Produkte* (Leipzig: Kammer der Technik/Fischkombinat Rostock, 1974), 15.

79. Dana L. Thomas, "It's an Ill Wind," *Barron's National Business and Financial Weekly* (March 4, 1963): 5; "News and Views of Investments: Record Earnings in Store This Year at H. J. Heinz," *Barron's National Business and Financial Weekly* (August 16, 1965): 8.

80. "Pfizer 1st Quarter Net Set Record," *Wall Street Journal* (April 28, 1964): 23; "Pfizer, Big Drug Concern, Goes into Fishing Business," *Wall Street Journal* (April 15, 1966): 18; "International Proteins Seeks to Acquire Ralston Facilities," *Wall Street Journal* (October 21, 1968): 5.

81. Linear programming emerged in the field of mathematics in the late 1940s; animal feed commodities, because of their narrow profit margins, were one of the most potentially profitable applications. See Frederick V. Waugh, "The Minimum-Cost Dairy Feed (An Application of 'Linear Programming')," *Journal of Farm*

Economics 33, no. 3 (1951): 299–310; A. E. Chappell, "Linear Programming Cuts Costs in Production of Animal Feeds," *Journal of the Operational Research Society* 25, no. 1 (1974): 19–26.

CHAPTER THREE. PROTEIN FROM THE SEA

1. Historian Amy Staples refers to this civil service movement as the "new internationalism." Amy L. Staples, *The Birth of Development: How the World Bank, Food and Agriculture Organization, and World Health Organization Changed the World, 1945–1965* (Kent, OH: Kent State University Press, 2006), 2, 6.

2. ASIPES and Luis Salvo González, *Historia de la industria pesquera en la región del Bío Bío, siglo XVI–siglo XX* (Santiago: LOM/ASIPES, 2000), 63.

3. See especially Robert E. Coker, "The Fisheries and the Guano Industry of Peru," paper presented at the Fourth International Fishery Congress, Washington, DC (1908); Coker, "Ocean Temperatures off the Coast of Peru," *Geographical Review* 5, no. 2 (1918): 127–35; Robert Cushman Murphy, "Fisheries Resources in Peru," *The Scientific Monthly* 16, no. 6 (1923): 594–607.

4. Murphy, "Fisheries Resources in Peru," 598.

5. "Notas sobre pesca," *El Mercurio* (April 18, 1943): 3.

6. The dependence on Norwegian fishmeal was of particular concern to individuals in the fish business; see *Die Fischwirtschaft* (Okt. 1925): 93–95; (Nov. 1925): 112–14; (Dez. 1925): 124–28. On other international research and collaboration in herring fishery research, see C. Heinrici, "Die Tätigkeit der Deutschen Wissenschaftlichen Kommission für Meeresforschung im Haushaltsjahr 1926," *Sonderdruck aus dem Jahresbericht für die deutsche Fischerei 1926* (Berlin: Gebr. Mann, 1926): 1–8.

7. David H. Cushing, *The Provident Sea* (Cambridge: Cambridge University Press, 1988), 234.

8. Pedro Golusda (Asesor Tecnico de la Dir. Gen de Pesca y Caza), "La industria pesquera en Chile," Trabajo presentado al Primer Congreso Marítimo de la Liga Marítima de Chile (Santiago, Chile), 1941, 14.

9. Murphy, "Fisheries Resources in Peru," 594.

10. Antonio López Villar, "Pescado Barato" [Letter to the Editor], *El Mercurio*, (January 2, 1937): 3; Benjamin Orlove, "Meat and Strength: The Moral Economy of a Chilean Food Riot," *Cultural Anthropology* 12, no. 2 (1997): 234–68.

11. League of Nations, Mixed Committee on the Problem of Nutrition, *Final Report on the Relation of Nutrition to Health, Agriculture, and Economic Policy* (Geneva, 1937): 63.

12. Staples, *The Birth of Development*, 74; see also League of Nations, *Final Report*, 34–35.

13. One of the first recommendations the Chilean National Nutrition Council made was for the construction of cold-storage infrastructure, which explicitly aimed to stimulate cattle ranching in the extreme southern region of Magallanes. Eduardo Cruz Coke, "Plans of the Chilean Government for Improving the Nutrition of the

People," trans. *Boletín de la Oficina Sanitaria Panamericana,* 1937, see especially 1151, 1154; Eduardo Cruz Coke/Consejo Nacional de Alimentación, "Plan de gobierno presentado por el Ministro de Salubridad," *Suplemento de la revista chilena de higiene y medicina preventiva* 1 (Santiago, Chile: Impr. Universo, 1937): 3, 9.

14. CAG published regular bulletins and annual reports with detailed information about the state of the industry and its development. Representative examples include: Erwin Schweigger, "Informe anual del experto en pesqurería," *Boletín de la Compañía Administradora del Guano* (October 1930): 569–74; F. Ballen, "La industria de la fabricación de harina de pescado en el Perú," *Boletín de la Compañía Administradora del Guano,* 14, no. 11 (1940): 339–42.

15. Reginald H. Fiedler, Norman D. Jarvis, and Milton J. Lobell, *La pesca y las industrias pesqueras en el Peru* (Lima: CAG, 1943); the report is summarized in English in Reginald H. Fiedler, "The Peruvian Fisheries," *The Geographical Review* (1944): 96–119.

16. United States Department of the Interior, Fish and Wildlife Service (USFW), and Corporación de Fomento de la Producción (CORFO), *Misión pesquera norteamericana en Chile: Un informe preliminar sobre la situación pesquera en Chile,* Santiago, Chile (1945); Milton A. Hill, "Comments on Current Events, No. 169," February 19, 1945; File no. 800.00, RG 84, NARA.

17. Mogens Jul, "Fomento de la pesca en America Latina" (Rome: FAO, 1951), Cuadro 7: Ejemplos del progreso en la industria del pescado, 30. FAO Archive-Rome.

18. Fiedler, "The Peruvian Fisheries," 119.

19. The SCIPA was signed in 1943 and extended through at least 1948. Fiedler, "The Peruvian Fisheries," 119. See also US Sec. of State to Peruvian Min. of Finance and Commerce, May 7, 1942, in US Department of State, *Treaties and Other International Agreements of the United States of America,* 1776–1949, compiled by Charles I. Bevans, vol. 13, (Washington, DC: US Government Printing Office), 1198–1201, 1243–49. The cannery was constructed in 1945 with financing from the Foreign Economic Administration. "Statement of Reasons why Fishery Products Should be Stricken from the List of Items to be Considered for Negotiation at Torquay Conference," August 30, 1950; W. M. Chapman Papers, Box 14, Folder 18, UW Special Collections.

20. See M. C. Finley, *All the Fish in the Sea: Maximum Sustainable Yield and the Failure of Fisheries Management* (Chicago: University of Chicago Press, 2011).

21. Cushman, *Guano and the Opening of the Pacific World,* 293.

22. Staples, *The Birth of Development,* 77.

23. Staples, *The Birth of Development,* 76–78, 98.

24. The study excluded subsistence-oriented fishers and vessels, which would have been numerous along these coasts. The reported data for Brazil—31,283 boats including 309 motorized—was more recent (1948) than the Peru-Chile data (1946) and included foreign vessels, making it a somewhat lopsided comparison. Jul, "Fomento de la Pesca," see *Cuadro 2: Producción de pescado, número de pescadores, número de barcos, etc., en América Latina y en países seleccionados,* 6, FAO Archive-Rome.

25. Mogens Jul, *Interview Reports on Fisheries—Peru* (1949); FAO Archive-Rome.

26. Jul, *Interview Reports*, Interview #35 (Sr. Arturo Madueño), n.p., and Interview #98 (Charles Bridgett, Assistant Commercial Attaché, U.S. Embassy, Lima), 2.

27. Fiedler, "The Peruvian Fisheries," 117.

28. Jul, *Interview Reports*, Interview #36 (Sr. Epifanio Azofra), n.p.

29. Jul, *Interview Reports on Fisheries—Chile* (1949), Interview #91 (Rodolfo Ravanol), Interview #95 (Julio Luna Sauvat).

30. Jul, *Interview Reports* (Ravanol), 1.

31. *Boletín Informativo*, Dir. Gen Pesca y Caza, no. 13 (August 1954), 4, Ministerio de Agricultura, V. 1085, ARNAD.

32. Finn Einarssen, to Osorio y Tafall, May 4, 1950, RG 14m FAO Archive-Rome.

33. B. F. Osorio y Tafall to Kask, [Untitled report on fisheries tour of Latin America], Doc. 0051909, 19 May 1950; Memo from B. F. Osorio y Tafall to D. B. Finn, "Establishment of the Latin American Fishery Council," July 24, 1950, 1, FAO Archive-Rome; Susana Pinar, "La genética española en el exilio y su repercusión en la ciencia mexicana," in *De Madrid a México: El exilio español y su impacto sobre el pensamiento, la ciencia y el sistema educativo mexicano*, ed. A. Sánchez Andrés and S. Figueroa Zamadio (Morelia, México: Univ. Michoacana de San Nicolás de Hidalgo, 2001).

34. Bibiano Fernandez Osorio y Tafall, "Preliminary report of my South American trip," February 1950, 1; FAO Archive-Rome.

35. Jul, *Interview Reports* (Ravanol), 2.

36. Osorio y Tafall to Kask, [Untitled report].

37. Osorio y Tafall, "Preliminary Report," and Memo from Osorio y Tafall to D. B. Finn, "Establishment of the Latin American Fishery Council," July 24, 1950, 1, FAO Archive-Rome.

38. Letter from A. G. Sandoval to Dr. Wahlen and Dr. Osorio y Tafall, Latin American Regional Fisheries Council Meeting, June 8, 1951, FAO Archive-Rome.

39. In the 1950s and '60s (peak years 1959–61) on-shore processing stations in both countries were active in processing thousands annually (sperm, baleen, blue, sei). In 1953, two joint ventures (one German-Peruvian, one US-Peruvian) established new whaling operations on the Peruvian coast, in Pisco and Lima, respectively, and in 1957 a third (US-Peruvian) venture opened in Paita. These activities produced further tensions with the IWC (which Peru and Chile did not join until 1979), as they reduced the effectiveness of the Antarctic quotas that had been set to protect the migratory species. Without the voluntary cooperation of these enterprises and the states that harbored them, whose coasts offered important breeding grounds for several whale species, such activities continued with few restrictions until Peruvian fishmeal and oil production—particularly near the peak of the fishmeal boom in 1970–71—made whale oil prices fluctuate wildly and at times prohibitively low for the costs involved in production. The 1973 nationalization of the fishing industry included the state takeover of the three whaling plants, by then majority owned by Chr. Salvesen & Co. through the firm Propesca Peruana;

J. N. Tønnessen and A. O. Johnsen, *The History of Modern Whaling*, trans. R. I. Christophersen (Berkeley: University of California Press, 1982), 651–52.

40. L. C. Norris, "The Need for Fish or Other Animal Derived Products in Poultry Rations," *Fish Meal and Oil Industry, International Yearbook* (1951): 20.

41. Osorio y Tafall to Kask, [Untitled report]. The report also noted that FAO was involved in experiments and demonstrations using fishmeal in livestock feed in rural areas.

42. Jul, *Interview Reports* (Sauvat). The interview notes do not indicate the precise sizes of each vessel but do indicate the measurements for a typical vessel as noted above, which employed a crew of nine.

43. Jul, *Interview Reports* (Sauvat).

44. Julio Luna Sauvat noted that there was "no export" of fishmeal (Jul interview, 2); statistics for Chile's fishmeal production and export from 1951 to 1959 are from FAO, *Position of Fish Meal Industry and Trade in Chile,* No. 61/C/2471, Report to the FAO International Meeting on Fish Meal, Rome, Italy (March 20–29), 1961, 2–4.

45. John Fridtjof, "Informe al gobierno de Chile sobre fomento del consumo de pescado," Informe FAO/ETAP No. 271 (1954), FAO Archive-Rome. On Lota during the Popular Front of the 1930s and 1940s, see Jody Pavilack, *Mining for the Nation: The Politics of Chile's Coal Communities from the Popular Front to the Cold War* (University Park: Penn State University Press, 2011).

46. Virginio Gomez, "Memorandum informativo a los comites pesqueros locales," April 13, 1954, 2, V. 1085, Ministerio de Agricultura, ARNAD; Willi Habich, "Betrachtungen über die Fischwirtschaft der Vereinigten Staaten von Nordamerika," *Die Fischwirtschaft* 4, no. 3 (1928): 33–38.

47. Fridtjof, "Informe al gobierno de Chile."

48. G. M. Gerhardsen, "Economic Development Projects in Fisheries," FAO-ETAP and the Government of Denmark Training Centre for Fishery Administrators (Denmark, 1955), 10, 12.

49. One year the use of Air Force planes to fly in ten tons of frozen tuna (purchased from the US-owned boat *Star Kist*) ended in a disastrous crash. N. E. Dodd, Outgoing letters to Chile, doc. 21, FAO-Archive-Rome.

50. B. R. Stillings and G. M. Knobl define fish protein concentrate as follows: "The concept of fish protein concentrate (FPC) is based on the more efficient use of our fishery resource by converting under-utilized fish to acceptable products for human consumption. FPC is not a single product. It is rather a family of products produced by different processes. Each member in the family of products has different characteristics and can be used for different purposes." B. R. Stillings and G. M. Knobl, "Fish Protein Concentrate: A New Source of Dietary Protein," *Journal of the American Oil Chemists' Society* 48, no. 8 (1971): 412–14.

51. Staff at the Chilean Nutrition Institute made various foods (soups, pastas, potatoes, beans, beet leaf pie, beef stew, and coffee cake), and served them to the employees to evaluate the taste, texture, and quality of the final product. A. Vergara, "Extensive Report on the Fish Flour Experiment in Chile," Doc. no. 053431 (1954),

FAO Archive-Rome. Marine Oil Refiners was one of two organizations involved in South African government–sponsored attempts starting in 1952 to manufacture fish flour for human consumption. E. R. Pariser, M. B. Wallerstein, C. J. Corkery, and N. L. Brown, *Fish Protein Concentrate: Panacea for Malnutrition?* (Cambridge, MA: MIT Press, 1978), 14.

52. In January 1954, FAO officials B. F. Osorio y Tafall (regional director) and A. Vergara (nutrition representative for Latin America) were in Chile to discuss the possibility of installing a plant to produce fish flour for human consumption. See Hugo Trivelli Faranzolini, Dir. Nac. de Ag. (Santiago), to Min. de Ag. (Santiago), REF: "Instalación de una fábrica de harina de pescado para consumo humano," No. 0416, January 25, 1954, Ministerio de Agricultura, V. 1085, ARNAD. The plant was later transferred to the Chilean government (to be managed by CORFO) and operated until 1964.

53. Pariser et al., *Fish Protein Concentrate,* 146–52, passim. Note, p. 196 of this source contradicts the claim on p. 151 that UNICEF-Quintero FPC supplied the British American Hospital project, indicating that the FPC for this study was provided by VioBin. The Quintero-UNICEF plant eventually closed in 1964, reportedly plagued by administrative problems.

54. The four experiments mentioned, conducted between 1953 and 1973, were only a handful of dozens of attempts to develop this product in experiments around the world throughout the late nineteenth and early twentieth centuries. Pariser et al., *Fish Protein Concentrate,* see chap. 8.

55. Chilean aviculturists and fishmeal producers agreed to set annual quotas for supplies of fishmeal to domestic chicken producers; Moises Hernandez Ponce, Dir. Gen. de Dir. de Pesca y Caza (Valparaíso), to Min. de Ag. (Santiago), REF: Memorandum sobre reuniones entre avicultores y fabricantes de harina del Estado, No. 740, May 29, 1954, Ministerio de Agricultura, V. 1085, ARNAD.

56. Gerhard Meseck, "World Fish Meal Production and Trade," Doc. No. IFIME-W/6, *Report to the International Meeting on Fish Meal* (March 20–29, 1961), 5–6, 9, 15–16. FAO Archive-Rome.

57. Meseck, "World Fish Meal."

58. Meseck, "World Fish Meal," 32.

59. Roger Horowitz, *Putting Meat on the American Table* (Baltimore: Johns Hopkins University Press, 2006), 132.

60. Wilfredo Peláez Gularte, "Pescado enlatado para los gatos debe ser especial: Estados Unidos primer comprador," (September 13,1977), CENDOPES Clippings File.

61. Many of the large poultry producers originated in the agricultural (rather than processing) side of the industry, hatching and feeding chicks, then contracting with growers to produce the broilers for slaughter. Glenn E. Bugos, "Intellectual Property Protection in the American Chicken-Breeding Industry," *Business History Review* 66, no. 1 (1992): 129, 147, 148, 148n35; Horowitz, *Putting Meat,* 114, 132.

62. See Frederick V. Waugh, "The Minimum-Cost Dairy Feed (An Application of 'Linear Programming')," *Journal of Farm Economics* 33, no. 3 (1951): 299–310;

A. E. Chappell, "Linear Programming Cuts Costs in Production of Animal Feeds," *Journal of the Operational Research Society* 25, no. 1 (1974): 19–26.

63. William Boyd, "Making Meat: Science, Technology, and the Industrialization of American Poultry Production," *Technology and Culture* 42 (2001): 646n5. See also Jaysuño Abramovich, *La industria pesquera en el Perú: Genesis, apogeo y crisis* (Lima: Universidad Nacional Federico Villarreal, Centro de Investigaciones Económicas y Sociales, 1973), 39–40.

64. V. A. Schlich, "Trash Fishing Highlights New England's Production Season," *Fish Meal and Oil Industry, International Yearbook* (1951): 13.

65. The FAO reports the peak harvest of 1936 at 791,100 tons, FAO, "Species Fact Sheet: *Sardinops caeruleus*," FAO internet resource, http://www.fao.org/fishery/species/2894/en; some California canneries operated until 1957 with fish trucked in from Southern California (E. Ueber and Alec MacCall, "The Rise and Fall of the California Sardine Empire," in *Climate Variability, Climate Change, and Fisheries*, ed. M. Glantz (Cambridge: Cambridge University Press, 2005) 39, 41); Milton J. Lobell (CORFO) to W. M. Chapman, Oct. 21, 1948; W. M. Chapman Papers, Box 12, Folder 26, UW Special Collections.

66. Van Camp listed eleven offices along the Pacific coast of the Americas, including six in California and one in Oregon, and the remaining four of them south of the US border. Advertisement for Van Camp Sea Foods, *Pacific Fishermen's News* 4, no. 12 (June 14, 1948): 7; W. M. Chapman Papers, Box 12, Folder 1, UW Special Collections.

67. The technology existed by 1949 but was not used widely until its introduction to the New England fleet several years later; "Nylon Nets Catch More Fish; May Revolutionize Industry," *Daily Boston Globe* (July 24, 1949): C38; A. E. Magnell, "Firm Cited for Process in Fish Nets," *The Hartford Courant* (March 7, 1954): B12; John Bunker, "Tuna Fleet Flies Flag of Optimism," *The Christian Science Monitor* (June 21, 1960): 13; "New Nets for old," *The Guardian* (September 5, 1961): 9; Floyd McCracken, "Tuna Fleet Sails into Sunnier Waters," *The Christian Science Monitor* (August 28, 1961): 10; "Industrial Textiles on the Water: New Fibres for Fishermen," *The Guardian* (September 3, 1963): 10.

68. M. Phister in personal letter to Chapman, November 25, 1950, 2; W. M. Chapman Papers, Box 14, Folder 3, UW Special Collections.

CHAPTER FOUR. THE GOLDEN ANCHOVETA

1. Emilio Romero, "La anchoveta personaje del mar," *El Comercio* (Lima) (December 2, 1964) (The author's description of phosphorescence is not referring to the phenomenon of bioluminescence, which occurs farther out in the open ocean.)

2. Victor Pezet, *Monografía de la Bahía de Chimbote* (Lima: N.p., 1912).

3. "Anchoveta: Oro que viene del mar," *La Prensa* (Lima) (January 2, 1965): 15–16; "En busca del pez de oro," *La Prensa* (Lima) (January 19, 1965): 14–15.

4. Government of Peru, *Peruvian National Census, Vol. III: Departments of Lambayeque/La Libertad/Ancash* (Lima: INE, 1940), 7; and *Peruvian National Census, Vol. II: Ancash* (Lima: INE, 1961), 6.

5. Ivo Tilic, *Capacidad de producción de la industria de harina de pescado en el Perú*, Informe No. 4 (Callao: Instituto de Investigación de los Recursos Marinos, 1962): 6; Ivo Tilic, *Información estadística sobre embarcaciones utilizadas en la pesca industrial en el Perú, 1953–1962*, Informe No. 8 (Callao: Instituto de Investigación de los Recursos Marinos, 1963): 11.

6. Tilic, *Capacidad*, 3.

7. During the mid-1960s, aside from Callao, the most important fishmeal-producing Peruvian towns were Chancay, Huacho, Supe, and Huarmey. Tilic, *Capacidad*, 5; W. F. Doucet and H. Einarsson, "A Brief Description of Peruvian Fisheries," *CalCOFI Reports* 11 (1966): 85.

8. For a thorough review of the oceanographic features of the Humboldt Current's three subsystems, see Vivian Montecino and Carina B. Lange, "The Humboldt Current System: Ecosystem Components and processes, fisheries, and sediment studies," *Progress in Oceanography* 83 (2009): 65–79.

9. Nathan Clarke, "Traces on the Peruvian Shore: The Environmental History of the Fishmeal Boom in Chimbote, Peru, 1940–1980" (PhD diss., University of Illinois, 2009), see especially 144–66.

10. "'Stinking City' Center of Key Peru Industry," *Los Angeles Times* (June 6, 1971): 8.

11. "'Stinking City.'"

12. Rubén Berrios, *Towards an Overview of Peru's Fishing Industry: Prospects and Problems* (Bogotá: International Development Research Center, Regional Office for Latin America and the Caribbean, 1983), 4. Michael Roemer estimated that in 1962, 63.9 percent of global fishmeal exports were Peru's (*Fishing for Growth: Export-Led Development in Peru, 1950–1967* [Cambridge, MA: Harvard University Press, 1970], table 5.4); Ivo Tilic estimated 70 percent that same year, *Capacidad*, 4.

13. Victor Pezet, *Monografía de la Bahía de Chimbote* (Lima: N.p., 1912); on Henry Meiggs, see Edward D. Melillo, *Strangers on Familiar Soil: Rediscovering the California-Chile Connection* (New Haven, CT: Yale University Press, 2015), especially 113–36.

14. In 1941, US consulting firm N.A. Brassert Co., having been commissioned by the Peruvian government to assess the iron ore deposits in Marcona (Ica province) and to determine the most suitable location for an industrial port, recommended Chimbote. "Historia: 50 años de la primera y más grande Siderúrgia," Empresa Siderúrgica del Perú S.A.A., available from http://www.sider.com.pe/sidernet/principal.html.

15. E.J. Clearly, "Chimbote: El Pittsburgh peruano en potencia," *Boletín de la Escuela Nacional de Ingenieros* (Lima), 3, no. 17 (1944): 3–27, trans. J.F. Aguilar Revoredo (originally published in *Engineering News-Record*, September 1944: 19).

16. Clearly, "El Pittsburgh peruano," 15.

17. The iron ore was shipped by sea from Marcona, while the coal was transported by train from the mountains. Clearly, "El Pittsburgh peruano."

18. Clearly, "El Pittsburgh peruano." Not all observers agreed with the plans to build an integrated steel mill in Peru. Some engineers advised the Peruvian government that a smaller operation based on domestic scrap would be more appropriate given the costs of operation and of first transporting iron ore and coal to the plant, then the finished steel to Lima: "For those who believe that a national steel industry is justifiable at any price," one 1959 article concluded, "Chimbote stands as a new El Dorado; for more dispassionate persons, however, the iron and steel plant at the mouth of the Santa is a costly monument to economic nationalism." C. Langdon White and Gary Chenkin, "Peru Moves onto the Iron and Steel Map of the Western Hemisphere," *Journal of Inter-American Studies* 1, no. 3 (1959): 386. The authors believed that in addition to high overall operating costs, Chimbote was not located close enough to any mass-consuming markets, and that the total output of the Siderperú mill—estimated at sixty thousand tons annually—was not sufficient to take advantage of the savings that large-scale production yields (384).

19. Clearly, "El Pittsburgh peruano," 3, 4, 17, 16.

20. "Chimbote: Plan Piloto Presentation Display," Folder B75T, Josep Lluís Sert Papers, Graduate School of Design, Harvard University. For background on the *Chimbote Project* in the context of Sert and Wiener's work with their firm, Town Planning Associates, see Eric Mumford, Hashim Sarkis, and Neyran Turan, eds., *Josep Lluís Sert: The Architect of Urban Design, 1953–1969* (New Haven, CT: Yale University Press and Cambridge, MA: Harvard University Press, 2008).

21. Government of Peru, Peruvian National Census, Vol. III: Departments of Lambayeque/La Libertad/Ancash (Lima: INE, 1940), 7; Peruvian National Census, Vol. II: Ancash (Lima: INE, 1961), 6.

22. Government of Peru, Peruvian National Census, Vol. II, 6.

23. "Gran Migración de Indígenas Crece a Diario en Chimbote," *La Prensa*, June 2, 1959, 8.

24. W. Peláez Gularte, "Chimbote, Ciudad-Problema," *La Prensa*, April 19, 1957, 8.

25. Robert E. Coker, "The Fisheries and the Guano Industry of Peru," *Bulletin of the U.S. Bureau of Fisheries* 28 (1908): 333–65.

26. One of Robert Cushman Murphy's most publicized studies was *El guano y la pesca de la anchoveta: Informe oficial al supremo gobierno* (Lima, 1954), cited in Cushman, *Guano*, 300.

27. A. Freyre, "Fishery Development in Peru," *Studies in Tropical Oceanography* 5 (1967): 392.

28. Gregory Cushman, "The Lords of Guano: Science and the Management of Peru's Marine Environment, 1800–1973" (PhD diss., University of Texas at Austin, 2003); W. G. Clark, "Lessons from the Peruvian anchoveta fishery," *CalCOFI Reports* 19 (1975–1976): 57.

29. Cushman, *Guano*, 291, says that CAG acquired a terrestrial fishmeal plant from California but, lacking capital, never produced any fishmeal before selling it to Italian-Peruvian entrepreneur Marcos Ghio in 1955. There is some disagreement as to the "first" functioning fishmeal plant: Jaysuño Abramovich claims that Peruvian industrialist Manuel Elguera began producing fishmeal in Chimbote in 1955 (see J. Abramovich, "La Industria Pesquera en el Perú: Genesis, Apogeo y Crisis" [Lima: Centro de Investigaciones Económicas y Sociales, Universidad Nacional Federico Villarreal, 1973]), but Michael Roemer notes that this plant was built in 1950 as a joint venture with Wilbur-Ellis; *Fishing for Growth*, 82–83.

30. Reginald H. Fiedler, Norman D. Jarvis, and Milton J. Lobell, "La pesca y las industrias pesqueras en el Peru," Informe de la Misión Pesquera Norteamericana (Lima: Compañía Administradora del Guano, 1943).

31. Cushman, *Guano*, 291; Fiedler et al., "La pesca."

32. David H. Cushing stated that the "modern form" of the purse seine originated in the mackerel fishery between Cape Hatteras and Nova Scotia; *The Provident Sea* (Cambridge: Cambridge University Press, 1988), 252. Although the first purse seines in the Peru-Chile zone arrived from the North American Pacific, CAG had reportedly studied the mackerel fishery between Virginia and North Carolina in 1940.

33. A tuna clipper is a specific type of purse seiner. These reconstructions took place at the Peruvian Steamship Company (Corporación Peruana de Vapores). "Pescadores sin barcos," *La Prensa* (Lima), nos. 79–80 (January 10, 1965): 21.

34. Maggiolo reportedly received an order for twelve motorized bolicheras in 1941, but their completion dates are unknown. "La técnica venció a la tradición," *La Prensa* (Lima), nos. 83–84 (January 12, 1965): 15–16; "La mayor flota pesquera de latinoamerica," *La Prensa* (Lima), nos. 85–86 (January 13, 1965): 16.

35. Backward linkages to the fishmeal industry also stimulated the production of nets, jute sacks, and other supply-side industries along the Peruvian coast; see Michael Roemer, *Fishing for Growth*, chap. 7.

36. Letter from A. G. Sandoval to Dr. Wahlen and Dr. Osorio-Tafall, Latin American Regional Fisheries Council Meeting, June 8, 1951, FAO Archive-Rome.

37. Mogens Jul, *Interview Reports on Fisheries—Peru* (1949); FAO Archive-Rome.

38. There are conflicting accounts of when this plant was actually built and when it began to operate. Roemer notes that the plant was built in 1950 (*Fishing for Growth*, 82–83). Jaysuño Abramovich claims that Peruvian industrialist Manuel Elguera began producing fishmeal in Chimbote in 1955 (*La industria pesquera en el Perú*).

39. Law 12283 (1955) extended to the fisheries sector the tax benefits of Law 10753, which applied to mineral and agricultural products; M. Arias Schreiber, "The Evolution of Legal Instruments and the Sustainability of the Peruvian Anchovy Fishery," *Marine Policy* 36, no. 1 (2012): 84.

40. Baltazar Caravedo Molinari, *Estado, pesca y burguesía, 1939–1973* (Lima: Teoría y Realidad, 1979), 40.

41. Of the ninety-eight plants installed in 1961, 66 percent were small-scale producers. Of a reported five hundred seventy thousand tons of fishmeal produced that year, only five thousand tons were from cannery offal. Only thirty thousand tons of fishmeal were consumed domestically in Peru (1960) for poultry and swine feeds. FAO, "Position of Fish Meal Industry and Trade in Peru," Doc. no. IFIME C/13, *Report to the International Meeting on Fish Meal* (1961), 1, 2, FAO-Archive, Rome.

42. Ivo Tilic's study, which accounted only for the first six months of production in 1962 at the time it was conducted, excluded plants still under construction or those that had not yet initiated operations. Tilic, *Capacidad* 5; Cuadro 2, 6.

43. In Peru in 1960, 83 percent used a power block (*macaco*), and 77 percent utilized the specially adapted hydraulic pump and hose (*absorbente*) developed by Peruvian firm Histrostal S.A.; Ivo Tilic, *Encuesta sobre las embarcaciones anchoveteras realizada en Junio de 1967*, Informe no. 23 (Callao: IMARPE, 1968), 27, 31; Roemer, *Fishing for Growth*, 84; Martin Stähle/Hidrostal S.A., Pump Impeller, US Patent 3156190A, filed 3/14/1963 (published 11/10/64), https://www.google.com/patents/US3156190.

44. FAO, "Position of Fish Meal Industry and Trade in Peru," Doc. no. IFIME C/13, International Meeting on Fish Meal (March 20–29, 1961), 1, FAO-Archive, Rome; "La mayor flota pesquera de latinoamerica,", 15.

45. Of the 489 new vessels, 254 were wooden, and 235 metal; these brought the estimated total number of vessels in operation to 935; Tilic, *Encuesta*," 6, 37. It is important to note that the researchers based their final numbers on a survey of 1,255 boats, and many vessels were likely operating informally, so it is difficult to ascertain how many of such vessels would have been beyond the scope of the researchers' enquiry.

46. Only 17 percent of respondents were independent owner-operators; the remaining 11 percent of owners did not specify; Tilic, "*Encuesta*," 6, 37.

47. Of the 1,536 vessels, an estimated 42 percent were wooden, 58 percent metal; Tilic, *Encuesta*, 6, 8, 37. N. Hellevang reported that 63 percent of Peruvian vessels were of steel construction—a large jump from the 1967 report estimate; N. Hellevang, "Recent Developments in the Peruvian Anchoveta Fishery," Proyecto UNDP/FAO 269, Paper presented at the Technical Conference on Fish Finding, Purse Seining and Aimed Trawling, Reykjavik, Iceland (May 24–30, 1970), 5.

48. Hellevang, "Recent Developments," 5.

49. U.S. Embassy (Santiago, Chile), Foreign Service Despatch to the U.S. State Department, No. 895 (June 7, 1960), RG 59, Box 2402, NARA.

50. Memorandum from D. W. Souter to B. Zunjic (Empresa Pesquera Perú S.A./Empresa Pesquera Ilo S.A./Cia. de Negocios de Ultramar S.A.), August 18, 1964, p.5; W. M. Chapman Papers, Box 59, Folder 20, UW Special Collections.

51. The article cited figures from the trade magazine *Pesca*. "Los riesgos del crecimiento," *La Prensa* (Lima), nos. 89–90 (January 15, 1965): 17–18.

52. "Los riesgos del crecimiento," ibid.; and "La mayor flota pesquera de latinoamerica," 16.

53. Hellevang, "Recent Developments," 5.
54. Hellevang, "Recent Developments," 5.
55. Letter from Hermann Einarsson (FAO fisheries expert at IMARPE) to Wilbert Chapman (c/o FAO-Rome), February 28, 1965, W.M. Chapman Papers, B9x 63, Folder 16, UW Special Collections.
56. On the other hand, only 10 percent of the fleet had the more modern sonar technology. Tilic, *Encuesta*, 25, 27; Hellevang, "Recent Developments," 1, 6.
57. Hellevang, "Recent Developments," 7.
58. Hellevang's figures (one hundred twenty thousand tons in 1956 and ten million tons in 1968–69) do not take into account the adjusted models for harvest data calculated by the *Sea Around Us* project, which are the data that this book uses for the appendixes.
59. Freyre, "Fishery Development in Peru," 398.
60. L.P. Leiva and C.T. Armas, *Movimiento sindical en Chimbote: Historia gráfica, 1940–1960* (Chimbote: Instituto de Promoción y Educación Popular, 1984), 18.
61. Maruja Barrig, Marcela Chuca, Ana María Yañez, *Anzuelo sin carnada: Obreras en la industria conservera de pescado* (Lima: Mosca Azul Editores/ADEC, 1985), 11.
62. Interview with Hernán Peralta Bouroncle, 2009.
63. Interview with Peralta, 2009; E. Ballón y J.M. Salcedo, "Reportaje a Chimbote," *Quehacer* 3 (Mayo 1980): 67.
64. Manuel Achurra Larraín, "Manpower in the Fisheries Sector of Peru: Present Status and Prospects of Education and Training," FAO Fisheries Report No. 93 (Rome: FAO, 1971), 4, 1.
65. Larraín, *Manpower*, 1, 11. Another estimate gives a total of 17,780 fishermen working on Peru's bolicheras during the boom years, most of whom were crew members; Jul, *Interview Reports*, Interview #35 (Sr. Arturo Madueño), n.p.
66. Larraín, *Manpower*, 11–12.
67. Tilic, "Cuadro 19: Embarcaciones y tripulantes," in *Encuesta*, 35. These are officially reported ratios; critics also complained of the persistent underreporting of catch, which would dramatically reduce the payments industrialists/owners made to their workers. Luis Delboy, "La cara oculta de la pesca," *Oiga* (Lima) No. 342 (September 19, 1969); Larrain, *Manpower*, 11–12.
68. Larraín, *Manpower*, 12.
69. "Gran migración de indígenas crece a diario en Chimbote," *La Prensa* (Lima) (June 2, 1959): 8.
70. Jul, *Interview Reports* (Madueño).
71. "Un día de pesca en una bolichera," *La Prensa* (Lima), nos. 93–94 (January 17, 1965): 14–15.
72. "El sindicato de pescadores pide a capitanía revisión de lanchas," *El Faro* (January 5, 1965): 1.
73. Luis Delboy, "La cara oculta de la pesca," *Oiga* (Lima) No. 342 (September 19, 1969).
74. Larraín, *Manpower*, 13.

75. Larraín, *Manpower*, 13.

76. Denis Sulmont, "La sociología francesa en el Perú," *Boletín del Instituto Francés de Estudios Andinos* 36, no. 1 (2007): 86; see also Denis Sulmont, "Chimbote: Constitución de un bloque popular regional," in *Jornadas de Balance de Estudios Urbano-Industriales* (December 13–18), Lima: Pontifcia Universidad Católica del Perú, 1982; "Conflictos laborales y movilización popular: Perú, 1968–1976," *Revista Mexicana de Sociología* 40, no. 2 (1978): 685–726; "El Boom Chimbote," Unpublished manuscript (1970).

77. D. Sulmont, "Chimbote," 1.

78. D. Sulmont, personal collection (Lima, Peru).

79. These characteristics were visible in many of the photographs of the Chimbote area from Sulmont's collection (Denis Sulmont, personal collection, Lima, Peru).

80. The Revolutionary Vanguard was founded in 1965 and based in Lima's intellectual and student movements. Its two primary spheres of action were in the fishing and mining sectors. Kenneth Roberts, *Deepening Democracy? The Modern Left and Social Movements in Chile and Peru* (Stanford, CA: Stanford University Press, 1998), 208; interview with Peralta, May 8, 2009.

81. Interview with Peralta, 2009.

82. Interview with Peralta, 2009.

83. More specifically, Marisol de la Cadena explains this as a kind of "multi-ontologism" that "saw the *necessity* of western reason and its *incapacity* to translate ... Andean ways of being." Marisol de la Cadena, "The Production of Other Knowledges and Its Tensions: From Andeanist Anthropology to Interculturalidad?" *Journal of the World Anthropology Network* 1 (2005): 20.

84. José María Arguedas, *El zorro de arriba y el zorro de abajo* (Lima: Editorial Horizonte, 1971).

85. J. M. Arguedas, letter to John Murra, 1 February 1967, in John Murra and M. López-Baralt, eds., *Las cartas de Arguedas* (Lima: Pontificia Universidad Católica del Perú, 1998), 142.

86. Arguedas himself wrote the first Spanish-Quechua bilingual version of the traditional tale, originally redacted by Spanish conquistador Francisco de Ávila in 1598 with the title *Dioses y hombres de Huarochirí* (IEP-Lima, 1966).

87. For example: Braschi, the industrialist whose money and power are behind the industry and its local mafia in the novel, is a reference to the Peruvian "fishmeal king" Luis Banchero Rossi. The "Crazy Moncada" character, who wandered around the city loudly denouncing the structures of power that governed the port, is said to represent a onetime resident of Chimbote during and after the time of Arguedas's residency there; his two sons were known as active participants in local politics during the early 1970s. Numerous other elements of the novel—including a Peace Corps volunteer named Maxwell—echoed processes, people, and events that had shaped both the natural and human ecosystems of the city.

88. José María Arguedas, *The Fox from Up Above and the Fox from Down Below*, trans. Frances Horning Barraclough (Pittsburgh: Pittsburgh University Press, 2000), 43.

89. J. Guzmán Aranda, "Presentación," in *Los Hervores de Chimbote*, ed. A. Cornejo Polar, Gonzalo Portocarrero, Julio Ortega, and Alberto Flores Galindo (Chimbote: Río Santa Editores, 2006), 13.

90. Cited in J. P. Robin and F. C. Terzo, *Urbanization in Peru*, International Urbanization Survey (New York: The Ford Foundation, 1972), 58.

91. Robin and Terzo, *Urbanization in Peru*, 61.

92. For a detailed account of the reconstruction process, see Nathan Clarke, "Revolutionizing the Tragic City: Rebuilding Chimbote, Peru, after the 1970 Earthquake," *Journal of Urban History* 41, no. 1 (2015): 93–115.

93. César N. Caviedes, "The Latin American Boom-Town in the Literary View of José María Arguedas," in W. E. Mallory and P. Simpson-Housley, eds., *Geography and Literature: A Meeting of the Disciplines* (Syracuse, NY: Syracuse University Press, 1986), 59.

94. J. M. Arguedas to J. Murra, 14 April 1967, in Murra and López-Baralt, *Las cartas*, 181.

CHAPTER FIVE. STATES OF UNCERTAINTY

1. Amy Bentley, *Inventing Baby Food: Taste, Health, and the Industrialization of the American Diet* (Oakland: University of California Press, 2014), 75.

2. This food revolution has been more thoroughly studied in the US context than elsewhere. See, for example, Roger Horowitz, *Putting Meat on the American Table* (Baltimore: Johns Hopkins University Press, 2006); Marion Nestle, *Food Politics: How the Food Industry Influences Nutrition and Health* (Berkeley: University of California Press, 2013); Thomas Reardon and C. Peter Timmer, "The Economics of the Food System Revolution," *Annual Review of Resource Economics* 4 (2012): 225–64.

3. "Van Camp Sea Food Buys 4 Fish Processors in Peru and 1 in U.S.," *Wall Street Journal* (July 10, 1962): 9; Dana L. Thomas, "It's an Ill Wind," *Barron's National Business and Financial Weekly* 43, no. 9 (March 4, 1963): 5.

4. Harry N. Scheiber, "Pacific Ocean Resources, Science, and Law of the Sea: Wilbert M. Chapman and the Pacific Fisheries, 1945–70," *Ecology Law Quarterly* 13, no. 3 (1986): 383–534.

5. "Fishmeal Futures Soar as Peru's Government Takes Over Marketing," *Wall Street Journal* (April 21, 1970): 32; Peter Milius, "Farm Prices Soar 5.7%," *Washington Post* (January 10, 1973): A1; "Peru Seizes Fishmeal Industry, U.S. Firms Hit," *Los Angeles Times* (May 9, 1973): A26; Robert A. Jones, "Anchovies Return: Boon for Poor, Bane for Farmers," *Washington Post* (April 22, 1974): A1; Paul G. Edwards, "Fishermen Watch Price of Soybeans," *Washington Post* (August 7, 1974): B1.

6. The United States, United Kingdom, Federal Republic of Germany, and Netherlands consumed about 65 percent of the world's total fishmeal in 1959. Gerhard Meseck, "World Fish Meal Production and Trade," Doc. No. IFIME-W/6, *Report to the International Meeting on Fish Meal* (March 20–29, 1961), 30–31, FAO Archive-Rome.

7. FAO, "Position of Fish Meal Industry and Trade in Peru," Doc. no. IFIME C/13, *Report to the International Meeting on Fish Meal* (March 20–29, 1961), 1, FAO Archive-Rome; "Triunfó la anchoveta en Paris," *Pesca* 1, no. 2 (1960): 29–31; Michael Roemer, *Fishing for Growth: Export-Led Development in Peru, 1950–1967* (Cambridge, MA: Harvard University Press, 1970), 76.

8. See, for example, William R. Lux, "The Peruvian Fishing Industry: A Case Study in Capitalism at Work," *Revista de Historia de América* 71 (1971): 144.

9. Meseck, "World Fish Meal Production and Trade," 12; FAO, "Position of Fish Meal Industry and Trade in Peru," 2.

10. Meseck, "World Fish Meal Production and Trade," 31.

11. FAO, "Position of Fish Meal Industry and Trade in Peru," 1; Other members of the FEO included Norway, Iceland, Angola, South Africa, and Chile. Roemer, *Fishing for Growth*, 75.

12. "Triunfó la anchoveta en Paris," 29–31.

13. Vicente Cerro Cebrián, "Position of Fish Meal Industry and Trade in Peru," *Report to the International Meeting on Fish Meal* (March 20–29, 1961): *Addendum 2*, FAO Archive-Rome.

14. Meseck, "World Fish Meal Production and Trade," 31.

15. M. Dickey-Collas et al., "Lessons Learned from Stock Collapse and Recovery of North Sea Herring: A Review," *ICES Journal of Marine Science* 67, no. 9 (2010): 1875–86; Jean Hewitt, "Where Have Herring Gone?" *New York Times* (February 14, 1970): 30.

16. Letter from J. Steele Culbertson to W. M. Chapman, October 28, 1966, W. M. Chapman Papers, Box 86, Folder 7, UW Special Collections.

17. Mexico reportedly requested aid and technical assistance from Germany for the expansion of fisheries. Meseck, "World Fish Meal Production and Trade," 13.

18. Biographical Note, Wilbert McLeod Chapman Papers, Special Collections at the University of Washington-Seattle, http://archiveswest.orbiscascade.org/ark:/80444/xv73548#bioghistID.

19. He plainly said as much: "The prime need of the fisherman from the scientist and technologist is the capability of being able to guess better than he now can how these ever shifting currents will trend and how they will shift the location and density of fish he intends to harvest." Wilbert M. Chapman, "Industry and the Economy of the Sea," *California and the World Ocean,* Conference proceedings (1964): 64.

20. Memo from W. M. Chapman to Ocean Committee (Ralston Purina), Re: "The United States Navy and the Bureau of Commercial Fisheries and the Fish Business," July 8, 1967; W. M. Chapman Papers, Folder 85, Box 7, UW Special Collections.

21. Biographical Note, Wilbert M. Chapman Papers, UW Special Collections.

22. Chapman, "Industry and the Economy of the Sea," 63, 64.

23. Chapman, "Industry and the Economy of the Sea," 70. That year [1964], the California Cooperative Oceanic Fisheries Investigations (CalCOFI) Committee presented a proposal to fish anchovy as a way of encouraging the recuperation of sardine stocks, as scientists believed the two were competitors within the ecosystem.

California authorities issued a limited number of permits for anchovy fishing under an experimental management program in 1965; James D. Messersmith, "The Northern Anchovy (*Engraulis mordax*) and Its Fishery, 1965–1968," State of California Department of Fish and Game, *Fisheries Bulletin* 147 (1969): 8, 10.

24. L. A. Hammergren, "Peruvian Political and Administrative Responses to El Niño: Organizational, Ideological and Political Constraints on Policy Change," in *Resource Management and Environmental Uncertainty: Lessons from Coastal Upwelling Fisheries*, ed. M. H. Glantz and J. D. Thompson (New York: John Wiley and Sons, 1981), 328; Baltazar Caravedo Molinari, *Estado, pesca y burguesía, 1939–1973* (Lima: Teoría y Realidad, 1979), 40.

25. Roemer, *Fishing for Growth*, 74.

26. Roemer, *Fishing for Growth*, 75–76.

27. "Aparatoso incidente puso fin a sesión de Comisión Revisora de Legislación de Pesquería," *El Comercio* (April 4, 1967): 4.

28. "Aparatoso incidente."

29. "Por una soberanía real y no de papel," *Oiga* (1969): 9, 10, 36, CENDOPES clippings file.

30. Harry N. Scheiber, "California Marine Research and the Founding of Modern Fisheries Oceanography: CALCOFI's Early Years, 1947–1964," *CALCOFI Reports* 31 (1990): 67.

31. M. B. Schaefer to A. C. Burd, June 13, 1969; Milner B. Schaefer Papers, Folder Sociedad Nacional de Pesquería—Proposal and Some Correspondence, SIO Archive.

32. Detailed historical SST data are available from 1854 to the present at Boyin Huang et al., "NOAA Extended Reconstructed Sea Surface Temperature (ERSST), Version 5," NOAA National Centers for Environmental Information, 2017, https://www.ncdc.noaa.gov/data-access/marineocean-data/extended-reconstructed-sea-surface-temperature-ersst-v5.

33. Emilio Delboy and Angel Maldonado/Comité Nacional de la Protección a la Naturaleza, "Que se declare a la anchoveta Reserva Natural," *La Nación* (Lima) (September 24, 1954): 2, 10.

34. Ecosystem-based management recognizes that marine ecosystems are adaptive and "linked across multiple scales by flows of water and species." The Commission for the Conservation of Antarctic Marine Living Resources (CCAMLR) first formally applied this principle as a fishery management practice in 1982. Mary Ruckelshaus et al., "Marine Ecosystem-based Management in Practice: Scientific and Governance Challenges," *BioScience* 58, no. 1 (2008): 53–63.

35. Delboy and Maldonado, "Que se declare a la anchoveta Reserva Natural," 10.

36. Francisco Pulgar Vidal, "La importancia de la anchoveta," *La Prensa* (Lima) (June 30, 1959): 13.

37. Letter from Max Cohen (International Proteins Corporation) to Wilbert Chapman (Ralston Purina), August 8, 1969. W. M. Chapman Papers, Box 61, Folder 7, UW Special Collections.

38. Memo from D. W. Souter to B. Zunjic, August 18, 1964, p.5 ; Wilbert M. Chapman Papers, Box 59, Folder 20, UW Special Collections.

39. Letter from Hermann Einarsson (FAO fisheries expert at IMARPE) to Sidney Holt (Chief fishery biologst, FAO-Rome), January 11, 1965, p1-2; W. M. Chapman Papers, Box 63, Folder 16, UW Special Collections.

40. Sociedad Nacional de Pesquería, *Si esta crisis no se arregla, quedaremos así* (Lima, Peru: SNP, 1967).

41. Letters Popper to Chapman, 1963–64, Wilbert M. Chapman papers, Box 101, Folder 19, UW Special Collections. IMARPE was established in 1960 with FAO-UNDP funds; see Consejo de Investigaciones Hidrobiologicas, *Plan of Operation for a Marine Resources Research Institute of Peru*, 1960, FAO Archive-Rome.

42. Einarsson noted that attempts to limit the *peladilla* catch during 1964 had been ineffective, but he did not reference the specific law in this regard, nor does such a measure appear in Schreiber's list of secondary regulations enacted on the anchoveta fishery during the 1960s. Letter from Hermann Einarsson to Wilbert Chapman (c/o FAO-Rome), February 28, 1965; W. M. Chapman Papers, Box 63, Folder 16, UW Special Collections; see also Milena Arias Schreiber, "The Evolution of Legal Instruments and the Sustainability of the Peruvian Anchovy Fishery," *Marine Policy* 36 (2012): 81, table 1.

43. Law No. 13825 (1961) levied a 14 percent tax on fishmeal exports; Law No. 15048 (1964) established a new tax system in part for contribution to the operating costs of IMARPE. M. Arias Schreiber, "The Evolution of Legal Instruments," table 1; Letter from Hermann Einarsson to Wilbert Chapman (c/o FAO-Rome), February 28, 1965, p2; W. M. Chapman Papers, Box 63, Folder 16, UW Special Collections.

44. Letter from Hermann Einarsson to Wilbert Chapman (c/o FAO-Rome), February 28, 1965, p2; W. M. Chapman Papers, Box 63, Folder 16, UW Special Collections.

45. Schreiber refers to these measures as "secondary legislation" since they were not comprehensive. Schreiber, "The Evolution of Legal Instruments."

46. Letter from Hermann Einarsson to Wilbert Chapman (c/o FAO-Rome), February 28, 1965; W. M. Chapman Papers, Box 63, Folder 16, UW Special Collections.

47. Decreto Supremo 05-65; Schreiber, "The Evolution of Legal Instruments," table 1, 81; J. A. Gulland et al., *Report of the Expert Panel on the Economic Effects of Alternative Regulatory Measures in the Peruvian Anchoveta Fishery*, IMARPE Informe No. 34 (Callao, Peru: IMARPE, 1970), 33.

48. Gulland et al., *Report of the Expert Panel*, 37. There was a minor dip in 1965 landings, but 1966 they seemed to rebound. John A. Gulland, "Letters to the Editor: Peruvian Anchoveta—Optimal Management," *Marine Policy* 4, no. 1 (1980): 78.

49. Gulland et al., *"Report of the Expert Panel*, 12.

50. Law no. 16694; Schreiber, "The Evolution of Legal Instruments," table 1; Gulland et al., *Report of the Expert Panel*, 33; Editorial, "La estatización de la pesca," *Oiga*, (May 11, 1973): 9.

51. Although numbers were unconfirmed by the time of the 1970 report, this trend continued until the first fishing season of 1970. Gulland et al., *Report of the Expert Panel*, 8.

52. Gulland et al., *Report of the Expert Panel*, 6.

53. Gulland et al., *Report of the Expert Panel*, 16, 17, 22, 25, 30. The concept of "maximum sustainable yield" has been thoroughly reviewed by Carmel Finley in *All the Fish in the Sea: Maximum Sustainable Yield and the Failure of Fisheries Management* (Chicago: Chicago University Press, 2011).

54. Gulland et al., *Report of the Expert Panel*, 11.

55. Decree Law 18121 (January 27, 1971) *Ley Orgánica del Sector Pesquero*, created EPSEP; Decree Law 18253 (1970), created EPCHAP. "Ministro Tantaleán dice que no es necesario estatizar industria pesquera en el Perú," *La Prensa* (Lima) (February 6, 1970): 2; "Fishmeal Futures Soar as Peru's Government Takes Over Marketing," *Wall Street Journal* (April 21, 1970): 32.

56. Decree Law 180261 (December 17, 1969) established the Ministry of Fisheries; Schreiber, "The Evolution of Legal Instruments," table 1, 81; "General Tantaleán juró Ministerio de Pesquería," *La Prensa* February 4, 1970, 1; "Ministro dice se impulsará más la industria pesquera del país," *La Prensa* February 4, 1970, 2; Javier Tantaleán Vanini, Prólogo, *Revista del Ministerio de Pesquería* (Lima, Perú), 1, no. 1 (1970): frontmatter.

57. Gulland et al., *Report of the Expert Panel*, 28.

58. Hammergren, "Peruvian Political and Administrative Responses," 330; Ministerio de Pesquería (Perú), Oficina Sectorial de Planificación, *Plan sectorial de pesquería, 1971–1975* (Lima: MIPE, 1971).

59. Decree Law 18810 (1971); Schreiber, "The Evolution of Legal Instruments," 81.

60. Hammergren, "Peruvian Political and Administrative Responses," 335.; "Hombres de mar tendran estabilidad en trabajo," *Expreso* (September 23, 1972), CENDOPES clippings file.

61. Hammergren, "Peruvian Political and Administrative Responses," 331.

62. "30 milliones de dólares en créditos para pesca daría Japon al Peru," *Expreso* (April 20, 1971) : 2; "Peru daría preferencia a industrias japonesas en el campo de la pesca," (April 20, 1971), CENDOPES clippings file.

63. Hammergren, "Peruvian Political and Administrative Responses," notes that the number of employees in the MIPE alone grew from less than two hundred initially to thirteen hundred by 1973 (329, 333).

64. William G. Clark, "The Lessons of the Peruvian Anchoveta Fishery," *CalCOFI Reports* 19 (1977): 62; see also "Peru Fish Go Wrong Way, Peril Industry," *Los Angeles Times* (June 14, 1972): K3; David F. Belnap, "Pungent Fishmeal Odor Like Perfume to Peru," *Los Angeles Times* (April 8, 1973): 17.

65. Belnap, "Pungent Fishmeal Odor."

66. Decree Law 19999 (May 7, 1973) created PescaPerú to take over fishing and processing.

67. "International Proteins Buys Shrimp Units, Peru Lets Profits Be Taken," *Wall Street Journal* (March 4, 1971): 17; "Peru Takes Over Declining Fisheries," *New York Times* (May 9, 1973): 3.

68. "El gobierno asume monopolio de la industria pesquera," *Expreso* (Lima) (May 8, 1973): 3.
69. Editorial, "La estatización de la pesca," *OIGA* (May 11, 1973): 9–15, 38–40.
70. *Expreso* (May 13, 1973), CENDOPES clippings file.
71. Gulland et al., *Report of the Expert Panel*, 28.
72. Front cover of *Oiga* No. 524 (May 11, 1973). The cover photo showed the minister gazing into the distance, as if to invoke the Velasco regime's "westward march" slogan, which promoted the expansion of the Peruvian empire toward the Pacific.
73. Decree Law 21558 (1976) stipulated the return of nationalized fleet to private ownership, and Decree Law 22329 (1978) repealed the rights of fishermen to share ownership, management and profits; see Schreiber, "The Evolution of Legal Instruments," 83; "Transferencia de la flota anchovetera de PescaPeru a pequeñas empresas," *Boletín PescaPerú* 10 (1977): n.p.
74. "EPSEP: Acción para difundir el consumo," *Boletín PescaPerú* 12 (1977): n.p.
75. E. Loayza, "Aprovechamiento de la anchoveta para el consumo humano en el Peru," Doc. no. FII: FP/73/E-43, paper presented at the FAO Technical Conference on Fishery Products, Tokyo (December 4–11, 1973), Rome: FAO, 1973.
76. "Chile elevó producción de harina por veda en nuestro litoral sur," *El Comercio* (November 11, 1980), CENDOPES clippings file.
77. "Peru: Convenio pesquero con la URSS," *Boletín Pesquero* 60 (1985): 28–29.
78. Decree Law 24790; Schreiber, "The Evolution of Legal Instruments," 83.
79. Schreiber explains that the use of *rational* translates to English "sustainable" prior to the latter's popularity after the 1992 Rio accords ("The Evolution of Legal Instruments," 82).
80. Sally Bowen, "Peru Aims to Feed on Fish Farming Expansion," *Financial Times* (February 22, 1991): I26.
81. Decree Law 25977 (1992), Schreiber, "The Evolution of Legal Instruments," 83.
82. Bowen, "Peru Aims."

CHAPTER SIX. THE TRANSLOCAL HISTORY
OF INDUSTRIAL FISHERIES IN IQUIQUE
AND TALCAHUANO, CHILE

1. Juan Carlos Castilla, "Fisheries in Chile: Small Pelagics, Management, Rights, and Sea Zoning," *Bulletin of Marine Science* 86, no. 2 (2010): 221–34; Kailin Kroetz et al., "Evaluation of the Chilean Jack Mackerel ITQ System," *Marine Resource Economics* 32, no. 2 (2017): 217–41; Sarah Schumann, "Co-management and 'Consciousness': Fishers' Assimilation of Management Principles in Chile," *Marine Policy* 31, no. 2 (2007): 101–11.
2. David W. Cushing, *The Provident Sea* (Cambridge: Cambridge University Press, 1988), 243.

3. MacCall, "The Sardine-Anchovy Puzzle," in *Shifting Baselines: The Past and the Future of Ocean Fisheries*, ed. Jeremy B. Jackson, Karen E. Alexander, and Enric Sala. New York: Island Press, 2011.52–54; Cushing, *The Provident Sea*, 253.

4. Recent literature labels these ecosystem-wide changes in fish populations "regime shifts." See MacCall, "The Sardine-Anchovy Puzzle," 52; Jürgen Alheit and Miguel Niquen, "Regime Shifts in the Humboldt Current Ecosystem," *Progress in Oceanography* 60, nos. 2–4 (2004): 201–22.

5. "Chile, primer productor de harina de pescado en el mundo; desplazó a Perú," *El Diario* (Lima) (November 10, 1980), CENDOPES clippings file.

6. The northern upwelling subsystem off Peru (near Chimbote) is the most abundant of the three subsystems; Vivian Montecino and Carina B. Lange, "The Humboldt Current System: Ecosystem Components and Processes, Fisheries, and Sediment Studies," *Progress in Oceanography* 83, nos. 1–4 (2009): 65.

7. Alheit and Niquen, "Regime Shifts," 208, 210.

8. Gregory T. Cushman, *Guano and the Opening of the Pacific World* (Cambridge: Cambridge University Press, 2013), 65; R. A. F. Penrose Jr., "The Nitrate Deposits of Chile," *Journal of Geology* 18, no. 1 (1910): 31.

9. Cushman, *Guano*, 67 and 67n114; William Bollaert, "Observations on the Geography of Southern Peru, Including Survey of the Province of Tarapacá, and Route to Chile by the Coast of the Desert of Atacama," *The Journal of the Royal Geographical Society of London* 21 (1851): 99–130; see also Luis Castro Castro et al., "William Bollaert y sus descripciones geográficas, cartográficas y antropológicas sobre la provincia de Tarapacá en la etapa inicial de la formación republicana del Perú, 1827–1854," *HiSTOReLo: Revista de Historia Regional y Local* 9, no. 18 (2017): 123–63.

10. Frank M. Chapman, "Darwin's Chile," *Geographical Journal* 68, no. 5 (1926): 371.

11. Cushman, *Guano*, 67, 155.

12. The 1883 Treaty of Ancón established the terrestrial boundary at the Sama River, north of the formerly Peruvian Tacna and Arica provinces, but the description in the treaty text later gave rise to a dispute over the precise location of this boundary. In 1922 the two countries submitted the dispute for international arbitration. The Arbitrator, US president Calvin Coolidge, determined in 1925 "that the Southern boundary of the territory covered by Article 3 of the Treaty of Ancon is the provincial boundary between the Peruvian provinces of Arica and Tarapaca as they stood on 20 October 1883," but in 1929 Chile and Peru signed the Treaty of Lima, with the assistance of US president Herbert Hoover, giving Tacna to Peru and Arica to Chile. See *Reports of International Arbitral Awards*, vol. 2, 921–58, cited in FAO Legal Office, "Summary of Decisions by International Tribunals including Arbitral Awards, Section 4.2.5. Tacna-Arica Case," in Food and Agricultural Organization of the United Nations (FAO), Legal Office, *Sources of International Water Law*, FAO Legislative Study 65 (1998), 246, available from ftp://ftp.fao.org/docrep/fao/005/w9549E/w9549E00.pdf. The region between approx. 19–26°S was reported to be the zone richest in nitrates; Penrose, "Nitrate Deposits," 1.

13. Philip W. Rundel, "Ecological Relationships of Desert Fog Zone Lichens," *The Bryologist* 81, no. 2 (1978): 277–93.

14. Robert Cushman Murphy, citing his nineteenth-century predecessors Delano and Morrell (1817 and 1832, respectively), *Oceanic Birds of South America* (New York: Macmillan, 1936), 2:902.

15. Rodolfo Disi Pavlic, "Explicando los resultados de los conflictos asimétricos: La Guerra de Arauco," *Estudios Internacionales* 50, no. 189 (2018): 97–119.

16. Asociación de Industriales Pesqueros Región del Bío Bío (ASIPES) and Luis Salvo González, *Historia de la industria pesquera en la región del Bío Bío* (Santiago: LOM Ediciones, 2000), 64–65; John J. Johnson, "Talcahuano and Concepción as Seen by the Forty-Niners," *Hispanic American Historical Review* 26, no. 2 (1946): 251.

17. William Bollaert, "Observations on the Coal Formation in Chile, S. America," *Journal of the Royal Geographical Society of London* 25 (1855): 173; Carlos Vivallos Espinoza and Alejandra Brito Peña, "Inmigración y sectores populares en las minas de carbón de Lota y Coronel (Chile, 1850–1900)," *Atenea (Concepción)* 501 (2010): 73–94; see also Jody Pavilack, *Mining for the Nation: The Politics of Chile's Coal Communities from the Popular Front to the Cold War* (University Park: Penn State University Press, 2011).

18. Johnson, "Talcahuano," 261.

19. Pablo Camus Gayán and Rodrigo Hidalgo Dattwyler, "'Y serán desplayados': Recorrido histórico sobre los bienes comunes, pescadores artesanales y control legal del litoral en Chile," *Historia Crítica (Bogotá)* 63 (2017): 106.

20. At least one fishermen's cooperative was active locally at the time. "Notas sobre pesca," *El Mercurio* (April 18, 1943): 3.

21. "Improvement of Fishing Industry in Chile," Edward A. Dow, American Consul General, to Secretary of State, Washington, DC (April 27, 1936); Santiago Consular General Records, RG 84, NARA (College Park, MD).

22. E. Yáñez, M. A. Barbieri, and L. Santillan, "Long-Term Environmental Variability and Pelagic Fisheries in Talcahuano, Chile," *South African Journal of Marine Science* 12, no. 1 (1992): 175–88.

23. "Notas sobre pesca," 3.

24. In 1950 Osorio-Tafall lamented the high proportion of hake being used for fishmeal. B. F. Osorio-Tafall to Kask, [Report on fisheries tour of Latin America], Doc. 0051909 (5/19/1950), RG 14, FAO Archive-Rome.

25. Angelini's first fishmeal enterprise was Pesquera Eperva, established in Arica in 1956.

26. W. M. Chapman to Fred E. Taylor, Letter (April 2, 1959); Foreign Report Chile No. 59-1, Appendix I, p. 3; W. M. Chapman Papers, Box 50, Folder 9, UW Special Collections.

27. Carl A. Hedreen to File, Memorandum re: "Luncheon meeting with Dr. Popovich of the Instituto de Estudios de Recursos Marinos," October 16, 1963; W. M. Chapman Papers, Box 59, Folder 20, UW Special Collections.

28. Governments of Peru, Chile, and Ecuador, *Agreement on the Special Maritime Boundary Zone,* December 4, 1954, http://www.un.org/depts/los/LEGISLATION ANDTREATIES/STATEFILES/CHL.htm.

29. Both Chilean and Peruvian boats were accused of and/or caught fishing on the other side of the maritime boundary. J. Manuel Casanueva R., "Sobre violación de aguas peruanas or embarcaciones pesqueras chilenas," February 23, 1961, Ministerio de Agricultura, vol. 1482, ARNAD; J. Manuel Casanueva R., "Ref: Oficio confidencial No. 21 sobre pesca de embarcaciones chilenas en aguas peruanas," August 9, 1961, Ministerio de Agricultura, vol. 1482, ARNAD; Ministro de Defensa (Chile) to Ministro del Interior (Chile), "Obj: R/c. medidas que se adoptan con pesqueros extranjeros por transgression disposiciones vigentes," October 4, 1961, Ministerio de Agricultura, Vol. 1482, ARNAD.

30. For a summary review of the boundary dispute and its legal and historical precedents, see International Court of Justice, Summaries of Judgments, Advisory Opinions and Orders of the ICJ—Maritime Dispute (Peru v. Chile) – Judgment of Jan. 27, 2014, http://legal.un.org/icjsummaries/documents/english/206_e.pdf.

31. "El hambre, el hombre, y el mar," *El Nacional* (Lima) (January 28, 1990), CENDOPES clippings file.

32. FAO, "Position of Fish Meal Industry and Trade in Chile," Doc. no. IFIME C/28. *Report to the FAO International Meeting on Fish Meal* (Rome, Italy, March 1961), 2, FAO Archive-Rome. A report to the US State Department estimated twenty-nine fishmeal factories in 1959. Victor Algrant, Commercial Attaché of U.S. Embassy (Santiago, Chile) to US Department of State (Washington, DC), "Chilean Fishmeal Industry," June 10, 1960, Box 2402 (Chile 1960–63), NARA. Alagrant noted that the cost of the hake-based fishmeal was far above the global norm, reflecting short supplies in local markets.

33. US Embassy (Santiago, Chile) to US Department of State (Washington, DC), "Subject: Fisheries of Chile," Foreign Service Dispatch No. 895 (6/7/1960), 4, NARA.

34. FAO, *Position of Fish Meal Industry,* 3.

35. US Embassy (Santiago, Chile) to US Department of State (Washington, DC), "Subject: Fisheries of Chile," Foreign Service Dispatch No. 895 (June 7, 1960), 1, NARA.

36. Humberto Díaz C. [Gerente General], CORFO, "Gerencia de Operaciones," *Plan de Fomento Pesquero para Iquique,* Acuerdo No. 5598 (March 25, 1960), 2, BNCH.

37. Díaz C., "Gerencia de Operaciones."

38. CORFO, Secretaría General, *Plan de Fomento Pesquero para Iquique,* Acuerdo No. 5598 (March 25, 1960), BNCH.

39. CORFO, *Plan de Fomento Pesquero,* 34.

40. Algrant, "Chilean Fishmeal."

41. FAO, *Position of Fish Meal Industry,* 4.

42. The statistics cited in this source do not indicate how much of the industrially processed fish was made into fishmeal. Between 1950 and 1960, Talcahuano

supplied only 15–25 percent of total fish landings for direct human consumption, suggesting that the majority of the fish landed there became fishmeal. "Talcahuano: Primer puerto pesquero," *Chile Pesquero* No. 11 (1962): 14.

43. "Una nueva area industrial se levantaría en Iquique," *El Tarapacá* (Iquique) (March 10, 1963): 1; "Bodega para 15.000 tns. de harina de pescado quedará habilitada en este puerto," *El Tarapacá* (Iquique)(March 23, 1963): 5.

44. Edward C. Burks, "Fish Meal a Boon to Port in Chile: New Export Trade Revives Dormant City of Iquique," *New York Times* (May 5, 1963): 4; "Chile's Fisheries Expanding Fleet: Foreign Capital Is Attracted by Booming Industry," *New York Times* (July 28, 1963): 96.

45. "Enormes cargamentos de harina de pescado, se han registrado," *El Tarapacá* (Iquique) (March 21, 1963): 1.

46. Bernardo Guerrero Jiménez, *Del chumbeque a la zofri: Los aromas de nuestra identidad cultural* (Iquique: Universidad Arturo Prat, 1999), 51–52.

47. Burks, "Fish Meal a Boon," 4.

48. Solange Duhart and Jacqueline Weinstein, *Pesca industrial: Sector estratégico y de alto riesgo* (Santiago, Chile: Academía de Humanismo Cristiano, 1988), 48.

49. "Chile's Fisheries Expanding Fleet."

50. As quoted in the original article, which did not mention the scientist's name. "Chile's Fisheries Expanding Fleet."

51. Julio Peña-Torres, "Regulación pesquera en Chile: Una perspectiva histórica," *Cuadernos de Economía* 33, no. 100 (1996): 369.

52. Number of vessels from J. R. Serra, "Changes in Abundance of Pelagic Resources along the Chilean Coast," *FAO Fisheries Reports* 291, nos. 2–3 (1983): 236, 239.

53. "Chile's fisheries;" Burks, "Fish Meal a Boon."

54. "4 modernas goletas pesqueras trajo ayer el Sr. Harvey Smith," *El Tarapacá* (Iquique) (March 23, 1963): 1.

55. "Pfizer 1st Quarter Net Set Record; Sales Rose from Like '63 Period," *Wall Street Journal* (April 28, 1964), 23; "Pfizer, Big Drug Concern, Goes into Fishing Business," *Wall Street Journal* (April 15, 1966): 18. The boats had 140-ton holds and could be filled within twenty-four hours when fishing at only fifteen to twenty miles offshore. The plant had a capacity of twenty-five thousand tons and was operated by Pfizer's Chilean subsidiary, Pfizer del Mar.

56. "Goletas pescan sardinas por falta de anchovetas," *El Tarapacá* (December 11, 1966): 3.

57. "Trading in Fishmeal Futures set to Begin Today," *Wall Street Journal* (April 12, 1967): 26.

58. "Chilean Fishing Town Seeks to Become a Divorce Resort," *Washington Post* (June 10, 1967): A12.

59. Chile had no legal divorce until 2004, but it is unclear how this would work on a practical legal level, or whether this experiment was ever attempted. In order to obtain the divorce, couples would, in completing the residency requirement, spend money on hotels, restaurants, and local entertainment. "Chilean Fishing Town Seeks."

60. A.S., interview with the author, 2009; Yáñez et al., "Long-Term Environmental Variability," 181.

61. Serra, "Changes in Abundance," 241.

62. "Hoy entregarán los pesqueros soviéticos," *Diario El Color* (January 26, 1972): 9. See also "Chile: Senate Discussion of the Chile-Union of Soviet Socialist Republics Contract for the Use of Soviet Vessels for Fishing Operations," *International Legal Materials* 11, no .5 (1972): 1156–68.

63. "Soviet Salesmen Find More Customers among the Nations of Latin America," *Wall Street Journal* (March 13, 1972): 9.

64. Fernando Carrasco Herrera, "Instalación recuperadora agua de cola proveniente de industrias pesqueras de Talcahuano" (April 25, 1975), CORFO Files, vol. 125, ARNAD.

65. Serra, "Changes in Abundance," 235; Yáñez et al. also note the 1976 collapse of anchoveta and sardine populations off Talcahuano and note the increasing harvest of jack mackerel beginning in 1974 ("Long-Term Environmental Variability," 185).

66. A.S., interview.

67. Serra, "Changes in Abundance," 235.

68. A.S., interview.

69. Yáñez et al., "Long-Term Environmental Variability," 185. The authors date the increasing abundance of jack mackerel beginning in 1974, although this contradicts the personal narrative Saldivia offered in the interview as well as informal accounts from my fieldwork in Talcahuano.

70. M. L. Stevenson, "Trawl Survey of the West Coast of the South Island and Tasman and Golden Bays," March–April 2003 (KAH0304), *New Zealand Fisheries Assessment Report* 2004/4; cited in FishBase, eds. R. Froese and D. Pauly, www .fishbase.org.

71. Yáñez et al., "Long-Term Environmental Variability," 185–86.

72. See Serra, "Changes in Abundance," 235, 238; Yáñez et al., "Long-Term Environmental Variability," 185. Pacific sardine populations became the most important fishery in the northern zone by the end of the decade, far surpassing the production of the 1960s.

73. This measure reversed a 1962 decree that permitted foreign factory ships supplying the Chilean market. "Chile's 200-mile zone fishing controls," *BBC Summary of World Broadcasts: Latin America,* V/6212/i (September 6, 1979).

74. The area between 25° and 41°S was the primary location of the Soviet fishery. Soviet long-distance fleets began prospecting South Pacific marine resources during the 1960s. A. A. Elizarov, "Prefacio," in *Biología y pesca comercial del jurel en el Pacífico Sur,* ed. Dagoberto Arcos and Alexander S. Grechina (Talcahuano, Chile: Instituto de Investigación Pesquera, 1994), 7.

75. Everett Martin, "Vanishing Anchovy Is Hurting, Changing Fish-Meal Production in Chile and Peru," *Wall Street Journal* (July 3, 1979): 20.

76. "Chile, primer productor de harina de pescado en el mundo; desplazó a Perú," *El Diario* (Lima) (November 10, 1980), CENDOPES clippings file.

77. "Chile elevó producción de harina por veda en nuestro litoral sur," *El Comercio* (Santiago) (November 11, 1980), CENDOPES clippings file.

78. "Chile elevó producción."

79. K. Turner, "Carelessness Cuts into Peru Fishing Industry," *The Telegraph* (London) (January 9, 1981): 13.

80. However, significant clandestine production occurred.

81. An October 1985 decree prohibited the use of white fish (*"pesca blanca"*) for fishmeal production, but allowed at least nine species to be used, including hake. "Chile: Reglamentan elaboración de harina de pescado," *Boletín Pesquero* no. 56 (1985): 1–3.

82. Magdalena Echeverria, "Radiografía de algunos de los grandes grupos pesqueros de Chile," *Economia y Negocios/El Mercurio* (July 13, 2007); Paola Damiani Quintanilla, Carolina Pino González, and Claudia Sanhueza González, "Analisis al desempeño de los grupos empresariales en Chile," Tesis para Lic. Ingeniería Comercial (Universidad de Chile, 2005).

83. "Chile: Estado actual y proyecciones de la actividad extractiva," *Boletín Pesquero* no. 3 (1984): 14–20.

84. "Chile elevó producción"; "Sin novedad regresaron dos goletas pesqueras," *El Pampino* (Iquique, Chile) (March 10, 1989): 7.

85. The outdated 1970s technology remained in use at least through the mid-1990s. "Empresas productivas del norte peruano tiene retraso tecnológico de 25 años," *El Comercio* (Lima) (January 19, 1994), CENDOPES clippings file.

86. "Gobierno suspenda venta de fábricas pesqueras a Chile: Investigan denuncia sobre utilización ilegal de CERTEX," *La República* (Lima) (June 24, 1983): 2, CENDOPES clippings file. In 2010, the fishmeal plant I visited in Guayaquil, Ecuador, used Peruvian machinery as well as steam dryers produced in Chile during the 1980s. A 1984 article also cites "Panama and countries of the Middle East and Africa" as purchasers of the Peruvian fleet. "Peru: Se recupera producción pesquera," *Boletín Pesquero* no. 1 (1984): 9–10; Duhart and Weinstein, *Pesca industrial,* 1:47.

87. Serra, "Changes in Abundance," 239, 241.

88. The Norwegian boats were more stable and powerful in waves and introduced other technological improvements such as setting the net without a panga (small skiff used for the setting maneuver in American-style models) and using nets specially designed to sink faster around the school in a shift to mid-water trawling for jack mackerel (Duhart and Weinstein, *Pesca industrial,* 1:49); interview with industry executive Coronel, Chile, 2009.

89. José Muga Alvarez, Randolfo Sanhueza Ward, Luis Eduardo Toro Alvarez, and Nelson Salas Pulgar, "Perspectivas de desarrollo del sector pesquero industrial" (Cuadro 14), in *Seminario sobre las perspectivas del desarrollo del sector pesquero chileno* (Valparaíso: Ediciones Universitarias de Valparaíso, 1974), 241. In 1985, the Chilean fleet included 439 vessels and 11 factory ships; "Nuevos barcos pesqueros," *Boletín Pesquero* no. 56 (1985): 5.

90. Gonzalo Tobella, "Una alternativa para algunas industrias," *Chile Pesquero* 4 (1978): 36; "Chile: Estado actual y proyecciones de la actividad extractiva," *Boletín Pesquero* no. 3 (1984): 16.

91. This occurs because delicate chemical structures of the proteins and other nutrients remain intact when using the vapor drying method. A. Bermejo, "Chile harinero," *Expreso* August 25, 1990, CENDOPES clippings file.

92. "Empresas productivas del norte peruano tienen retraso tecnológico de 25 años," *El Comercio,* January 19, 1994.

93. Luis Pichott, "Los gatos: Peligroso robo organizado a la industria pesquera de Talcahuano," *Chile Pesquero* (August 1985).

94. "Los malos olores," *El Pampino* (Iquique, Chile) (February 25, 1989): 5; "En San Vicente: Vecinos reclaman por el mal olor de pesqueras," *El Sur* (Concepción, Chile) (March 1, 1993): 13.

95. "En San Vicente."

96. "Desastre en San Vicente: El puerto en llamas," *El Sur* (Concepción, Chile) (March 7, 1993): 1; "Port fire," *Lloyd's List* (March 9, 1993): 10; "Chile," *Miami Herald* (March 8, 1993): A6.

97. Rachel A. Schurman, "Shuckers, Sorters, Headers, and Gutters: Labor in the Fisheries Sector," in *Victims of the Chilean Miracle: Workers and Neoliberalism in the Pinochet Era, 1973–2002*, ed. Peter Winn (Durham, NC: Duke University Press, 2004), 298–336.

98. A.S. interview.

99. Peña-Torres, "Regulacion pesquera, 376.

100. Jorge Valenzuela Ocampo, "Observaciones al proyecto ley de pesca: Exposición del subsector artesanal cooperativo pesquero," in *El desafío pesquero chileno: La explotación racional de nuestras riquezas marinas*, ed. Eduardo Bitrán (Santiago, Chile: Hachette, 1989), 373; Humberto Chamorro Alvarez, "Planteamientos del Consejo Nacional de los Pescadores Artesanales de Chile acerca de la ley de pesca," in Bitrán, ed. *El desafío pesquero chileno*, 411.

101. Ernesto Tironi B., "La necesidad de regular la pesca en Chile," *El desafío pesquero chileno*, 325. The discussion that preceded the implementation of this law was extensive in Chile, and it included a careful consideration of other nations' experiences with similar regulations.

102. Leslie Crawford, "Chile No Longer Has Plenty More Fish in the Sea," *Financial Times* (July 19, 1991): 28.

103. "New Law Could Boost Orders," *Lloyd's List* (February 25, 1991): 4 (Lexis Nexis).

104. Julio Peña-Torres, Jorge Dresdner, and Felipe Vasquez, "El Niño and Fishing Location Decisions: The Chilean Straddling Jack Mackerel Fishery," *Marine Resource Economics* 32, no. 3 (2017): 249–75.

105. For example, Chilean bio-economist Álvaro Espinoza argued that the fishery was unstable at its current harvest levels, warning against the potential disaster of continued pressure on stocks. See Álvaro Andrés Espinoza Muñoz, "Sustentabilidad de la pesquería del jurel en la región del Bío Bío" (PhD diss., Universidad de Concepción, 1993). On uncertainty surrounding jack mackerel fisheries biology, see Dagoberto F. Arcos, Luis A. Cubillos, and Sergio P. Núñez, "The Jack Mackerel Fishery and El Niño 1997–98 Effects Off Chile," *Progress in Oceanography* 49

(2001): 613; Sergio Núñez et al., "Distribution of Early Developmental Stages of Jack Mackerel in the Southeastern Pacific Ocean," Paper no. 2, *South Pacific RFMO Chilean Jack Mackerel Workshop* (2009).

106. "Fish Exporting Booms in Chile, Peru," *The Globe and Mail* (Canada) (March 13, 1995).

107. For an environmental-historical study of the industry's development in southern Chile, see Andrew W. Gerhart, "An Environmental and Social History of the Chilean Salmon Farming Industry, 1976–2009" (PhD diss., Stanford University, 2014).

108. On salmon as a new natural resource export in the context of neoliberal policies, see Rachel A. Schurman, "Snails, Southern Hake and Sustainability: Neoliberalism and Natural Resource Exports in Chile," *World Development* 24, no. 11 (1996): 1695–709. The industry was highly vulnerable to disease outbreaks and suffered a major crisis in 2008–10; see Andrew Gerhart, "Petri Dishes of an Archipelago: The Ecological Rubble of the Chilean Salmon Farming Industry," *Journal of Political Ecology* 24, no. 1 (2017): 726–42; John Soluri, "Something Fishy: Chile's Blue Revolution, Commodity Diseases, and the Problem of Sustainability," *Latin American Research Review* 46 (2011): 32–54.

109. Arcos et al., "The Jack Mackerel Fishery and El Niño.

110. Castilla, "Fisheries in Chile"; Kroetz et al., "Evaluation of the Chilean Jack Mackerel ITQ System"; Sarah Schumann, "Co-management and 'Consciousness.'"

CONCLUSION

1. "Special product fish meals ... are distinguished from standard fish meals by being prepared from fresh raw material using low temperature conditions of processing." International Fishmeal and Oil Manufacturers Association, *Tests to Predict the Quality of Fish Meals for Special Uses*, Research Report Number 1993-1 (London: IFOMA, 1993), 1.

2. "Chile elevó producción de harina por veda en nuestro litoral sur," *El Comercio* (Lima) (November 11, 1980), CENDOPES clippings file.

3. "Chile: Solo la pesca creció en periodo de recesión," *Boletín Pesquero* 83 (1985): 1–2.

4. Sally Bowen, "Peru Aims to Feed on Fish Farming Expansion," *Financial Times* (London) (February 22, 1991): I26.

5. Sigbjørn Tveterås and Ragnar Tveterås, "The Global Competition for Wild Fish Resources between Livestock and Agriculture," *Journal of Agricultural Economics* 61, no. 2 (2010): 381–97, cited in Pierre Fréon et al., "Harvesting for Food versus Feed: A Review of Peruvian Fisheries in Global Context," *Review in Fish Biology and Fisheries* 24 (2014): 382.

6. Bowen, "Peru Aims."

7. Alec D. MacCall, "The Sardine-Anchovy Puzzle," in *Shifting Baselines: The Past and the Future of Ocean Fisheries*, ed. Jeremy B. C. Jackson et al. (New York: Island Press, 2011), 55; Fréon et al., "Harvesting for Food versus Feed," 389.

8. For a list of ENSO events and their intensities 1871–2008, see especially table 2 in Benjamin S. Giese and Sulagna Ray, "El Niño Variability in Simple Ocean Data Assimilation (SODA), 1871–2008," *Journal of Geophysical Research: Oceans* 116, no. C2 (2011), https://doi.org/10.1029/2010JC006695.

9. Edward J. Balleisen and Elizabeth K. Brake, "Historical Perspective and Better Regulatory Governance: An Agenda for Institutional Reform," *Regulation & Governance* 8 (2014): 222–45.

10. David H. Cushing, *The Provident Sea* (Cambridge: Cambridge University Press, 1988), 253.

11. MacCall, "The Sardine-Anchovy Puzzle," 48.

12. Cushman, *Guano and the Opening of the Pacific World: A Global Ecological History* (Cambridge: Cambridge University Press, 2013), 337.

13. Raymond J. H. Beverton and David H. Cushing, "John Alan Gulland, 16 September 1926–24 June 1990," *Biographical Memoirs of Fellows of the Royal Society* 38 (1992): 176.

14. MacCall, "The Sardine-Anchovy Puzzle," 52, citing J. D. Isaacs, "Some Ideas and Frustrations about Fisheries Science," *CalCOFI Reports* 18 (1976): 34.

15. MacCall, "The Sardine-Anchovy Puzzle," 56.

16. Michael H. Glantz, "Science, Politics, and the Economics of the Peruvian Anchoveta Fishery," *Marine Policy* (1979): 201–10; William Safire, "El Niño," *New York Times* (August 30, 1973): 33.

17. MacCall, "The Sardine-Anchovy Puzzle," 56.

18. J. Alheit and M. Ñiquen, "Regime Shifts in the Humboldt Current Ecosystem," *Progress in Oceanography* 60, nos. 2–4 (2004): 201–22; Alec MacCall discusses this debate in the context of the California sardine collapse, "The Sardine-Anchovy Puzzle," 57.

19. Fan Jia et al., "Weakening Atlantic Niño-Pacific Connection under Greenhouse Warming," *Science Advances* 5, no. 8 (2019); S. W. Yeh et al., "El Niño in a Changing Climate," *Nature* 461, no. 7263 (2009): 511.

20. Ivan J. Ramírez and Fernando Briones, "Understanding the El Niño Costero of 2017: The Definition Problem and Challenges of Climate Forecasting and Disaster Responses," *International Journal of Disaster Risk Sciences* 8 (2017): 489.

21. Yoo-Geun Ham, Jeong-Hwan Kim, and Jing-Jia Luo, "Deep Learning for Multi-year ENSO Forecasts," *Nature* 573, no. 7775 (2019), https://doi.org/10.1038/s41586-019-1559-7; Markus Reichstein et al., "Deep Learning and Process Understanding for Data-Driven Earth System Science," *Nature* 566, no. 7743 (2019): 195–204.

22. Ramírez and Briones, "Understanding the El Niño Costero of 2017," 489.

23. Ramírez and Briones, "Understanding the El Niño Costero of 2017," 490; see also Giese and Ray, "El Niño variability," table 2.

24. This is calculated as an average range of sea surface temperatures (SSTs) during the preceding thirty-year period.

25. Frank Uekötter and Uwe Lübken, *Managing the Unknown: Essays on Environmental Ignorance* (New York: Berghahn, 2014), 1–2.

26. Reg Watson and Daniel Pauly, "Systematic Distortions in World Fisheries Catch Trends," *Nature* 414, no. 6863 (2001): 534–36.

27. H. Scott Gordon, "The Economic Theory of a Common-Property Resource: The Fishery," *Journal of Political Economy* 62, no. 2 (1954): 124.

28. Gordon, "The Economic Theory of a Common-Property Resource," 129. Anthony Scott noted that Gordon's theory laid the foundations for individual property rights in fisheries regimes via individual quota systems; see Anthony Scott, "The Fishery: The Objectives of Sole Ownership," *Journal of Political Economy* 63, no. 2 (1955): 116–24; and "The Pedigree of Fishery Economics," *Marine Resource Economics* 26, no. 1 (2011): 75–85.

29. Garrett Hardin, "Tragedy of the Commons," *Science* 162, no. 3859 (1968): 1243–48.

30. A detailed review of the vast literature on the "tragedy of the commons" debate is beyond the scope of this book, but one of the most important contributors was the Nobel-winning political scientist Elinor Ostrom, whose critique pointed to cases of collective action and cooperation in common-property regimes, most substantively in her monograph *Governing the Commons: The Evolution of Institutions for Collective Action* (Cambridge: Cambridge University Press, 1990). Craig Johnson provides a thorough review of the literature through the early twenty-first century in, "Uncommon Ground: The 'Poverty of History' in Common Property Discourse," *Development and Change* 35, no. 3 (2004): 407–33. Johnson poignantly highlights the divergence between "deductive models of individual decision-making and rational choice to explain the ways in which different types of property rights arrangements emerge and change over time, and one whose questions, aims and methods are more modest, and historically-specific" (407). For a recent critique of the debate from an interdisciplinary perspective, and a see David Bollier, who proposes instead a "tragedy of the market," in: *Think Like a Commoner: A Short Life of the Commons* (Gabriola Island, BC: New Society Publishers, 2014), see especially chapter 2; thanks to Keith McNeal for this reference.

31. Joaquim Radkau, *Nature and Power: A Global History of the Environment* (Cambridge: Cambridge University Press, 2008), 72–73.

32. Johnson, "Uncommon Ground," 419; see also Ian Scoones, "New Ecology and the Social Sciences: What Prospects for Fruitful Engagement?" *Annual Review of Anthropology* 28 (1999): 479–507.

33. Amy Sinden, "The Tragedy of the Commons and the Myth of a Private Property Solution," *University of Colorado Law Review* 78 (2007): 612; see also Mary C. Stiner and Gillian Feeley-Harnik, "Energy and Ecosystems," in Andrew Shyrock and Daniel Lord Smail, eds., *Deep History: The Architecture of Past and Present* (Berkeley: University of California Press, 2011), 97

34. In behavioral economics, "rational choice" is a model for individual decision-making in which "the process of determining what options are available and then choosing the most preferred one according to some consistent criterion," usually the "optimization" or maximization of utility; Jonathan Levin and Paul Milgrom, "Introduction to Choice Theory," Stanford University Working Paper

(2004), 1, available from https://web.stanford.edu/~jdlevin/Econ%20202/Choice%20Theory.pdf.

35. Proposing that the relationship between fishing effort and yield was not simply linear, this concept of "marginal yield" stood in contrast to Milner Schaefer's theory of "maximum sustainable yield." Raymond J. H. Beverton and David H. Cushing, "John Alan Gulland, 16 September 1926–24 June 1990," *Biographical Memoirs of Fellows of the Royal Society* 38 (1992): 176, citing Gulland, "Science and Fishery Management," *Journal du Conseil Permanent International pour l'Exploration de la Mer* 33 (1971): 471–77.

36. John A. Gulland, "Letters to the editor: Peruvian anchoveta—optimal management," *Marine Policy* (1980): 78.

37. Development studies scholar Craig Johnson, for example, argues for "an inductive methodology that searches for commonalities and connections to broader historical trends and problems" while also accounting for contextual specificity; *Arresting Development: The Power of Knowledge for Social Change* (New York: Routledge, 2008).

38. The historical, transnational process of the relocation of capital in pursuit of lower production costs—specifically in electronics manufacturing—was chronicled by Jefferson Cowie in *Capital Moves: RCA's 70-Year Quest for Cheap Labor* (New York: New Press, 2001).

39. Andy Thorpe and Elizabeth Bennett, "Globalisation and the Sustainability of World Fisheries: A View from Latin America," *Marine Resource Economics* 16 (2001): 144.

40. Sophie Bertrand et al., "Scale-Invariant Movements of Fishermen: The Same Foraging Strategy as Natural Predators," *Ecological Applications* 17, no. 2 (2007): 331–37.

41. Julio Peña-Torres, Jorge Dresdner, and Felipe Vasquez, *"El Niño* and Fishing Location Decisions: The Chilean Straddling Jack Mackerel Fishery," *Marine Resource Economics* 32, no. 3 (2017): 249–75.

42. Lisa M. Campbell et al., "Global Oceans Governance: New and Emerging Issues," *Annual Review of Environment and Resources* 41 (2016): 523.

43. Campbell et al., "Global Oceans Governance," 523, citing Kevin St. Martin and Madeleine Hall-Arber, "The Missing Layer: Geo-Technologies, Communities, and Implications for Marine Spatial Planning," *Marine Policy* 32, no. 5 (2008): 779–86.

44. James Joseph, "The Management of Highly Migratory Species: Some Important Concepts," *Marine Policy* 1, no. 4 (1977): 275–88.

45. For a detailed study of the Law of the Sea and its history, see David Attard et al., eds., *The IMLI Manual on International Maritime Law: Volume I: The Law of the Sea* (Oxford, 2014); for a nuanced review of the Law of the Sea in the context of geopolitics and the evolution of international law, see Bernard H. Oxman, "The Territorial Temptation: A Siren Song at Sea," *The American Journal of International Law* 100, no. 4 (2006): 830–51.

46. For a comprehensive, if somewhat dated, legal history of the EEZ concept, see David Attard, *The Exclusive Economic Zone in International Law* (Oxford, 1987).

47. For more on the role of these and other Latin American nations in the legal codification of the EEZ, see Alexandre Pereira da Silva, "From the First Claims to the Exclusive Economic Zone: Reviewing Latin America's 200-Mile Sea Seventy Years On," *Ocean Yearbook Online* 33, no. 1 (2019): 131–60.

48. See Guillaume Long, "Ecuador en el mar: Materialismo, seguridad e identidad en la política exterior de un país periférico," in Beatriz Zepeda, ed., *Ecuador: Relaciones exteriores a la luz del bicentenario* (Quito: FLACSO, 2009), 331–64; David C. Loring, "The United States–Peruvian 'Fisheries' Dispute," *Stanford Law Review* 23, no. 3 (1971): 391–453.

49. A. A. Elizarov, "Prefacio," in Dagoberto Arcos and Alexander S. Grechina, eds., *Biología y pesca comercial del jurel en el Pacífico Sur* (Talcahuano, Chile: Instituto de Investigación Pesquera, 1994), 7; Bernie Napp, "Charting Ocean Life, an Unknown Frontier," *The Evening Post* (Wellington, NZ) (November 14, 2001).

50. South Pacific Regional Fisheries Management Organisation, SPRFMO, http://www.southpacificrfmo.org/.

51. For more on Chile's "Presential Sea" doctrine and its critiques, see: Paul Stanton Kibel, "Alone at Sea: Chile's Presential Ocean Policy," *Journal of Environmental Law* 12, no. 1 (2000): 43–63; Francisco Orrego Vicuña, "Toward an Effective Management of High Seas Fisheries and the Settlement of the Pending Issues of the Law of the Sea," *Ocean Development and International Law* 24, no. 1 (1993): 81–92; Thomas A. Clingan Jr., "Mar Presencial (the Presential Sea): Déjà Vu All Over Again?—A Response to Francisco Orrego Vicuña," *Ocean Development and International Law* 24, no. 1 (1993): 93–97.

52. Rebecca Bratspies, "Finessing King Neptune: Fisheries Management and the Limits of International Law," *Harvard Environmental Law Review* 25 (2001): 213; Lawrence Juda, "The 1995 United Nations Agreement on Straddling Fish Stocks and Highly Migratory Fish Stocks: A Critique," *Ocean Development and International Law* 28, no. 2 (1997): 146–66; José Antonio de Yturriaga, *The International Regime of Fisheries: From UNCLOS 1982 to the Presential Sea* (Leiden, Netherlands: Martinus Nijhoff Publishers, 1997), 228; Christopher C. Joyner and Peter N. De Cola, "Chile's Presential Sea Proposal: Implications for Straddling Stocks and the International Law of Fisheries," *Ocean Development and International Law* 24, no. 1 (1993): 99–121.

53. Uzma S. Burney, "International Court of Justice Defines Maritime Boundary between Peru and Chile," *ASIL Insights* 18, no. 3 (February 10, 2014), https://www.asil.org/insights/volume/18/issue/3/international-court-justice-defines-maritime-boundary-between-peru-and; for the full legal documentation, see International Court of Justice, Maritime Dispute (Peru v. Chile), Judgment (January 27, 2014), http://legal.un.org/icjsummaries/documents/english/206_e.pdf; EFE-EPA, "Peruvian Trawler Caught in Chilean Waters with 4 Tons of Shark," *EFE-EPA* (,March 6, 2018), https://www.efe.com/efe/english/world/peruvian-trawler-caught-in-chilean-waters-withg-4-tons-of-shark/50000262-3544716

54. Stiner and Feeley-Harnik, "Energy and Ecosystems," 98.

55. For a comprehensive discussion of global value chain (GVC) analysis and methodology, see Stefano Ponte, Gary Gereffi, and Gale Raj-Reichert, eds., *Handbook*

on Global Value Chains (Cheltenham, UK: Edward Elgar Publishing, 2019), https://doi.org/10.4337/9781788113779; for recent applications of this framework to global fisheries and seafood, see: Steven W. Purcell et al., "Distribution of Economic Returns in Small-Scale Fisheries for International Markets: A Value-Chain Analysis," *Marine Policy* 86 (2017): 9–16; Steven Adolf, Simon R. Bush, and Sietze Vellema, "Reinserting State Agency in Global Value Chains: The Case of MSC Certified Skipjack Tuna," *Fisheries Research* 182 (2016): 79–87; Natasha Hamilton-Hart and Christina Stringer, "Upgrading and Exploitation in the Fishing Industry: Contributions of Value Chain Analysis," *Marine Policy* 63 (2016): 166–71.

56. Ian Scoones, "The Politics of Sustainability and Development," *Annual Review of Environment and Resources* 41 (2016): 309.

57. Fridolin Krausman et al., "Material Flow Accounting: Measuring Global Material Use for Sustainable Development," *Annual Review of Environment and Resources* 42 (2017): 649.

58. A 2017 study examined the geographical distribution of agriculture, livestock, and aquaculture operations globally and the relative values of their nutrient contributions to the total food supply, finding that large-scale farms now produce the majority of sugar crops and oils. Mario Herrero et al., "Farming and the Geography of Nutrient Production for Human Use: A Transdisciplinary Analysis," *The Lancet* 1 (2017): 33–42.

59. Notably, between 1961 and 2013, Peru experienced a relative overall decline in per capita consumption of beef, pork, and seafood supplies at the same time that poultry and egg supplies increased; FAOSTAT Food Commodity Supply and Consumption statistical series (2017), http://www.fao.org/faostat/.

60. In the twenty-first century, and particularly during the past fifteen years, environmental activists around the world who attempt to speak out against the encroachment of agribusiness and mining operations increasingly risk violence and death. Nathalie Butt et al., "The Supply Chain of Violence," *Nature Sustainability* 2 (2019): 742–47.

61. Stiner and Feeley-Harnik, "Energy and Ecosystems," 98.

62. "New Food for a Hungry World," *Los Angeles Times* (February 13, 1967): A4; US Department of Commerce, "More People Need More Protein—FPC: It's for People," US Department of Commerce booklet (1971), reprinted in Kenneth J. Carpenter, *Protein and Energy: A Study of Changing Ideas in Nutrition* (Cambridge: Cambridge University Press, 1994), Fig. 9.1, 166; Ernst R. Pariser, Christopher J. Corkery, Mitchel B. Wallerstein, and Norman L. Brown, *Fish Protein Concentrate: Panacea for Malnutrition?* (Cambridge, MA: MIT Press, 1978).

63. Daniel Pauly, "Fish as Food: A Love Affair, Issues Included," *Huffington Post* (November 12, 2009).

64. Tim Cashion et al., "Most Fish Destined for Fishmeal Production Are Food-Grade Fish," *Fish and Fisheries* 18, no. 5 (2017): 839.

65. Fréon et al., "Harvesting for Food versus Feed," 383.

66. By 2010, Chile's global importance as a fishmeal and oil producer had even increased slightly (to 16.5%) relative to the sixty-year average the authors calculated

for Chile's contribution during the period 1950–2010 (14.9%). Cashion et al., "Most Fish Destined," table 1, 841.

67. Jennifer Jacquet et al., "Conserving Wild Fish in a Sea of Market-Based Efforts," *Oryx* (2009): 1–12.

68. Fréon et al., "Harvesting for Food versus Feed," 383.

69. Kristin Wintersteen, "Sustainable Gastronomy: A Market-Based Approach to Improving Environmental Sustainability in the Peruvian Anchoveta Fishery," in *Environmental Leadership: A Reference Handbook*, Vol. 2, edited by D. Gallagher (Los Angeles: Sage, 2012), 626–34.

70. Fréon et al., "Harvesting for Food versus Feed," 385.

71. Fréon et al., "Harvesting for Food versus Feed," 394.

72. Excluding capital investments, Fréon et al. calculated a nearly 30 percent difference between industrial and food fisheries in Peru; "Harvesting for Food versus Feed," 387, table 2.

73. On aquaculture's demand for fishmeal, see Ragnar L. Olsen and Mohammad R. Hasan, "A Limited Supply of Fishmeal: Impact on Future Increases in Global Aquaculture Production," *Trends in Food Science and Technology* 27 (2012): 120–128; Lisa Deutsch et al., "Feeding Aquaculture Growth through Globalization: Exploitation of Marine Ecosystems for Fishmeal," *Global Environmental Change* 17, no. 2 (2007): 238–49; Tveterås and Tveterås, "The Global Competition for Wild Fish Resources." On the "Blue Revolution," see Cushman, *Guano*, 21–22; John Soluri, "Something Fishy," *Latin American Research Review* 46 (2011); Andrew Gerhart, "An Environmental and Social History of the Chilean Salmon Farming Industry, 1976–2009," PhD diss. (Stanford University, 2014).

74. Jonathan Barton, "The Political Ecology of Chilean Salmon Aquaculture, 1982–2010: A Trajectory from Economic Development to Global Sustainability," *Global Environmental Change* 20, no. 4 (2010): 739–52; Andrew Gerhart, "Petri Dishes of an Archipelago: The Ecological Rubble of the Chilean Salmon Farming Industry," *Journal of Political Ecology* 24, no. 1 (2017); Soluri, "Something Fishy."

75. Jessica A. Gephart et al., "Shocks to Fish Production: Identification, Trends, and Consequences," *Global Environmental Change* 42 (2017): 28; on the history of disease in monocultural banana plantations, see John Soluri, *Banana Cultures: Agriculture, Consumption, and Environmental Change in Honduras and the United States* (Austin: University of Texas Press, 2005).

76. Chris Bogan, "Grinding Away the Rust: The Legacy of Iceland's Herring Oil and Meal Factories," *Gastronomica* 4, no. 2 (2004): 51.

77. Bogan, "Grinding Away the Rust," 56.

78. John F. Harris, "[Virginia town] Wrangling over the Smell of Success," *Washington Post* (June 10, 1991): D1.

79. J. B. Dalgaard et al., "Fatal Poisoning and Other Health Hazards Connected with Industrial Fishing," *British Journal of Industrial Medicine* 29 (1972): 307–16.

80. Maria Diná Afonso and Rodrigo Bórquez, "Review of the Treatment of Seafood Processing Wastewaters and Recovery of Proteins Therein by Membrane

Separation Processes—Prospects of the Ultrafiltration of Wastewaters from the Fish Meal Industry," *Desalination* 142 (2002): 29–45.

81. Afonso and Bórquez, "Review of the Treatment," 37–38.

82. For example, Chile's IFOP published a study on technologies for recuperating "stickwater" in 1967: Christopher Molteno, James Steel, Hilarion Gomez, "Sistema de recuperación de agua de cola mediante evaporadores de llama sumergida," Pub. no. 43, Santiago: IFOP, 1967.

83. Tim Cashion, Peter Tyedmers, and Robert W. R. Parker, "Global Reduction Fisheries and Their Products in the Context of Sustainable Limits," *Fish and Fisheries* 18, no. 6 (2017): 1026–37.

84. In recent years, studies evaluating the impact of the quota systems in Peru and Chile have begun to appear. See especially Kailin Kroetz et al., "Examination of the Peruvian Anchovy Individual Vessel Quota (IVQ) System," *Marine Policy* 101 (2019): 150–24; and Kroetz et al., "Evaluation of the Chilean Jack Mackerel ITQ System," *Marine Resource Economics* 32, no. 2 (2017): 217–41.

85. "Chile Bans Bottom Sea Trawling in 98% of Its Exclusive Economic Zone," *Santiago Times* December 18, 2017), https://santiagotimes.cl/2017/12/18/chile-bans-bottom-sea-trawling-in-98-of-its-exclusive-economic-zone/.

86. Samantha Emmert, "Peru's Vessel Tracking Data Now Publicly Available through Global Fishing Watch," Global Fishing Watch Press Release (October 25, 2018), https://globalfishingwatch.org/press-release/perus-vessel-tracking-data-now-publicly-available/; Eloy Aroni, "World's Largest Commercial Fishery Publicly Tracked on Global Fishing Watch Map," *Global Fishing Watch News & Views* (May 3, 2019), https://globalfishingwatch.org/news-views/worlds-largest-commercial-fishery-publicly-tracked-on-global-fishing-watch-map/. The interactive map is available from Global Fishing Watch at https://globalfishingwatch.org/map/.

87. For an examination of this concept in the context of Brazilian labor history and working-class history, see John D. French, *Drowning in Laws: Labor Law and Brazilian Political Culture* (Chapel Hill: University of North Carolina Press, 2004).

88. Tony J. Pitcher and Mimi E. Lam, "Fishful Thinking: Rhetoric, Reality, and the Sea Before Us," *Ecology and Society* 15, no. 2 (2010): 12, http://www.ecologyandsociety.org/vol15/iss2/art12/.

89. Exequiel González-Poblete, Vladimir Kaczynski, and Andrea Méndez Arias, "Marine Coastal Resources as an Engine of Development for the Lafkenche and Williche Populations of Southern Chile," *Ocean Development and International Law* (2019): 1–26.

90. Pablo Camus Gayán and Rodrigo Hidalgo Dattwyler, "'Y serán desplayados': Recorrido histórico sobre los bienes comunes, pescadores artesanales y control legal del litoral en Chile," *Historia Crítica* (Bogotá) 63 (2017): 113.

91. Pitcher and Lam, "Fishful Thinking."

92. Dirk Zeller and Daniel Pauly, "Viewpoint: Back to the Future for Fisheries, Where Will We Choose to Go?" *Global Sustainability* 2, no. e11 (2019): 1–8. Capacity-enhancing subsidies include those that fund boat construction or modernization, the development of ports and infrastructure, tax exemptions, and access privileges; recent

estimates suggest that up to 90 percent of such subsidies support industrial, rather than small-scale, fisheries. Anna Schuhbauer et al., "How Subsidies Affect the Economic Viability of Small-Scale Fisheries," *Marine Policy* 82 (2017): 117.

93. Zeller and Pauly, "Back to the Future;" see also Purcell et al., "Distribution of Economic Returns."

94. Steve Dow, "'Such Brutality': Tricked into Slavery in the Thai Fishing Industry," *The Guardian* (September 21, 2019), https://www.theguardian.com/world/2019/sep/21/such-brutality-tricked-into-slavery-in-the-thai-fishing-industry; Ian Urbina, "'Sea Slaves': The Human Misery That Feeds Pets and Livestock," *New York Times* (July 27, 2015), https://www.nytimes.com/2015/07/27/world/outlaw-ocean-thailand-fishing-sea-slaves-pets.html

95. Judith E. Fan, "Can Ideas about Food Inspire Real Social Change? The Case of Peruvian Gastronomy," *Gastronomica* 13, no. 2 (2013): 32, 35–36; Laura M. Pereira et al., "Chefs as Change-Makers from the Kitchen: Indigenous Knowledge and Traditional Food as Sustainability Innovations," *Global Sustainability* 2, no. e16 (2019): 1–9; Wintersteen, "Sustainable Gastronomy"; for critiques of the commercialization and marketing of Peruvian gastronomy, see especially María Elena García, "The Taste of Conquest: Colonialism, Cosmopolitics, and the Dark Side of Peru's Gastronomic Boom," *Journal of Latin American and Caribbean Anthropology* 18, no. 3 (2013): 505–24; Raúl Matta, "Cocinando una nación de consumidores: El Perú como marca global," *Revista Consensus* 17, no. 1 (2012): 49–60; Matta, "Food Incursions into Global Heritage: Peruvian Cuisine's Slippery Road to UNESCO," *Social Anthropology* 24, no. 3 (2016): 338–52.

96. "New Peruvian Plant to Produce 'Marine Beef,'" *Marine Fisheries Review* 47, no. 2 (1985): 106–7.

97. Alex Beggs, "Don't Call 'Em Trash Fish," *Bon Appétit* (September 19, 2019), https://www.bonappetit.com/story/trash-fish.

98. Lester R. Brown, "A World without Borders," *Washington Post* (November 12, 1972): B1.

99. Ian Scoones, "New Ecology and the Social Sciences: What Prospects for a Fruitful Engagement?" *Annual Review of Anthropology* 28 (1999): 479.

100. Scoones, "The Politics of Sustainability," 293, 295.

APPENDIX A

1. R. Froese and D. Pauly, eds., *FishBase*, www.fishbase.org (2019); Robert Cushman Murphy, *Oceanic Birds of South America*, 2 vols. (New York: Macmillan, 1936).

2. FAO, "FAO Species Fact Sheet: *Engraulis ringens*," http://www.fao.org/fishery/species/2917/en.

3. Murphy, *Oceanic Birds*, 2:840.

4. Murphy, *Oceanic Birds*, 2:849.

5. D. M. Cohen, et al., *Gadiform Fishes of the World (Order Gadiformes): An Annotated and Illustrated Catalogue of Cods, Hakes, Grenadiers and Other Gadiform*

Fishes Known to Date, FAO species catalogue, Vol. 10, FAO Fisheries Synopsis 125 (Rome: FAO, 1990), cited in Froese and Pauly, *FishBase.*

6. Murphy, citing Robert E. Coker (1919), in *Oceanic Birds,* 2:900.

7. Leonard J. V. Compagno, *Sharks of the World,* FAO Species Catalogue Vol. 4, Pt. 2, FAO Fisheries Synopsis 125 (Rome: FAO, 1984), 251–655; cited in Froese and Pauly, *FishBase.*

8. M. Espino, R. Castillo, and F. Fernandez, "Biology and Fisheries of Peruvian Hake (*M. gayi peruanus*)," in *Hake: Biology, Fisheries, and Markets,* ed. J. Alheit and T. J. Pitcher (London: Chapman and Hall, 1995), 339–63, cited in Froese and Pauly, *FishBase.*

9. Cohen, et al., *Gadiform Fishes of the World,* cited in Froese and Pauly, *FishBase.*

10. J. R. Norman, "A New Fish of the Genus *Clupea* from Chile," *Annals and Magazine of Natural History,* Series 10, 17, no. 100 (1936): 491–92, cited in R. Fricke, W. N. Eschmeyer, and R. Van der Laan *Eschmeyer's Catalog of Fishes* (Species *Clupea bentincki*), http://researcharchive.calacademy.org/research/ichthyology/catalog/fishcatmain.asp.

11. Quote from "Katsuwonus pelamis/Skipjack tuna," in Froese and Pauly, *FishBase.*

12. Johan Nicolay Tønnessen and Arne Johnsen, *The History of Modern Whaling,* trans. R. I. Christophersen (Berkeley: University of California Press, 1982), 3, 5, 118.

13. Hal Whitehead, "Sperm Whales in Ocean Ecosystems," in *Whales, Whaling, and Ocean Ecosystems,* ed. Estes, et al. (Berkeley: University of California Press, 2006), 324–25.

14. Whitehead, "Sperm Whales," 329.

BIBLIOGRAPHY

ARCHIVES AND SPECIAL LIBRARY COLLECTIONS

Chile

Archivo Nacional de la Documentación (ARNAD), Santiago
Biblioteca del Congreso de Chile, Santiago and Valparaíso
Biblioteca Nacional de Chile (BNCH), Santiago
Collección Museo Histórico Nacional, Santiago
Corporación del Fomento (CORFO), Santiago
Facultad Latinoamericana de Ciencias Sociales (FLACSO), Santiago
Food and Agricultural Organization of the United Nations (FAO), Regional Office Library, Santiago
Hernán Santa Cruz Library, Economic Commission for Latin America (ECLA), Santiago
Instituto de Fomento Pesquero (IFOP), Valparaíso and Talcahuano

Ecuador

Biblioteca Municipal de Guayaquil
Comisión Permanente del Pacífico Sur (CPPS), Guayaquil

Germany

Bundesamt für Hydrographie, Hamburg
Deutsches Literaturarchiv (DLA), Marbach
GEOMAR Helmholtz-Zentrum für Ozeanforschung, Kiel
Ibero-Amerikanisches Institut, Berlin

Italy

David Lubin Memorial Library, Food and Agricultural Organization of the United Nations (FAO), Rome

Peru

Biblioteca Nacional del Perú, Lima
Centro Para la Documentación Pesquera (CENDOPES), Lima
Instituto del Mar del Perú (IMARPE), Callao
Instituto Natura, Chimbote
Personal archive of Denis Sulmont, Lima
Pontificia Universidad Católica del Perú, Lima

United States

American Geographical Society Library, University of Wisconsin-Milwaukee Libraries
Loeb Library, Graduate School of Design, Harvard University, Cambridge, Massachusetts
National Archives and Records Administration (NARA), College Park, Maryland
Scripps Institution of Oceanography (SIO), Special Collections, University of California-San Diego, La Jolla, California
United States Department of Agriculture (USDA), National Agricultural Library, Beltsville, Maryland
United States Library of Congress, Prints and Photographs Division,
University of Washington (UW), Special Collections, Seattle, Washington

ELECTRONIC DATABASES AND DIGITAL ARCHIVES

Biodiversity Heritage Library. http://www.biodiversitylibrary.org
California Cooperative Oceanic Fisheries Investigations (CalCOFI) Reports, PDF Library. https://www.calcofi.org/ccpublications/ccreports/calcofi-reports-pdf.html
CGSpace: A Repository of Agricultural Research Outputs. http://cgspace.cgiar.org
Food and Agricultural Organization of the United Nations (FAO), Fisheries and Aquaculture Department, Fishery Statistical Collections: Consumption of

Fish and Fishery Products. http://www.fao.org/fishery/statistics/global-consumption/en

Fricke, R., W. N. Eschmeyer, and R. Van der Laan, eds. Eschmeyer's Catalog of Fishes. http://researcharchive.calacademy.org/research/ichthyology/catalog/fishcatmain.asp

Froese, R., and D. Pauly, eds. FishBase (Version 4/2019). http://www.fishbase.org

Google Scholar. http://scholar.google.com

HathiTrust Digital Library. http://www.hathitrust.org

Hein Online. http://home.heinonline.org

Huang, Boyin, Peter W. Thorne, Viva F. Banzon, Tim Boyer, Gennady Chepurin, Jay H. Lawrimore, Matthew J. Menne, Thomas M. Smith, Russell S. Vose, and Huai-Min Zhang. "NOAA Extended Reconstructed Sea Surface Temperature (ERSST), Version 5." NOAA National Centers for Environmental Information (2017). https://www.ncdc.noaa.gov/data-access/marineocean-data/extended-reconstructed-sea-surface-temperature-ersst-v5

Instituto del Mar del Perú (IMARPE), Repositorio Digital. http://biblioimarpe.imarpe.gob.pe

Internet Archive. http://archive.org

JSTOR. https://www.jstor.org

LexisNexis Academic. https://www.lexisnexis.com/en-us/academic-and-library/library-research.page

National Geophysical Data Center/World Data Service (NGDC/WDS). Global Historical Tsunami Database, 2100 BC to Present. doi:10.7289/V5PN93H7

Oceanic Niño Index (ONI) Data Series, NOAA and U.S. National Weather Service. https://origin.cpc.ncep.noaa.gov/products/analysis_monitoring/ensostuff/ONI_v5.php

Pauly, D., and D. Zeller, eds. *Sea Around Us: Concepts, Design, and Data* (2015) http://seaaroundus.org

ProQuest Historical Newspapers. https://www.proquest.com/libraries/academic/news-newspapers/

Scientific Electronic Library Online (SciElo). https://scielo.org

SeaBase. http://seabase.core.cli.mbl.edu

Web of Science. https://www.webofknowledge.com

NEWSPAPERS, PERIODICALS, AND SERIES

Ambiente y Desarrollo (Santiago, Chile)
Boletín PescaPerú (Lima, Peru)

Boletín Pesquero (Santiago, Chile)
Chile Pesquero (Santiago, Chile)
Die Fischwirtschaft (Hamburg, Germany)
El Comercio (Lima, Peru)
El Mercurio (Santiago, Chile)
En Viaje (Santiago, Chile)
IMARPE Boletín (Lima, Peru)
La Prensa (Lima, Peru)
Marcha Hacia El Oeste (Lima, Peru)
Oiga (Lima, Peru)
Pesca (Lima, Peru)
Revista Documenta (Lima, Peru)
USDA Bulletin (College Park, MD)

THESES AND DISSERTATIONS

Clarke, Nathan. "Traces on the Peruvian Shore: The Environmental History of the Fishmeal Boom in Chimbote, Peru, 1940–1980." PhD dissertation, University of Illinois, 2009.

Cushman, Gregory T. "The Lords of Guano: Science and the Management of Peru's Marine Environment, 1800–1973." PhD dissertation, University of Texas at Austin, 2003.

Espinoza Muñoz, Álvaro Andrés. "Sustentabilidad de la pesquería del jurel en la región del Bío Bío." PhD dissertation, Universidad de Concepción-Chile, 1993.

Gerhart, Andrew W. "An Environmental and Social History of the Chilean Salmon Farming Industry, 1976–2009." PhD dissertation, Stanford University, 2014.

Murra, John. "The Economic Organization of the Inca State." Ph.D. dissertation, University of Chicago, 1956.

Quintanilla, Damiani, Paola, Carolina Pino González, and Claudia Sanhueza González. "Analisis al desempeño de los grupos empresariales en Chile," Tesis para Lic. Ingeniería Comercial, Universidad de Chile, 2005.

GOVERNMENT, INTERNATIONAL AGENCY, AND NONGOVERNMENTAL ORGANIZATION REPORTS

Ashbrook, Frank G. "Fish Meal as a Feed for Swine." *USDA Bulletin* 610 (1917): 1–9.

Carr, George C. "International Trade in Fish Meal." Foodstuffs Division of the US Bureau of Foreign and Domestic Commerce, 1931.

Clark, William G. "The Lessons of the Peruvian Anchoveta Fishery." *CalCOFI Reports* 19 (1977): 57–63.

Cohen, D. M., T. Inada, T. Iwamoto, and N. Scialabba, *Gadiform Fishes of the World (Order Gadiformes): An Annotated and Illustrated Catalogue of Cods, Hakes, Grenadiers and Other Gadiform Fishes Known to Date*. FAO species catalogue, Vol. 10. FAO Fisheries Synopsis 125. Rome: FAO, 1990.

Coke, Eduardo Cruz. "Plans of the Chilean Government for Improving the Nutrition of the People." *Boletín de la Oficina Sanitaria Panamericana*, 1937.

Coke, Eduardo Cruz, and Consejo Nacional de Alimentación. "Plan de gobierno presentado por el Ministro de Salubridad." In *Suplemento de la revista chilena de higiene y medicina preventiva* 1. Santiago, Chile: Impr. Universo, 1937.

Coker, Robert E. "The Fisheries and the Guano Industry of Peru." *Bulletin of the U.S. Bureau of Fisheries* 28 (1908): 333–65. https://www.st.nmfs.noaa.gov/spo/FishBull/28-1/coker.pdf.

Compagno, Leonard J. V. *Sharks of the World: An Annotated and Illustrated Catalogue of Shark Species Known to Date*. FAO Species Catalogue, Vol. 4, Part 2. FAO Fisheries Synopsis 125. Rome: FAO, 1984. http://www.fao.org/3/ad123e/ad123e00.htm.

Consejo de Investigaciones Hidrobiológicas (Perú). "Plan of Operation for a Marine Resources Research Institute of Peru [English Text]." Ministerio de Marina, Government of Peru, 1960.

Doucet, W. F., and H. Einarsson. "A Brief Description of Peruvian Fisheries." *CalCOFI Reports* 11 (1966): 82–87.

Espino, M., R. Castillo, and F. Fernandez. "Biology and Fisheries of Peruvian Hake (*M. gayi peruanus*)." In *Hake: Biology, Fisheries, and Markets*, edited by J. Alheit and T. J. Pitcher, 339–63. London: Chapman and Hall, 1995.

Fiedler, Reginald H., Norman D. Jarvis, and Milton J. Lobell. *La pesca y las industrias pesqueras en el Perú*. Informe de la Misión Pesquera Norteamericana. Lima, Perú: Compañía Administradora del Guano, 1943.

Food and Agricultural Organization of the United Nations (FAO), "Position of Fish Meal Industry and Trade in Chile." Doc. no. IFIME C/28. *Report to the International Meeting on Fish Meal*. Rome: FAO, 1961.

———. "Position of Fish Meal Industry and Trade in Peru." Doc. no. IFIME C/13. *Report to the International Meeting on Fish Meal*. Rome: FAO, 1961.

Food and Agricultural Organization of the United Nations (FAO), Legal Office. *Sources of International Water Law*. FAO Legislative Study 65. Rome: FAO, 1998.

Fridtjof, John. "Informe al gobierno de Chile sobre fomento del consumo de pescado." Informe FAO/ETAP no. 271, 1954.

Government of Peru. *Peruvian National Census, Vol. III: Departments of Lambayeque/La Libertad/Ancash*. Lima: INE, 1940.

———. *Peruvian National Census, Vol. II: Ancash*. Lima: INE, 1961.

Gulland, J. A., A. Holmsen, A. Laing, C. J. Paulik, F. E. Popper, H. Watzinger, and IMARPE. *Report of the Expert Panel on the Economic Effects of Alternative Regulatory Measures in the Peruvian Anchoveta Fishery.* IMARPE Informe No. 34. Callao, Peru: IMARPE, 1970.

Heinrici, Carl. "Die Tätigkeit der Deutschen Wissenschaftlichen Kommission für Meeresforschung im Haushaltsjahr 1926," *Sonderdruck aus dem Jahresbericht für die deutsche Fischerei 1926* (Berlin: Gebr. Mann, 1926): 1–8.

Hellevang, N. "Recent Developments in the Peruvian Anchoveta Fishery." Proyecto UNDP/FAO 269. Paper presented at the Technical Conference on Fish Finding, Purse Seining and Aimed Trawling, Reykjavik, Iceland, 1970.

International Fishmeal and Oil Manufacturers Association. *Tests to Predict the Quality of Fish Meals for Special Uses.* Research Report No. 1993-1. London: IFOMA, 1993.

Isaacs, John D. "Some Ideas and Frustrations about Fisheries Science." *CalCOFI Reports* 18 (1976): 34–43.

Joseph, James. "The Management of Highly Migratory Species: Some Important Concepts." *Marine Policy* 1, no. 4 (1977): 275–88.

Larraín, Manuel Achurra. "Report on Manpower in the Fisheries Sector of Peru: Present Status and Prospects of Education and Training." FAO Fisheries Report No. 93. Rome: FAO, 1971.

League of Nations, Mixed Committee on the Problem of Nutrition. *Final Report on the Relation of Nutrition to Health, Agriculture, and Economic Policy.* Geneva, 1937.

Loayza, E. "Aprovechamiento de la anchoveta para el consumo humano en el Peru." Doc. no. FII: FP/73/E-43. Paper presented at the FAO Technical Conference on Fishery Products, Tokyo (December 4–11, 1973). Rome: FAO, 1973.

Lobell, Milton J., Albert J. Byer, Boris O. Knake, and James R. Westman. *Misión pesquera norteamericana en Chile: Un informe preliminar sobre la situación pesquera en Chile.* Santiago, Chile: CORFO, 1945.

Messersmith, James D. "The Northern Anchovy (*Engraulis mordax*) and Its Fishery, 1965–1968." State of California Department of Fish and Game, *Fisheries Bulletin* 147 (1969): 1–102.

Ministerio de Pesquería (Perú). *Plan Sectorial de Pesquería, 1971–1975.* Lima: Ministerio de Pesquería, Oficina Sectorial de Planificación, 1971.

Molteno, Christopher, James Steel, Hilarion Gomez. "Sistema de recuperación de agua de cola mediante evaporadores de llama sumergida." Pub. no. 43. Santiago: IFOP, 1967.

Murphy, Robert Cushman. *El guano y la pesca de anchoveta: Informe oficial al supremo gobierno.* Lima, Peru, 1954.

———. "Fisheries Resources in Peru." *The Scientific Monthly* 16, no. 6 (1923), 594–607.

———. "Notes on the Findings of the 'William Scoresby' in the Peru Coastal Current." *Geographical Review* 27, no. 2 (1937): 295–300.

———. *Oceanic Birds of South America*, 2 vols. New York: Macmillan, 1936.

Nandan, S. N. "The Exclusive Economic Zone: A Historical Perspective." Rome: FAO, 1987.

Núñez, Sergio, Sebastián Vásquez, Patricia Ruiz, and Aquiles Sepúlveda. "Distribution of Early Developmental Stages of Jack Mackerel in the Southeastern Pacific Ocean." Paper No. 2, *South Pacific RFMO Chilean Jack Mackerel Workshop*, 2009.

Robin, J. P., and F. C. Terzo. *Urbanization in Peru*. International Urbanization Survey. New York: The Ford Foundation, 1972.

Scheiber, Harry. "California Marine Research and the Founding of Modern Fisheries Oceanography: CalCOFI's Early Years, 1947–1964." *CalCOFI Reports* 31 (1990): 63–83.

Schlich, V. A. "Trash Fishing Highlights New England's Production Season." *Fish Meal and Oil Industry, International Yearbook*, 1951.

Serra, J. R. "Changes in Abundance of Pelagic Resources along the Chilean Coast." *FAO Fisheries Reports* 291, nos. 2–3 (1983).

Steinfeld, Henning, Pierre Gerber, T. D. Wassenaar, Vincent Castel, Mauricio Rosales, and Cees de Haan. *Livestock's Long Shadow: Environmental Issues and Options*. Rome: FAO, 2006.

Stevenson, Charles H. "Aquatic Products in Arts and Industries." US Fisheries Commission, Report by the Commissioner of Fish and Fisheries, 1902.

Tilic, Ivo. *Capacidad de producción de la industria de harina de pescado en el Perú*. Informe No. 4. Callao: Instituto de Investigación de los Recursos Marinos, 1962.

———. *Encuesta sobre las embarcaciones anchoveteras realizada en Junio de 1967*, Informe No. 23. Callao: Instituto del Mar del Peru, 1968.

———. *Información estadística sobre embarcaciones utilizadas en la pesca industrial en el Perú, 1953–1962*. Informe No. 8. Callao: Instituto de Investigación de los Recursos Marinos, 1963.

United States Department of the Interior, Fish and Wildlife Service (USFW), and Corporación de Fomento de la Producción (CORFO). *Misión pesquera norteamericana en Chile: Un informe preliminar sobre la situación pesquera en Chile*, Santiago, Chile, 1945.

United States Department of State, *Treaties and Other International Agreements of the United States of America, 1776–1949*. Compiled by Charles I Bevans. Vol. 13. Washington, DC: US Government Printing Office. Record available at: https://lccn.loc.gov/70600742.

Weber, Frederick C. "Fish Meal: Its Use as a Stock and Poultry Food." *USDA Bulletin* 378 (1916): 1–21.

OTHER PUBLISHED PRIMARY SOURCES

Arguedas, José María. *El zorro de arriba y el zorro de abajo*. Lima: Editorial Horizonte, 1971.

———. *The Fox from Up Above and the Fox from Down Below*. Translated by Frances Horning Barraclough. Pittsburgh: University of Pittsburgh Press, 2000.

Berghaus, Heinrich. *Physikalischer Atlas Oder Sammlung von Karten*. Justus Perthes, 1845 [1838].
Bollaert, William. "Observations on the Coal Formation in Chile, S. America." *Journal of the Royal Geographical Society of London* 25 (1855): 172–85.
———. "Observations on the Geography of Southern Peru, Including Survey of the Province of Tarapacá, and Route to Chile by the Coast of the Desert Atacama." *Journal of the Royal Geographical Society of London* 21 (1851): 99–130.
Carson, Rachel L. "Under the Sea-Wind." In *The Sea*. London: Readers Union, 1965 [1941].
Chapman, Frank M. "Darwin's Chile." *Geographical Journal* 68, no. 5 (1926): 369–81.
Chapman, Wilbert M. "Industry and the Economy of the Sea." *California and the World Ocean*. Conference proceedings. Los Angeles: California Museum of Science and Industry, 1964.
Cieza De León, Pedro de. *Crónica del Perú: El señorío de los Incas. Primera parte*. Edited by Franklin Pease. Ayacucho: Fundación Biblioteca Ayacucho, 2005.
———. *The Discovery and Conquest of Peru, Part Three*. Edited by Alexandra Parma Cook and Noble David Cook. Durham, NC: Duke University Press, 1999.
de Acosta, José. *The Naturall and Morall Historie of the East and West Indies, No. 60*. London, 1880 [1604].
de Tessan, Urbain Dortet. *Voyage autour du monde sur la frégate* la Vénus *pendant les années 1836–1839, vol. X*. Paris, 1844.
Fiedler, Reginald H. "The Peruvian Fisheries." *Geographical Review* 34, no. 1 (1944): 96–119.
Frezier, A. F. *Relation du voyage de la Mer du Sud aux côtes du Chily et du Perou, fait pendant les années 1712, 1713, 1714*. Paris/London, 1717 [1716].
Funnel, W. *A Voyage Round the World: Being an Account of Capt. William Dampier's Expedition into the South Seas in the Ship* St George. London: James Knapton, 1729.
Golusda, Pedro. "La industria pesquera en Chile." Trabajo presentado al Primer Congreso Marítimo de la Liga Marítima de Chile. Santiago, Chile, 1941.
Governments of Peru, Chile, and Ecuador, *Agreement on the Special Maritime Boundary Zone*, December 4, 1954, http://www.un.org/depts/los/LEGISLATION ANDTREATIES/STATEFILES/CHL.htm.
Hutchinson, E. N. "Food for Plant Life Is Food for Beast," *Better Fruit* 24, no. 8 (1930): 39.
International Court of Justice, Summaries of Judgments, Advisory Opinions and Orders of the ICJ—Maritime Dispute (Peru v. Chile) – Judgment of Jan. 27, 2014, http://legal.un.org/icjsummaries/documents/english/206_e.pdf.
Jenness, Burt Franklin. "The 'Callao Painter.'" In *Sea Lanes and Other Poems*, 27–28. Boston: Cornhill Publishing Company, 1921.
Jenyns, Leonard. "*Engraulis ringens*." In *The Works of Charles Darwin, Volume 6: The Zoology of the Voyage of H.M.S. Beagle*, edited by Paul H. Barrett and R. B. Freeman, 202–3. New York: New York University Press, 1987 [1842].

Juan y Santacilla, J., and A. de Ulloa. *Relacion historica del viage a la America meridional hecho de orden de S. Mag. para medir algunos grados de Meridiano Terrestre, y venir por ellos en conocimiento de la verdadera Figura, y Magnitud de la Tierra, con otras varias Observaciones Astronomicas y Phisicas*. Madrid/London, 1807 [1748].

Lehmann, F. "Die Eignung von Fischmehl als Futtermittel," *Hannoversche Land- und Forstwirtschaftliche Zeitung* (1892–1893).

———. "Tierische Mehle und Futtermittel aus Niederen Tieren." In *Handbuch der Ernährung und des Stoffwechsels der Landwirtschaftlichen Nutztiere als Grundlagen der Fütterungslehre, Erster Band: Nährstoffe und Futtermittel*, edited by E. Mangold. Berlin: Springer Verlag, 1929.

Leitner, Ulrike, and Eberhard Knobloch, eds. *Alexander von Humboldt und Cotta, Briefwechsel*. Berlin: Akademie Verlag, 2009.

Meakin, Edgar T. "Apparatus for Producing Fish Meal." U.S. Patent No. 1,421,283A. Issued June 27, 1922. https://patents.google.com/patent/US1421283A/en.

Murphy, Robert Cushman. "Fisheries Resources in Peru." *Scientific Monthly* 16, no. 6 (1923): 594–607.

———. "Notes on the Findings of the 'William Scoresby' in the Peru Coastal Current." *Geographical Review* 27, no. 2 (1937): 295–300.

———. *Oceanic Birds of South America*. 2 vols. Washington, DC: American Museum of Natural History, 1936.

Murra, John, and M. López-Baralt, eds. *Las cartas de Arguedas*. Lima: Pontificia Universidad Católica del Perú, 1998.

Norman, J. R. "A New Fish of the Genus *Clupea* from Chile." *Journal of Natural History* 17, no. 100 (1936): 491–92.

Penrose, R. A. F. Jr. "The Nitrate Deposits of Chile." *Journal of Geology* 18, no. 1 (1910): 1–32.

Pezet, Victor. *Monografía de la Bahía de Chimbote*. Lima: N.p., 1912.

Poeppig, Eduard. *Reise in Chile, Peru und auf dem Amazonenstrome, Während der Jahre 1827–1832, Erster Band*. Leipzig: Friedrich Fleischer, 1835.

Ruiz, Hipólito. *The Journals of Hipólito Ruiz, Spanish Botanist in Peru and Chile, 1777–88*. Translated by Richard Evans Schultes and Maria Jose Nemry von Thenen de Jaramillo-Arango. Portland, OR: Timber Press, 1998.

———. *Relación histórica del viage, que hizo a los reynos del Perú y Chile el botánico D. Hipolito Ruiz en el año de 1777 hasta el de 1788, en cuya época regresó a Madrid, Tomo I*, 2nd. ed. Madrid: Talleres Gráficos Bermejo, 1952.

Soldán, Mateo Paz, with Mariano Felipe Paz Soldán, eds., *Geografía del Perú*. Paris: F. Didot, 1862.

Stähle, Martin, and Hidrostal (Lima, Peru). "Pump Impeller." U.S. Patent No. 3,156,190A. Issued Nov. 10, 1964. https://patents.google.com/patent/US3156190A/en.

Von Humboldt, Alexander. *Alexander von Humboldt en el Perú: Diario de viaje y otros escritos*. Edited by Estuardo Núñez and Georg Petersen. Lima: Banco Central de la Reserva del Perú, 2002.

---. *Cosmos: A Sketch of a Physical Description of the Universe*, Vol. I. Translated by E. C. Otté. London: H.G. Bohn, 1849.

---. *Recuil d'observations astronomiques, d'opérations trigonométriques et de mesures barométriques, faites pendant le cours d'un voyage aux régions équinoxiales du nouveau continent, depuis 1799 jusqu'en 1803*, I. Paris, 1810.

Von Liebig, Justus. *Die Organische Chemie in Ihrer Anwendung auf Agricultur und Physiologie*. Braunschweig, 1840.

Walter, Richard. *A Voyage Round the World in the Years 1740–1744 by George Anson Esq.* London: Knapton, 1748.

BOOKS, CHAPTERS, AND ARTICLES

Abe, K. "Size of Great Earthquakes of 1837–1974 Inferred from Tsunami Data." *Journal of Geophysical Research* 84, no. B4 (1979): 1561–68.

Abramovich, Jaysuño. *La Industria Pesquera en el Perú: Genesis, Apogeo y Crisis.* Lima: Universidad Nacional Federico Villarreal, Centro de Investigaciones Económicas y Sociales, 1973.

Adams, William Y. "On the Argument from Ceramics to History: A Challenge Based on Evidence from Medieval Nubia." *Current Anthropology* 20, no. 4 (1979): 727–44.

Adolf, Steven, Simon R. Bush, and Sietze Vellema. "Reinserting State Agency in Global Value Chains: The Case of MSC Certified Skipjack Tuna." *Fisheries Research* 182 (2016): 79–87.

Afonso, Maria Diná, and Rodrigo Bórquez. "Review of the Treatment of Seafood Processing Wastewaters and Recovery of Proteins Therein by Membrane Separation Processes—Prospects of the Ultrafiltration of Eastewaters from the Fish Meal Industry." *Desalination* 142 (2002): 29–45.

Alder, Jacqueline, and Brooke Campbell, Vasiliki Karpouzi, Kristin Kaschner, and Daniel Pauly. "Forage Fish: From Ecosystems to Markets." *Annual Review of Environment and Resources* 33 (2008): 153–66.

Alheit, Jurgen, and Michael Niquen. "Regime Shifts in the Humboldt Current Ecosystem." *Progress in Oceanography* 60, nos. 2–4 (2004): 201–22.

Aranda, J. Guzmán. "Presentación." In *Los Hervores de Chimbote*, edited by Antonio Cornejo Polar, Gonzalo Portocarrero, Julio Ortega, and Alberto Flores Galindo, 13. Chimbote: Río Santa Editores, 2006.

Arcos, Dagoberto F., Luis A. Cubillos, and Sergio P. Núñez. "The Jack Mackerel Fishery and El Niño 1997–98 Effects Off Chile." *Progress in Oceanography* 49 (2001): 597–617.

Asociación de Industriales Pesqueros Región del Bío Bío (ASIPES), and Luis Salvo González. *Historia de la industria pesquera en la región del Bío Bío*. Santiago: LOM Ediciones, 2000.

Attard, David. *The Exclusive Economic Zone in International Law*. New York: Oxford University Press, 1987.

Attard, David, Malgosia Fitzmaurice, and Norman A. Martinez Gutierrez, eds. *The IMLI Manual on International Maritime Law: Volume I: The Law of the Sea*. New York: Oxford University Press, 2014.

Balleisen, Edward J., and Elizabeth K. Brake. "Historical Perspective and Better Regulatory Governance: An Agenda for Institutional Reform." *Regulation & Governance* 8 (2014): 222–45.

Ballón, E., and J. M. Salcedo. "Reportaje a Chimbote." *Quehacer* 3 (Mayo 1980): 67.

Barrig, Maruja, Marcela Chueca, and Ana María Yañez. *Anzuelo sin carnada: Obreras en la industria de conserva de pescado*. Lima: Mosca Azul Editores/ADEC, 1985.

Barton, Jonathan R. "The Political Ecology of Chilean Salmon Aquaculture, 1982–2010: A Trajectory from Economic Development to Global Sustainability," *Global Environmental Change* 20, no. 4 (2010): 739–52.

Bentley, Amy. *Inventing Baby Food: Taste, Health, and the Industrialization of the American Diet*. Oakland: University of California Press, 2014.

Beresford-Jones, David, Alexander Pullen, George Chauca, Lauren Cadwaller, Maria García, Isabel Salvatierra, Oliver Whaley, Víctor Vásquez, Susana Arce, Kevin Lane, and Charles French. "Refining the Maritime Foundations of Andean Civilization: How Plant Fiber Technology Drove Social Complexity during the Preceramic Period," *Journal of Archaeological Method & Theory* 25, no. 2 (2018): 393–425.

Berrios, Rubén. *Towards an Overview of Peru's Fishing Industry: Prospects and Problems*. Bogotá: International Development Research Center, Regional Office for Latin America and the Caribbean, 1983.

Bertrand, Arnaud, Marceliano Segura, Mariano Gutiérrez, and Luis Vásquez. "From Small-Scale Habitat Loopholes to Decadal Cycles: A Habitat-Based Hypothesis Explaining Fluctuation in Pelagic Fish Populations Off Peru." *Fish and Fisheries* 5 (2004): 296–316.

Bertrand, Sophie, Arnaud Bertrand, Renato Guevara-Carrasco, and François Gerlotto. "Scale-Invariant Movements of Fishermen: The Same Foraging Strategy as Natural Predators." *Ecological Applications* 17, no. 2 (2007): 331–37.

Beverton, Raymond J. H., and David H. Cushing. "John Alan Gulland, 16 September 1926–24 June 1990." *Biographical Memoirs of Fellows of the Royal Society* 38 (1992): 165–83.

Blench, Roger. "Two Vanished African Maritime Traditions and a Parallel from South America." *African Archaeological Review* 29 (2012): 273–92.

Bogan, Chris. "Grinding Away the Rust: The Legacy of Iceland's Herring Oil and Meal Factories," *Gastronomica* 4, no. 2 (2004): 51–57.

Bollier, David. *Think Like a Commoner: A Short Life of the Commons*. Gabriola Island, BC: New Society Publishers, 2014.

Boyd, William. "Making Meat: Science, Technology, and the Industrialization of American Poultry Production." *Technology and Culture* 42 (2001): 631–64.

Boyd, William, and Michael Watts. "Agro-Industrial Just-in-Time: The Chicken Industry and Postwar American Capitalism." In *Globalising Food: Agrarian Questions and Global Restructuring*, edited by D. Goodman and M. Watts, 150–82. New York: Routledge, 1997.

Bratspies, Rebecca. "Finessing King Neptune: Fisheries Management and the Limits of International Law." *Harvard Environmental Law Review* 25 (2001): 213.
Brown, Karen. "Tropical Medicine and Animal Diseases: Onderstepoort and the Development of Veterinary Science in South Africa, 1908–1950." *Journal of Southern African Studies* 31, no. 3 (2005): 513–29.
Bugos, Glenn E. "Intellectual Property Protection in the American Chicken-Breeding Industry." *Business History Review* 66, no. 1 (1992): 127–68.
Butt, Nathalie, Frances Lambrick, Mary Menton, and Anna Renwick. "The Supply Chain of Violence." *Nature Sustainability* 2 (2019): 742–47.
Calienes, Ruth. "Producción primaria en el ambiente marino en el Pacífico sudeste, Perú, 1960–2000." *Boletín IMARPE* 29, nos. 1–2 (2014): 8–307.
Campbell, Lisa M., Noella J. Gray, Luke Fairbanks, Jennifer J. Silver, Rebecca L. Gruby, Bradford A. Dubik, and Xavier Basurto. "Global Oceans Governance: New and Emerging Issues." *Annual Review of Environment and Resources* 41 (2016): 517–43.
Cañizares-Esguerra, Jorge. "How Derivative Was Humboldt? Microcosmic Narratives in Early Modern Spanish America and the (Other) Origins of Humboldt's Ecological Sensibilities." In *Nature, Empire, and Nation: Explorations of the History of Science in the Iberian World,* 112–28. Stanford, CA: Stanford University Press, 2006.
Carabias, D., N. Lira, and L. Adán. "Reflexiones en torno al uso de embarcaciones monóxilas en ambientes boscoso lacustres precordilleranos andinos, zona centro-sur de Chile." *Magallania (Chile)* 38, no. 1 (2010): 87–108.
Carpenter, Kenneth J. *Protein and Energy: A Study of Changing Ideas in Nutrition.* Cambridge: Cambridge University Press, 1994.
Cashion, Tim, Frédéric Le Manach, Dirk Zeller, and Daniel Pauly. "Most Fish Destined for Fishmeal Production Are Food-Grade Fish." *Fish and Fisheries* 18, no.5 (2017): 837–44.
Cashion, Tim, Peter Tyedmers, and Robert W. R. Parker, "Global Reduction Fisheries and Their Products in the Context of Sustainable Limits." *Fish and Fisheries* 18, no. 6 (2017): 1026–37.
Castilla, Juan Carlos. "Fisheries in Chile: Small Pelagics, Management, Rights, and Sea Zoning." *Bulletin of Marine Science* 86, no. 2 (2010): 221–34.
Castro Castro, Luis, Carolina Figueroa Cerna, Paglo Guerrero Oñate, and Benjamín Silva Torrealba. "William Bollaert y sus descripciones geográficas, cartográficas y antropológicas sobre la provincia de Tarapacá en la etapa inicial de la formación republicana del Perú, 1827–1854." *HiSTOReLo: Revista de Historia Regional y Local* 9, no. 18 (2017): 123–63.
Caviedes, César N. "The Latin American Boom-Town in the Literary View of José María Arguedas." In *Geography and Literature: A Meeting of the Disciplines*, edited by William E. Mallory and Paul Simpson-Housley, 56–77. Syracuse, NY: Syracuse University Press, 1986.
Chamorro Álvarez, Humberto. "Planteamientos del Consejo Nacional de los Pescadores Artesanales de Chile acerca de la ley de pesca." In *El desafío pesquero chileno: La explotación racional de nuestras riquezas marinas,* edited by Eduardo Bitrán, 407–12. Santiago, Chile: Hachette, 1989.

Chappell, A. E. "Linear Programming Cuts Costs in Production of Animal Feeds," *Journal of the Operational Research Society* 25, no. 1 (1974): 19–26.
Chavez, Francisco P., and Monique Messié. "A Comparison of Eastern Boundary Upwelling Ecosystems." *Progress in Oceanography: Eastern Boundary Upwelling Ecosystems Symposium* 83, nos. 1–4 (2009): 80–96.
Chavez, Francisco P., Arnaud Betrand, Renato Guevarra-Carrasco, Pierre Soler, and Jorge Csirke. "The Northern Humboldt Current System: Brief History, Present Status and a View towards the Future." *Progress in Oceanography: The Northern Humboldt Current System: Ocean Dynamics, Ecosystem Processes, and Fisheries*, 79, nos. 2–4 (2008): 95–105.
Clarke, Nathan. "Revolutionizing the Tragic City: Rebuilding Chimbote, Peru, after the 1970 Earthquake," *Journal of Urban History* 41, no. 1 (2015): 93–115.
Clearly, E. J. "Chimbote: El Pittsburgh peruano en potencia." *Boletín de la Escuela Nacional de Ingenieros [Lima, Peru]* 3, no. 17 (1944): 3–27. Translated by J. F. Aguilar Revoredo.
Clingan, Thomas A. Jr. "Mar Presencial (the Presential Sea): Déjà Vu All Over Again?—A Response to Francisco Orrego Vicuña," *Ocean Development and International Law* 24, no. 1 (1993): 93–97
Coker, Robert. "Ocean Temperatures Off the Coast of Peru." *Geographical Review* 5, no. 2 (1918), 127–35.
Conrad, Sebastian. *What Is Global History?* Princeton, NJ: Princeton University Press, 2016.
Cowie, Jefferson. *Capital Moves: RCA's 70-Year Quest for Cheap Labor.* New York: New Press, 2001.
Cushing, David H. "Enclave Vision: Foreign Networks in Peru and the Internationalization of El Niño Research During the 1920s." *History of Meteorology* 1, no. 1 (2004): 65–74.
———. *Guano and the Opening of the Pacific World: A Global Ecological History.* Cambridge: Cambridge University Press, 2013.
———. "Humboldtian Science, Creole Meteorology, and the Discovery of Human-Caused Climate Change in South America." *Osiris* 26, no. 1 (2011): 19–44.
———. *The Provident Sea.* Cambridge: Cambridge University Press, 1988.
Dalgaard, J. B., F. Dencker, B. Fallentin, P. Hansen, B. Kaempe, J. Steensberg, and P. Wilhardt. "Fatal Poisoning and other Health Hazards Connected with Industrial Fishing." *Occupational and Environmental Medicine* 29, no. 3 (1972): 307–16.
De la Cadena, Marisol. "The Production of Other Knowledges and Its Tensions: From Andeanist Anthropology to Interculturalidad?" *Journal of the World Anthropology Network* 1 (2005): 13–33.
Deacon, Margaret. *Scientists and the Sea, 1650–1900: A Study of Marine Science.* London: Academic Press, 1971.
Del Busto Duthurburu, José Antonio. *Túpac Yupanqui: Descubridor de Oceanía.* Lima: Fondo Editorial del Congreso del Perú, 2006.
Dettelbach, Michael. "Global Physics and Aesthetic Empire: Humboldt's Physical Portrait of the Tropics." In *Visions of Empire: Voyages, Botany, and Representations*

of Nature, edited by David Philip Miller and Peter Hanns Reill, 258–92. Cambridge: Cambridge University Press, 2011 [1996].

Deutsch, Lisa, Sara Gräslund, Carl Folke, Max Troell, Miriam Huitric, Nils Kautsky, and Louis Lebel. "Feeding Aquaculture Growth through Globalization: Exploitation of Marine Ecosystems for Fishmeal." *Global Environmental Change* 17, no. 2 (2007): 238–49.

Dezileau, Laurent, Osvaldo Ulloa, Dierk Hebbeln, Frank Lamy, Jean-Louis Reyss, and Michel Fontugne. "Iron Control of Past Productivity in the Coastal Upwelling System off the Atacama Desert, Chile." *Paleoceanography* 19, no. 3 (2004).

Dickey-Collas, Mark, Richard D. M. Nash, Thomas Brunel, Cindy J. G. Van Damme, C. Tara Marshall, Mark R. Payne, and Ad Corten. "Lessons Learned from Stock Collapse and Recovery of North Sea Herring: A Review." *ICES Journal of Marine Science* 67, no. 9 (2010): 1875–86.

Dickinson, W. R. "Geological Perspectives on the Monte Verde Archaeological Site in Chile and Pre-Clovis Coastal Migration in the Americas." *Quaternary Research* 76 (2011): 201–10.

Disi Pavlic, Rodolfo. "Explicando los resultados de los conflictos asimétricos: La Guera de Arauco." *Estudios Internacionales* 50, no. 189 (2018): 97–119.

Duhart, Solange, and Jacqueline Weinstein. *Pesca industrial: Sector estratégico y de alto riesgo.* 2 vols. Colección de Estudios Sectoriales No. 5. Santiago, Chile: Academía de Humanismo Cristiano, 1988.

Elizarov, A. A. "Preface." *Biología y pesca comercial del jurel en el Pacífico Sur,* edited by Dagoberto Arcos and Alexander S. Grechina. Talcahuano, Chile: Instituto de Investigación Pesquera, 1994.

Escribano, Ruben, and Carmen E. Morales. "Spatial and Temporal Scales of Variability in the Coastal Upwelling and Coastal Transition Zones off Central-Southern Chile (35–40°S)." *Progress in Oceanography: Variability of the Coastal Upwelling and Coastal Transition Zones off Central-Southern Chile* 92–95 (2012): 1–7.

Fan, Judith E. "Can Ideas about Food Inspire Real Social Change? The Case of Peruvian Gastronomy." *Gastronomica* 13, no. 2: 29–40.

Federico, Giovanni. *Feeding the World: An Economic History of Agriculture, 1800–2000.* Princeton, NJ: Princeton University Press, 2005.

Finlay, Mark R. "The German Agricultural Experiment Stations and the Beginnings of American Agricultural Research." *Agricultural History* 62, no. 2 (1988): 41–50.

Finley, Carmel. *All the Fish in the Sea: Maximum Sustainable Yield and the Failure of Fisheries Management.* Chicago: University of Chicago Press, 2011.

Franklin, H. Bruce. *The Most Important Fish in the Sea: Menhaden and America.* Washington, DC: Island Press, 2007.

French, John D. *Drowning in Laws: Labor Law and Brazilian Political Culture.* Chapel Hill: University of North Carolina Press, 2005.

Fréon, Pierre, Juan Carlos Sueiro, Federico Iriarte, and Oscar F. Miro Evar, Yuri Landa, Jean-François Mittaine, and Marilu Bichon. "Harvesting for Food versus Feed: A Review of Peruvian Fisheries in Global Context," *Review in Fish Biology and Fisheries* 24 (2014): 381–98.

Freyre, A. "Fishery Development in Peru." *Studies in Tropical Oceanography* 5 (1967): 391–411.
Galli-Olivier, Carlos. "Climate: A Primary Control of Sedimentation in the Peru-Chile Trench." *Geological Society of America Bulletin* 80, no. 9 (1969): 1849–52.
García, María Elena. "The Taste of Conquest: Colonialism, Cosmopolitics, and the Dark Side of Peru's Gastronomic Boom." *The Journal of Latin American and Caribbean Anthropology* 18, no. 3 (2013): 505–24.
Gayán, Pablo Camus, and Rodrigo Hidalgo Dattwyler. "'Y serán desplayados': Recorrido histórico sobre los bienes comunes, pescadores artesanales y control legal del litoral en Chile." *Historia Crítica* (Bogotá) 63 (2017): 97–117.
Gephart, Jessica A., Lisa Deutsch, Michael L. Pace, Max Troell, David A. Seekell. "Shocks to Fish Production: Identification, Trends, and Consequences." *Global Environmental Change* 42 (2017): 24–32.
Gerhart, Andrew. "Petri Dishes of an Archipelago: The Ecological Rubble of the Chilean Salmon Farming Industry." *Journal of Political Ecology* 24, no. 1 (2017): 726–42.
Giese, Benjamin S. and Sulagna Ray. "El Niño Variability in Simple Ocean Data Assimilation (SODA), 1871–2008." *Journal of Geophysical Research: Oceans* 116, no. C2 (2011).
Glantz, Michael H. "Science, Politics, and the Economics of the Peruvian Anchoveta Fishery." *Marine Policy* 3, no. 3 (1979): 201–10.
González-Poblete, Exequiel, Vladimir Kaczynski, and Andrea Méndez Arias. "Marine Coastal Resources as an Engine of Development for the Lafkenche and Williche Populations of Southern Chile." *Ocean Development and International Law* (2019): 1–26.
Gootenberg, Paul. *Between Silver and Guano: Commercial Policy and the State in Postindependence Peru*. Princeton, NJ: Princeton University Press, 1989.
Gordon, H. Scott. "The Economic Theory of a Common-Property Resource: The Fishery." *Journal of Political Economy* 62, no. 2 (1954): 124–42.
Gorman, Hugh. "Thinking in Cycles: Flows of Nitrogen and Sustainable Uses of the Environment." In *Managing the Unknown: Essays on Environmental Ignorance*, edited by F. Uekötter and U. Lübken, 32–52. New York Berghahn, 2014.
———. *The Story of N: A Social History of the Nitrogen Cycle and the Challenge of Sustainability*. New Brunswick, NJ: Rutgers University Press, 2013.
Guerrero Jiménez, Bernardo. *Del chumbeque a la zofri: Los aromas de nuestra identidad cultural*. Iquique, Chile: Universidad Arturo Prat, 1999.
Gulland, John A. "Letters to the Editor: Peruvian Anchoveta—Optimal Management." *Marine Policy* 4, no. 1 (1980): 78.
———. "Science and Fishery Management." *Journal du Conseil Permanent International pour l'Exploration de la Mer* 33 (1971): 471–77.
Gunther, E. R. "A Report on Oceanographical Investigations in the Peru Coastal Current." In *Discovery Reports, Vol. 13*, 109–276. Cambridge: Cambridge University Press, 1936.

———. "Variations in Behaviour of the Peru Coastal Current: With an Historical Introduction." *Geographical Journal* 88, no. 1 (1936): 37–61.
Ham, Yoo-Geun, Jeong-Hwan Kim, and Jing-Jia Luo. "Deep Learning for Multi-Year ENSO Forecasts," *Nature* 573, no. 7775 (2019): 568–72.
Hamilton-Hart, Natasha, and Christina Stringer. "Upgrading and Exploitation in The Fishing Industry: Contributions of Value Chain Analysis." *Marine Policy* 63 (2016): 166–71.
Hammergren, L. A. "Peruvian Political and Administrative Responses to El Niño: Organizational, Ideological and Political Constraints on Policy Change." In *Resource Management and Environmental Uncertainty: Lessons from Coastal Upwelling Fisheries*, edited by M. H. Glantz and J. D. Thompson, 317–50. New York: John Wiley and Sons, 1981.
Hardin, Garrett. "Tragedy of the Commons." *Science* 162, no. 3859 (1968): 682–83.
Hardy, Ronald W., and Albert G. J. Tacon. "Fish Meal: Historical Uses, Production Trends and Future Outlook for Sustainable Supplies." In *Responsible Marine Aquaculture*, edited by R. R. Stickney and J. P. McVey, 311–25. New York: CABI, 2002.
Hedgpeth, Joel W., and Harry S. Ladd, eds. *Treatise on Marine Ecology and Paleoecology*. 2 vols. Boulder, CO: Geological Society of America, 1957.
Henning, Brian G. "The Ethics of Food, Fuel, and Feed." *Daedalus* 144, no. 4 (2015): 90–98.
———. "'Standing in Livestock's Long Shadow': The Ethics of Eating Meat on a Small Planet." *Ethics and the Environment* 16, no. 2 (2011): 63–93.
Herrero, Mario, Philip K. Thornton, Brendan Power, Jessica R. Bogard, Roseline Remans, Steffen Fritz, James S. Gerber. "Farming and the Geography of Nutrient Production for Human Use: A Transdisciplinary Analysis." *The Lancet* 1, no. 1 (2017): e33–e42.
Heyerdahl, Thor. *American Indians in the Pacific: The Theory behind the Kon-Tiki Expedition*. London: George Allen and Unwin, 1952.
———. "Voyaging Distance and Voyaging Time in Pacific Migration." *Geographical Journal* 117, no. 1 (1951): 69–77.
Hidalgo, Jorge. "Los pescadores de la costa norte de Chile y su relación con los agricultores, siglos XVI y XVII." In *La arqueología y la etnohistoria: Un encuentro andino*, edited by John R. Topic, 143–99. Lima: Instituto de Estudios Peruanos, 2009.
Homburg, Ernst, Anthony S. Travis, and Harm G. Schröter, eds. *The Chemical Industry in Europe, 1850–1914: Industrial Growth, Pollution, and Professionalization*. Dordrecht, The Netherlands: Kluwer, 1998.
Horowitz, Roger. *Putting Meat on the American Table*. Baltimore: Johns Hopkins University Press, 2006.
Jackson, Jeremy B., Karen E. Alexander, and Enric Sala, eds. *Shifting Baselines: The Past and the Future of Ocean Fisheries*. New York: Island Press, 2011.
Jacquet, Jennifer, John Hocevar, Sherman Lai, Patricia Majluf, Nathan Pelletier, Tony Pitcher, Enric Sala, Rashid Sumaila, and Daniel Pauly. "Conserving Wild Fish in a Sea of Market-Based Efforts." *Oryx* 44, no. 1 (2009): 45–56.

Jia, Fan, Wenju Cai, Lixin Wu, Bolan Gan, Guojian Wang, Fred Kucharski, Ping Chang, and Noel Keenlyside. "Weakening Atlantic Niño-Pacific Connection under Greenhouse Warming." *Science Advances* 5, no. 8 (2019): eaax4111.

Johnson, Craig. *Arresting Development: The Power of Knowledge for Social Change.* New York: Routledge, 2008.

———. "Uncommon Ground: The 'Poverty of History' in Common Property Discourse." *Development and Change* 35, no. 3 (2004): 407–33.

Johnson, John J. "Early Relations of the United States with Chile." *Pacific Historical Review* 13, no. 3 (1944): 260–70.

———. "Talcahuano and Concepción as Seen by the Forty-Niners." *Hispanic American Historical Review* 26, no. 2 (1946): 251–62.

Johnson, LaDon J., William E. Dinusson, and Duane O. Erickson. "Nitrogen in Animal Production." *Farm Research* 37, no. 3 (1979): 30–36.

Joseph, James. "The Management of Highly Migratory Species: Some Important Concepts." *Marine Policy* 1, no. 4 (1977): 275–88.

Josephson, Paul. "The Ocean's Hot Dog: The Development of the Fish Stick." *Technology and Culture* 49, no. 1 (2008): 41–61.

Joyner, Christopher C., and Peter N. De Cola. "Chile's Presential Sea Proposal: Implications for Straddling Stocks and the International Law of Fisheries." *Ocean Development and International Law* 24, no. 1 (1993): 99–121.

Juda, Lawrence. "The 1995 United Nations Agreement on Straddling Fish Stocks and Highly Migratory Fish Stocks: A Critique." *Ocean Development and International Law* 28, no. 2 (1997): 146–66

Kibel, Paul Stanton. "Alone at Sea: Chile's Presential Ocean Policy." *Journal of Environmental Law* 12, no. 1 (2000): 43–63

Kleisner, K., H. Mansour, and D. Pauly. "The MTI and RMTI as tools for unmasking the fishing down phenomenon." University of British Columbia Fisheries Centre: Sea Around Us, 2015. http://www.seaaroundus.org/mti-fib-rmti/.

Kortum, Gerhard. "Humboldt und das Meer: Eine Ozeanographiegeschichtliche Bestandaufnahme." *Northeastern Naturalist* 8, no. 1 (2001): 91–108.

Krausman, Fridolin, Heinz Schandl, Nina Eisemenger, Stefan Giljum, and Tim Jackson. "Material Flow Accounting: Measuring Global Material Use for Sustainable Development." *Annual Review of Environment and Resources* 42 (2017): 647–75.

Kroetz, Kailin, James N. Sanchirico, Elsa Galarza Contreras, David Corderi Novoa, Nestor Collado, and Elaine W. Swiedler. "Examination of the Peruvian Anchovy Individual Vessel Quota (IVQ) System." *Marine Policy* 101 (2019): 150–24.

Kroetz, Kailin, James N. Sanchirico, Julio Peña-Torres, David Corderi Novoa. "Evaluation of the Chilean Jack Mackerel ITQ System." *Marine Resource Economics* 32, no. 2 (2017): 217–41.

Kubler, George. "Period, Style, and Meaning in Ancient American Art." *New Literary History* 1, no. 2 (1970): 127–44.

Lane, Kris. *Pillaging the Empire: Piracy in the Americas, 1500–1750.* London: M.E. Sharpe, 1998.

Lassen, Sven, E. Kyle Bacon, and H. J. Dunn. "Fish Reduction Process: Relation of Yields and Quality of Products to Freshness of Raw Material." *Journal of Industrial and Engineering Chemistry* 43, no. 9 (1951): 2082–87.

Leiva, Luis Pretel. Carmen Tocón Armas, and Roberto López. *Movimiento sindical en Chimbote: Historia gráfica, 1940–1960.* Chimbote: Instituto de Promoción y Educación Popular, 1984.

Levin, Jonathan, and Paul Milgrom. "Introduction to Choice Theory." Stanford University Working Paper (2004). https://web.stanford.edu/~jdlevin/Econ%20 202/Choice%20Theory.pdf.

Llagostera, Agostín. "Early Occupations and the Emergence of Fishermen on the Pacific Coast of South America." *Andean Past* 3, no. 1 (1992): 87–109.

Loftin, Horace. "Nature Ramblings: The Callao Painter." *Science News Letter* (September 22, 1956): 192.

Long, Guillaume. "Ecuador en el mar: Materialismo, seguridad e identidad en la politica exterior de un país periférico." In *Ecuador: Relaciones exteriores a la luz del bicentenario,* edited by Beatriz Zepeda, 331–64. Quito: FLACSO, 2009.

Loring, David C. "The United States–Peruvian "Fisheries" Dispute." *Stanford Law Review* 23, no. 3 (1971): 391–453.

Lux, William R. "The Peruvian Fishing Industry: A Case Study in Capitalism at Work." *Revista de Historia de América* 71 (1971): 137–46.

MacCall, Alec D. "The Sardine-Anchovy Puzzle." In *Shifting Baselines: The Past and the Future of Ocean Fisheries,* edited by Jeremy B. Jackson, Karen E. Alexander, and Enric Sala, 47–58. New York: Island Press, 2011.

Marcus, Joyce, Jeffrey D. Sommer, and Christopher P. Glew. "Fish and Mammals in the Economy of an Ancient Peruvian Kingdom." *Proceedings of the National Academy of Sciences* 96, no. 11 (1999): 6564–70.

Matsuda, Matt K. *Pacific Worlds: A History of Seas, Peoples, and Cultures.* Cambridge: Cambridge University Press, 2012.

Matta, Raúl. "Cocinando una nación de consumidores: El Perú como marca global." *Revista Consensus* 17, no. 1 (2012): 49–60.

———. "Food Incursions into Global Heritage: Peruvian Cuisine's Slippery Road to UNESCO." *Social Anthropology* 24, no. 3 (2016): 338–52.

Mayewski, Paul A., Eelco E. Rohling, J. Curt Stager, and Wibjörn Karlén. "Holocene Climate Variability." *Quaternary Research* 62, no. 3 (2004): 243–55.

McEvoy, Arthur F. *The Fisherman's Problem: Ecology and Law in the California Fisheries, 1850–1980.* Cambridge: Cambridge University Press, 1986.

McPhaden, Michael J., Stephen E. Zebiak, and Michael H. Glantz. "ENSO as an Integrating Concept in Earth Science." *Science* 314, no. 5806 (2006): 1740–45.

Mears, Eliot G. "The Callao Painter." *Scientific Monthly* 57, no. 4 (1943): 331–36.

Melillo, Edward D. *Strangers on Familiar Soil: Rediscovering the California-Chile Connection.* New Haven, CT: Yale University Press, 2015.

Méndez, César, Amalia Delaunay, and Ramiro Barberena. "New Perspectives in Archaeological Research of Marginal Deserts in South America." In *Futuro sostenible de la vida en el desierto*, edited by Nuria Sanz, 89–101. Mexico City: UNESCO, 2017.

Mendo, Jaime, and Claudia Wosnitza-Mendo. "Reconstruction of Total Marine Fisheries Catches for Peru: 1950–2010." University of British Columbia Fisheries Centre, Working Paper #2014-21 (2014): 1–23.

Meseck, Gerhard. "Erzeugung und Absatz von Fischmehl in der Welt." *Berichte über Landwirtschaft: Zeitschrift für Agrarpolitik und Landwirtschaft* 38, no. 4 (1960): 666–70.

Mills, Eric L. *The Fluid Envelope of Our Planet: How the Study of Ocean Currents Became a Science*. Toronto: University of Toronto Press, 2009.

Molinari, Baltazar Caravedo. *Estado, pesca y burguesía, 1939–1973*. Lima, Perú: Teoría y Realidad, 1979.

Montecino, Vivian, and Carina B. Lange. "The Humboldt Current System: Ecosystem Components and Processes, Fisheries, and Sediment Studies." *Progress in Oceanography: Eastern Boundary Upwelling Ecosystems Symposium* 83, nos. 1–4 (2009): 65–79.

Moreno, Karen, Juan Enrique Bostelmann, Cintia Macías, Ximena Navarro-Harris, Ricardo De Pol-Holz, and Mario Pino. "A Late Pleistocene Human Footprint from the Pilauco Archaeological Site, Northern Patagonia, Chile," *PLoS ONE* 14, no. 4 (2019): e0213572.

Moseley, M. E. *The Maritime Foundations of Andean Civilization*. Menlo Park, CA: Cummings, 1975.

Muga Alvarez, José, Randolfo Sanhueza Ward, Luis Eduardo Toro Alvarez, and Nelson Salas Pulgar. "Perspectivas de desarrollo del sector pesquero industrial." In *Seminario sobre las perspectivas del desarrollo del sector pesquero chileno*, edited by Asociación de Profesionales Pesqueros de Chile, 193–249. Valparaíso: Ediciones Universitarias de Valparaíso, 1974.

Mumford, Eric, Hashim Sarkis, and Neyran Turan, eds. *Josep Lluís Sert: The Architect of Urban Design, 1953–1969*. New Haven, CT and Cambridge, MA: Yale University Press and Harvard University Press, 2008.

Murra, John V. *El 'control vertical' de un máximo de pisos ecológicos en la economía de las sociedades andinas*. Huánuco, Peru: Universidad Hermilio Valdizán, 1972.

Nestle, Marion. *Food Politics: How the Food Industry Influences Nutrition and Health* Berkeley: University of California Press, 2013.

Norris, L. C. "The Need for Fish or Other Animal Derived Products in Poultry Rations." In *Fish Meal and Oil Industry, International Yearbook*, 1951.

Núñez, Lautaro, Martin Grosjean, and Isabel Cartajena. "Human Occupations and Climate Change in Puna de Atacama, Chile." *Science* 298, no. 5594 (2002): 821–824.

Olsen, Ragnar L., and Mohammad R. Hasan. "A Limited Supply of Fishmeal: Impact on Future Increases in Global Aquaculture Production." *Trends in Food Science and Technology* 27 (2012): 120–28.

Orlove, Benjamin. "Meat and Strength: The Moral Economy of a Chilean Food Riot." *Cultural Anthropology* 12, no. 2 (1997): 234–68.

Orrego Vicuña, Francisco. *The Exclusive Economic Zone: A Latin American Perspective.* Foreign Relations of the Third World Series, No. 1. Boulder, CO: Westview Press, 1984.

———. "Toward an Effective Management of High Seas Fisheries and the Settlement of the Pending Issues of the Law of the Sea," *Ocean Development and International Law* 24, no. 1 (1993): 81–92

Osterhammel, Jürgen. *The Transformation of the World: A Global History of the Nineteenth Century.* Princeton, NJ: Princeton University Press, 2014.

Ostrom, Elinor. *Governing the Commons: The Evolution of Institutions for Collective Action.* Cambridge: Cambridge University Press, 1990.

OxCal. "Radiocarbon Calibration." University of Oxford (updated July 26, 2019). https://c14.arch.ox.ac.uk/calibration.html.

Oxman, Bernard H. "The Territorial Temptation: A Siren Song at Sea." *The American Journal of International Law* 100, no. 4 (2006): 830–51.

Papenfuss, H., and K. Röpke. *Fischmehl, Fischöl und Andere Seetier Produkte.* Leipzig: Kammer der Technik/Fischkombinat Rostock, 1974.

Pariser, Ernst R., Christopher J. Corkery, Mitchel B. Wallerstein, and Norman L. Brown. *Fish Protein Concentrate: Panacea for Malnutrition?* Cambridge, MA: MIT Press, 1978.

Patel, Raj, and Philip McMichael. "A Political Economy of the Food Riot." *Review: A Journal of the Fernand Braudel Center* 32, no. 1 (2009): 9–35.

Pauly, Daniel. "Charles Darwin, Ichthyology and the Species Concept." *Fish and Fisheries* 3, no. 3 (2002): 146–50.

Pauly, Daniel, P. Muck, Jaime Mendo, and I. Tsukayama. *The Peruvian Upwelling Ecosystem: Dynamics and Interactions.* Manila: ICLARM, 1989.

Pavilack, Jody. *Mining for the Nation: The Politics of Chile's Coal Communities from the Popular Front to the Cold War.* University Park: Penn State University Press, 2011.

Peña-Torres, Julio. "Regulación pesquera en Chile: Una perspectiva histórica," *Cuadernos de Economía* 33, no. 100 (1996): 367–95.

Peña-Torres, Julio, Jorge Dresdner, and Felipe Vasquez, *"El Niño* and Fishing Location Decisions: The Chilean Straddling Jack Mackerel Fishery," *Marine Resource Economics* 32, no. 3 (2017): 249–75

Pereira, Laura M. Rafael Calderón-Contreras, Albert V. Norström, and Dulce Espinosa, Jenny Willis, Leonie Guerrero Lara, Zayaan Khan, Loubie Rusch, Eduardo Correa Palacios, and Ovidio Pérez Amaya. "Chefs as Change-Makers from the Kitchen: Indigenous Knowledge and Traditional Food as Sustainability Innovations." *Global Sustainability* 2.e16 (2019): 1–9.

Pereira da Silva, Alexandre. "From the First Claims to the Exclusive Economic Zone: Reviewing Latin America's 200-Mile Sea Seventy Years On." *Ocean Yearbook Online* 33, no. 1 (2019): 131–60.

Pickersgill, Barbara. "Domestication of Plants in the Americas: Insights from Mendelian and Molecular Genetics." *Annals of Botany* 100, no. 5 (2007): 925–40.

Pinar, Susana. "La genética española en el exilio y su repercusión en la ciencia mexicana." In *De Madrid a México: El exilio español y su impacto sobre el pensamiento, la ciencia y el sistema educativo mexicano,* edited by A. Sánchez Andrés and S. Figueroa Zamadio, 127–59. Morelia, México: Universidad Michoacana de San Nicolás de Hidalgo, 2001.

Pitcher, Tony J., and Mimi E. Lam. "Fishful Thinking: Rhetoric, Reality, and the Sea Before Us." *Ecology and Society* 15, no. 2 (2010): 12.

Ponte, Stefano, Gary Gereffi, and Gale Raj-Reichert, eds. *Handbook on Global Value Chains.* Cheltenham, UK: Edward Elgar Publishing, 2019.

Pozorski, Thomas, and Shelia Pozorski. "The Impact of the El Niño Phenomenon on Prehistoric Chimú Irrigation Systems of the Peruvian Coast." In *El Niño in Peru: Biology and Culture Over 10,000 Years,* edited by Jonathan Haas and Michael O. Dillon, 70–91. Chicago: Field Museum of Natural History, 2003.

Probyn, Elspeth. *Eating the Ocean.* Durham, NC: Duke University Press, 2016.

Proulx, Donald A. *A Sourcebook of Nasca Ceramic Iconography: Reading a Culture through Its Art.* Iowa City: University of Iowa Press, 2006.

Purcell, Steven W., Beatrice I. Crona, Watisoni Lalavanua, and Hampus Erikkson. "Distribution of Economic Returns in Small-Scale Fisheries for International Markets: A Value-Chain Analysis." *Marine Policy* 86 (2017): 9–16.

Radkau, Joaquín. *Nature and Power: A Global History of the Environment.* Translated by Thomas Dunlap. Cambridge: Cambridge University Press, 2008.

Ramírez, Ivan J., and Fernando Briones. "Understanding the El Niño Costero of 2017: The Definition Problem and Challenges of Climate Forecasting and Disaster Responses." *International Journal of Disaster Risk Sciences* 8 (2017): 489–92.

Reardon, Thomas, and C. Peter Timmer. "The Economics of the Food System Revolution." *Annual Review of Resource Economics* 4 (2012): 225–64.

———. "Whales and Walruses in the Northern Oceans." In *The Unending Frontier: An Environmental History of the Early Modern World,* 574–616. Berkeley: University of California Press, 2003.

Reichstein, Markus, Gustau Camps-Valls, Bjorn Stevens, Martin Jung, Joachim Denzler, Nuno Caravalhais, and Prabat. "Deep Learning and Process Understanding for Data-Driven Earth System Science." *Nature* 566, no. 7743 (2019): 195–204.

Roberts, Kenneth. *Deepening Democracy? The Modern Left and Social Movements in Chile and Peru.* Stanford, CA: Stanford University Press, 1998.

Roemer, Michael. *Fishing for Growth: Export-Led Development in Peru, 1950–1967.* Cambridge, MA: Harvard University Press, 1970.

Rostworowski de Diez Canseco, María. *Obras completas III: Costa peruana prehispánica.* Lima: Instituto de Estudios Peruanos, 2004.

———. *Recursos naturales renovables y pesca, siglos XVI–XVII: Curacas y sucesiones, costa norte: Obras completas, tomo IV.* Lima: Instituto de Estudios Peruanos, 2005.

Ruckelshaus, Mary, Terrie Klinger, Nancy Knowlton, and Douglas P. DeMaster. "Marine Ecosystem-Based Management in Practice: Scientific and Governance Challenges," *BioScience* 58, no. 1 (2008): 53–63.

Rundel, Philip W. "Ecological Relationships of Desert Fog Zone Lichens." *The Bryologist* 81, no. 2 (1978): 277–93.

Saccone, Elena. "Seafaring as a Key Element in the First Peopling of the Americas: A Perspective from the Southern Cone." *Journal of Maritime Archaeology* (2019): 1–16.

Sandweiss, Daniel H., Kirk A. Maasch, Fei Chai, C. Fred T. Andrus, and Elizabeth J. Reitz. "Geoarchaeological Evidence for Multidecadal Natural Climatic Variability and Ancient Peruvian Fisheries." *Quaternary Research* 61 (2004): 330–34.

Sandweiss, Daniel H., Ruth Shady Solís, Michael E. Moseley, David K. Keefer, Charles R. Ortloff. "Environmental Change and Economic Development in Coastal Peru between 5,800 and 3,600 years ago." *Proceedings of the National Academy of Sciences* 106, no. 5 (2009): 1359–63.

Scheiber, Harry N. "California Marine Research and the Founding of Modern Fisheries Oceanography: CALCOFI's Early Years, 1947–1964," *CALCOFI Reports* 31 (1990): 63–83.

———. "Ocean Governance and the Marine Fisheries Crisis: Two Decades of Innovation- and Frustration." *Virginia Journal of Environmental Law* 20 (2001): 119–39.

———. "Pacific Ocean Resources, Science, and Law of the Sea: Wilbert M. Chapman and the Pacific Fisheries, 1945–70." *Ecology Law Quarterly* 13, no. 3 (1986): 383–534.

Schling-Brodersen, Uschi. "Liebig's Role in the Establishment of Agricultural Chemistry." *Ambix* 39, no. 1 (1992): 21–31.

Schreiber, Milena Arias. "The Evolution of Legal Instruments and the Sustainability of the Peruvian Anchovy Fishery." *Marine Policy* 36, no. 1 (2012): 78–89.

Schreiner, Oswald, Albert R. Merz, and B. E. Brown, "Fertilizer Materials," *Yearbook of Fertilizer Materials* (1938): 487–521.

Schuhbauer, Anna, Ratana Chuenpagdee, William W. L. Chueng, Krista Greer, and U. Rashid Sumaila. "How Subsidies Affect the Economic Viability of Small-Scale Fisheries." *Marine Policy* 82 (2017): 114–21.

Schumann, Sarah. "Co-management and "Consciousness": Fishers Assimilation of Management Principles in Chile." *Marine Policy* 31, no. 2 (2007): 101–11.

Schurman, Rachel A. "Shuckers, Sorters, Headers, and Gutters: Labor in the Fisheries Sector." In *Victims of the Chilean Miracle: Workers and Neoliberalism in the Pinochet Era, 1973–2002*, edited by Peter Winn, 298–336. Durham, NC: Duke University Press, 2004.

———. "Snails, Southern Hake and Sustainability: Neoliberalism and Natural Resource Exports in Chile." *World Development* 24, no. 11 (1996): 1695–709.

Schweigger, Erwin. *El litoral peruano*, 2nd ed. Lima, Perú: Universidad Nacional Federico Villareal, 1964.

Scoones, Ian. "New Ecology and the Social Sciences: What Prospects for Fruitful Engagement?" *Annual Review of Anthropology* 28 (1999): 479–507.

———. "The Politics of Sustainability and Development." *Annual Review of Environment and Resources* 41 (2016): 293–319.

Scott, Anthony. "The Fishery: The Objectives of Sole Ownership." *Journal of Political Economy* 63, no. 2 (1955): 116–24.

———. "The Pedigree of Fishery Economics." *Marine Resource Economics* 26, no. 1 (2011): 75–85.

Shady Solís, Ruth. "Caral-Supe and the North-Central Area of Peru: The History of Maize in the Land Where Civilization Came into Being." In *Histories of Maize: Multidisciplinary Approaches to the Prehistory, Linguistics, Biogeography, Domestication and Evolution of Maize*, edited by John E. Staller, Robert H. Tykot, and Bruce F. Benz, 381–402. Cambridge, MA: Elsevier, 2006.

———. "Caral-Supe y su entorno natural y social en los origines de la civilizacion." *Investigaciones Sociales* 9 (2014): 89–120.

Sherman, Kenneth, Dann Sklarew, Igor Belkin, James Oliver, Marie-Christine Aquarone, and Sybil Seitzinger. "Policy Brief on Large Marine Ecosystems." Working Group on Large Marine Ecosystems, *Fourth Global Conference on Oceans, Coasts, and Islands*, 2008. https://globaloceanforumdotcom.files.wordpress.com/2013/03/lme-pb-june18.pdf.

Shryock, Andrew, and Daniel Lord Smail. *Deep History: The Architecture of Past and Present*. Berkeley: University of California Press, 2011.

Sinden, Amy. "The Tragedy of the Commons and the Myth of a Private Property Solution." *University of Colorado Law Review* 78 (2007): 533–615.

Sociedad Nacional de Pesquería (SNP). *Si esta crisis no se arregla, quedaremos así*. Lima: SNP, 1967.

Soloviev, S. L. and Ch. N. Go. "A Catalogue of Tsunamis on the Eastern Shore of the Pacific Ocean [dates include 1513–1968]." Academy of Sciences of the USSR (Moscow: Nauka Publishing House), translation no. 5078 of Canadian Translation of Fisheries and Aquatic Sciences serries. Ottawa: Canada Institute for Scientific and Technical Information, 1984.

Soluri, John. *Banana Cultures: Agriculture, Consumption, and Environmental Change in Honduras and the United States*. Austin: University of Texas Press, 2005.

———. "On Edge: Fur Seals and Hunters along the Patagonian Littoral, 1860–1930." In *Centering Animals in Latin American History*, edited by Martha Few and Zeb Tortorici, 243–69. Durham, NC: Duke University Press, 2013.

———. "Something Fishy: Chile's Blue Revolution, Commodity Diseases, and the Problem of Sustainability." *Latin American Research Review* 46 (2011): 32–54.

Spalding, Mark, Helen E. Fox, Gerald R. Allen, Nick Davidson, Zach A. Ferdaña, Max Finlayson, Benjamin B. Halpern, Miguel A. Jorge, Al Lombana, Sara A. Lourie, Kirsten D. Martin, Edmund McManus, Jennifer Molnar, Cheri A. Recchia, and James Robertson. "Marine Ecoregions of the World: A Bioregionalization of Coastal and Shelf Areas." *BioScience* 57, no. 7 (2007): 573–83.

Sparenberg, Ole. "Perception and Use of Marine Biological Resources under National Socialist Autarky Policy." In *Managing the Unknown: Essays on Environmental Ignorance*, edited by Frank Uekötter and Uwe Lübken, 91–121. New York: Berghahn Books, 2014.

Spate, O. H. K. "From 'South Sea' to the 'Pacific': A Note on Nomenclature." *Journal of Pacific History* 12, no. 4 (1977): 205–211.

———. *The Spanish Lake.* Cambridge: Cambridge University Press, 1977.
St. Martin, Kevin, and Madeleine Hall-Arber. "The Missing Layer: Geo-Technologies, Communities, and Implications for Marine Spatial Planning." *Marine Policy* 32, no. 5 (2008): 779–86.
Stansby, M. E. "Development of Fish Oil Industry in the United States." *Journal of the American Oil Chemists' Society* 55 (1978): 238–43.
Staples, Amy L. *The Birth of Development: How the World Bank, Food and Agriculture Organization, and World Health Organization Changed the World, 1945–1965.* Kent, OH: Kent State University Press, 2006.
Stillings, B. R., and G. M. Knobl Jr. "Fish Protein Concentrate: A New Source of Dietary Protein." *Journal of the American Oil Chemists Society* 48, no. 8 (1971): 412–14.
Stiner, Mary C., and Gillian Feeley-Harnik. "Energy and Ecosystems." In *Deep History: The Architecture of Past and Present*, edited by Andrew Shyrock and Daniel Lord Smail, 78–102. Berkeley: University of California Press, 2011.
Stone, Rebecca. *Art of the Andes: From Chavín to Inca*, 3rd ed. New York: Thames and Hudson, 2012.
Sulmont, Denis. "Chimbote: Constitución de un bloque popular regional." In *Jornadas de Balance de Estudios Urbano-Industriales* (December 13–18). Lima: Pontifícia Universidad Católica del Perú, 1982.
———. "Conflictos laborales y movilización popular: Perú, 1968–1976." *Revista Mexicana de Sociología* 40, no. 2 (1978): 685–726.
———. "El Boom Chimbote." Unpublished manuscript, 1970.
———. "La sociología francesa en el Perú." *Boletín del Instituto Francés de Estudios Andinos* 36, no. 1 (2007): 85–92.
Sundrum, A., K. Schneider, and U. Richter. "Report: Possibilities and Limitations of Poultry Supply in Organic Poultry and Pig Production," *Research to Support Revision of the EU Regulation on Organic Agriculture* (2005), 13. http://www.organic-revision.org/pub/Final_Report_EC_Revision.pdf.
Swenson, Edward, and Andrew Roddick. "Rethinking Temporality and Historicity from the Perspective of Andean Archaeology." In *Constructions of Time and History in the Pre-Columbian Andes*, edited by E. Swenson and A. Roddick, 11–34. Boulder: University Press of Colorado, 2018.
Thorpe, Andy, and Elizabeth Bennett. "Globalisation and the Sustainability of World Fisheries: A View from Latin America." *Marine Resource Economics* 16 (2001): 143–64.
Tilly, Louise A. "The Food Riot as a Form of Political Conflict in France." *Journal of Interdisciplinary History* 2, no. 1 (1971): 23–57.
Tironi B., Ernesto. "La necesidad de regular la pesca en Chile," in *El desafío pesquero chileno: La explotación racional de nuestras riquezas marinas,* edited by Eduardo Bitrán, 323–29. Santiago, Chile: Hachette, 1989.
Tønnessen, Johan Nicolay, and Arne Johnsen. *The History of Modern Whaling.* Translated by R. I. Christophersen. Berkeley: University of California Press, 1982.
Trawick, Paul. *The Struggle for Water in Peru: Comedy and Tragedy in the Andean Common.* Stanford, CA: Stanford University Press, 2003.

Tsing, Anna L. "Natural Resources and Capitalist Frontiers." *Economic and Political Weekly* 38, no. 48 (2003): 5101–6.
Turrentine, J. W. "The Menhaden Industry," *Journal of Industrial and Engineering Chemistry* 5, no. 5 (1913): 378–88.
Tveterås, Sigbjørn, and Ragnar Tveterås, "The Global Competition for Wild Fish Resources between Livestock and Agriculture," *Journal of Agricultural Economics* 61, no. 2 (2010): 381–97.
Udías, A., R. R. Madariaga, E. Buforn, D. Muñoz, and M. Ros. "The Large Chilean Historical Earthquakes of 1647, 1657, 1730, and 1751 from Contemporary Documents." *Bulletin of the Seismological Society of America* 102, no. 4 (2012): 1639–53.
Ueber, E., and Alec McCall. "The Rise and Fall of the California Sardine Empire." In *Climate Variability, Climate Change, and Fisheries*, edited by M. Glantz, 31–47. Cambridge: Cambridge University Press, 2005.
Uekötter, Frank. *Die Wahrheit ist auf dem Feld: Eine Wissensgeschichte der deutschen Landwirtschaft*. Göttingen: Vandenhoeck & Ruprecht, 2010.
———. "Rise, Fall, and Permanence: Issues in the Environmental History of the Global Plantation." In *Comparing Apples, Oranges, and Cotton: Environmental Histories of the Global Plantation*, edited by F. Uekötter, 7–26. Frankfurt: Campus Verlag, 2014.
———. "Why Panaceas Work: Recasting Science, Knowledge, and Fertilizer Interests in German Agriculture." *Agricultural History* 88, no. 1 (2014): 68–86.
Uekötter, Frank, and Uwe Lübken, eds. *Managing the Unknown: Essays on Environmental Ignorance*. New York: Berghahn Books, 2014.
Valenzuela Ocampo, Jorge. "Observaciones al proyecto ley de pesca: Exposición del subsector artesanal cooperativo pesquero." In *El desafío pesquero chileno: La explotación racional de nuestras riquezas marinas*, edited by Eduardo Bitrán, 371–81. Santiago, Chile: Hachette, 1989.
Van Buren, Mary. "Rethinking the Vertical Archipelago: Ethnicity, Exchange, and History in the South Central Andes." *American Anthropologist* 98, no. 2 (1996): 338–51.
Van der Meer, Liesbeth, H. Arancibia., K. Zylich, and D. Zeller. "Reconstruction of Total Marine Fisheries Catches for Mainland Chile (1950–2010)." University of British Columbia Fisheries Centre, Working Paper #2015-91 (2015): 1–15.
Velásquez, Jorge Gamboa, and Jason Nesbitt. "La ocupación Moche en la margen norte del valle bajo de Moche, costa norte del Perú." *Arqueología y Sociedad*, no. 25 (2012): 115–42.
Vivallos Espinoza, Carlos, and Alejandra Brito Peña. "Inmigración y sectores populares en las minas de carbón de Lota y Coronel (Chile, 1850–1900)." *Atenea (Concepción)* 501 (2010): 73–94.
Von Huene, Roland, Erwin Suess, and Kay-Christian Emeis. "Convergent Tectonics and Coastal Upwelling: A History of the Peru Continental Margin." *Episode* 10, no. 2 (1987): 87–93.
Walker, Charles. *Shaky Colonialism: The 1746 Earthquake-Tsunami in Lima, Peru, and Its Long Aftermath*. Durham, NC: Duke University Press, 2008.

Walls, Laura D. *The Passage to Cosmos: Alexander Von Humboldt and the Shaping of America*. Chicago: University of Chicago Press, 2009.

Watson, Reg, and Daniel Pauly. "Systematic Distortions in World Fisheries Catch Trends." *Nature* 414, no. 6863 (2001): 534–36.

Waugh, Frederick V. "The Minimum-Cost Dairy Feed (An Application of 'Linear Programming')." *Journal of Farm Economics* 33, no. 3 (1951): 299–310.

Wells, Lisa Esquivel, and Jay Stratton Noller. "Holocene Coevolution of the Physical Landscape and Human Settlement in Northern Coastal Peru." *Geoarchaeology: An International Journal* 14, no. 8 (1999): 757–58.

Westengen, O. T., Z. Huamán, and M. Heun. "Genetic Diversity and Geographic Pattern in Early South American Cotton Domestication." *Theoretical and Applied Genetics* 110 (2005): 392–402.

White, C. Langdon, and Gary Chenkin. "Peru Moves onto the Iron and Steel Map of the Western Hemisphere." *Journal of Inter-American Studies* 1, no. 3 (1959): 377–86.

Whitehead, Hal. "Sperm Whales in Ocean Ecosystems." In *Whales, Whaling, and Ocean Ecosystems*, edited by James A. Estes, et al. Berkeley: University of California Press, 2006, 324–34.

Wintersteen, Kristin. "Sustainable Gastronomy: A Market-Based Approach to Improving Environmental Sustainability in the Peruvian Anchoveta Fishery." In *Environmental Leadership: A Reference Handbook*, Vol. 2, edited by D. Gallagher, 626–34. Los Angeles: Sage, 2012.

Yáñez, E., M. A. Barbieri, and L. Santillan. "Long-Term Environmental Variability and Pelagic Fisheries in Talcahuano, Chile." *South African Journal of Marine Science* 12, no. 1 (1992): 175–88.

Yeh, Sang-Wook, Jong-Seong Kug, Boris Dewitte, Min-Ho Kwon, Ben P. Kirtman, and Fei-Fei Jin. "El Niño in a Changing Climate," *Nature* 461, no. 7263 (2009): 511.

Yturriaga, José Antonio de. *The International Regime of Fisheries: From UNCLOS 1982 to the Presential Sea*. Leiden, Netherlands: Martinus Nijhoff Publishers, 1997.

Zeller, Dirk, M. L. D. Palomares, A. Tavakolie, M. Ang, D. Belhabib, W. W. L. Cheung, V. W. Y. Lam, E. Sy, G. Tsui, K. Zylich, and D. Pauly. "Still Catching Attention: *Sea Around Us* Reconstructed Global Catch Data, Their Spatial Expression and Public Accessibility." *Marine Policy* 70 (2016): 145–52.

Zeller, Dirk, and Daniel Pauly, "Viewpoint: Back to the Future for Fisheries, Where Will We Choose to Go?" *Global Sustainability* 2, no. e11 (2019): 1–8.

Zevallos, Enrique Amayo. "Proyecciones Andinas en el Pacífico: Del pasado al presente." In *Geopolítica Latinoamericana y del Caribe*, edited by Leopoldo Zea and Mario Magallón. México City: Fondo de Cultura Económica, 1999.

INDEX

Note: figures and maps are indicated by page numbers followed by *fig.* and *map*.

agricultural chemistry, 36–37
agricultural systems: agribusiness and, 45, 119, 184n60; chemical fertilizers and, 30, 119; distribution of animal proteins, 119–20, 184n58; in Germany, 36–37; guano fertilizer and, 31, 35; indigenous peoples, 6, 18–19, 22; industrial fishing and, 31–32; lack of diversity in food production, 119; marine proteins in, 13; market access to, 76; modernization of, 30, 32, 119; nutrient contributions of, 119, 184n58; post-world war, 119; understanding of nitrogen cycle, 31–32; use of fish as fertilizer, 22, 32, 35
Allende Gossens, Salvador, 102–3
anchoveta (*Engraulis ringens*): abundant populations of, 1–3, 29, 100–101, 137n3; behavior of, 67–68; calls for protection of, 82–83; diet of, 82; exploitation of, 5, 11, 111; fishery collapse, 14, 74–75, 77, 89, 92, 102, 104, 112; fishmeal production and, 5, 10, 13, 60–61, 65, 120; Humboldt Current ecosystem and, 1–2, 60, 64, 87*fig.*, 92, 112, 131*fig.*; impact of El Niño on, 6, 8–9, 89, 101–2; indigenous peoples and, 3, 121; industrial fishing and, 59–60, 64–67, 67*fig.*; Little Ice Age climate changes and, 28; local fisheries and, 96; location of seabirds and, 68; overfishing and, 85–86; overview, 127; *peladilla* landings, 85; Peruvian landings, 86; Peruvian promotion of, 121; Peruvian state management of, 84–86, 88; rates of abundance, 84–85; resilience of, 123
anchovies (*Engraulidae*): combination model vessels for, 106; dominating phases of, 92, 112; fishery collapses, 112; food production of, 40; Inca-period trade in, 20; marine ecosystems and, 28; North Pacific, 81; purse seine fishing and, 5; upwelling ecosystems and, 9; usage restrictions on, 81
Andes Mountains, 17–18
Angelini, Anacleto, 97–98, 105
animal farming: consumption of food crops, 30–31; distribution of animal proteins, 119–20; fishmeal/oil and, 3; high-protein commodities and, 31–32, 44; increase in, 30; industrial ecology of, 32–33, 36, 43–44. *See also* poultry
animal feeds: costs of, 30; fishmeal in, 3, 31–32, 38, 40, 42, 44, 54, 57, 110; food-grade fish and, 4; formulation of, 57; marine proteins in, 31–32, 37, 43–44; mathematical models for, 44, 58, 153n81; protein sources, 31–32, 37, 44
aquaculture production: ecological consequences of, 121–22; expansion of, 108; female labor force, 109; fishmeal/oil demand and, 109, 111, 121; salmon and, 91, 109, 121

Araucanía, 95
Araucanian herring (*Clupea bentincki*), 87*fig.*, 96, 104, 128
Arauco Fishing Company (*Compañía Pesquera Arauco*), 54, 96, 102
Arauco War (1536–1883), 95
Arequipa, 22
Arguedas, José María, 13, 71–73, 165n86, 165n87
Arica, Chile, 100*fig.*, 103
Ashbrook, Frank, 38
Atacama Desert, 18, 46, 94
Atlantic bluefin tuna (*Thunnus thynnus*), 10, 129

Banchero Rossi, Luis, 81, 85
Barker, Christopher, 35
Belnap, David, 89
Bío Bío River, 95
blue-footed booby (*Sula nebouxii*), 127
blue whale (*Balaenoptera musculus*), 130
bolicheras: capacity of, 66; Peruvian industrial fishing and, 64–69, 89, 162n34, 163n45; re-privatization of, 90, 171n73; technological modernization of, 66–67; working conditions on, 70
Bolivia, 94
Bollaert, William, 46, 94
bonito (*Sarda chiliensis chiliensis*), 49–50, 64, 79, 103, 131*fig.*
Booth, F. E., 40
Bosch, Carl, 37
Bridgett, Charles, 51
Burks, Edward C., 99

Caja de Beneficios del Pescador, 70
California: canneries in, 40; collapse of sardine industry, 41–42, 46, 63, 79, 89; fishmeal production and, 40, 64; industrial fishing in, 5, 11, 80; poultry producers in, 57; Southeast Pacific resources and, 58, 76, 79–80; tuna fishing in, 117; usage restrictions on sardines, 40, 105
California Cooperative Oceanic Fisheries Investigations (CalCOFI) Committee, 167n23
California Current, 9, 41, 132*map*
Callao, 25

Callao Painter, 15
canneries: bonito and, 49, 61, 64, 79; in Chimbote, Peru, 59, 68; dangerous working conditions in, 69; *enganchados* (migrants) and, 59, 68; female labor force, 69; fish scrap and, 31, 40, 57, 65; impact of US tariffs on, 50, 79; local infrastructure and, 47; in Peru, 49, 77; tuna and, 77
Caral, 18–19
Cargill, 89
Carrasco Herrera, Fernando, 103
Carson, Rachel, 137n3
Cerro Azul, Peru, 20
Cerro Cebrián, Vicente, 79
Chancay, 22
Chan Chan, 20
Chapman, Frank, 94
Chapman, Wilbert, 58, 80–81, 97
Chile: border disputes, 94, 172n12; canned goods production, 49; economic crisis in, 107; environment of, 95; FAO and, 51–56; fisheries law in, 107–9; fishermen's unions in, 107; fishmeal/oil production, 4–6; fish processing in, 50*fig.*; food riots in, 47; independence of, 25; indigenous fisher rights, 124; industrial development in, 45, 99; industrial fishing in, 3–6, 14, 47–49, 51–53, 98–99, 104–5; local fisheries and, 45–47, 52, 55*fig.*, 99; marine protections and, 123; maritime boundaries and, 97, 105, 111, 118; mining in, 94; national nutrition committees, 48, 154n13; national sovereignty and, 117; nutrition campaigns, 48, 56; salmon aquaculture and, 109; state's role in fisheries management, 102–5, 176n73. *See also* Chilean fishmeal industry; Iquique, Chile; Peru-Chile coast; Talcahuano, Chile
Chilean Development Corporation (CORFO), 54, 93, 96, 98, 101, 103
Chilean Fishing Company (*Compañía Pesquera Chilena*), 100
Chilean fishmeal industry: abundance and decline cycles, 14; agricultural commodity production, 110; in Arica, 100*fig.*; boom years in, 57; Coquimbo, 101*fig.*;

environmental burden of, 103, 106–7; expansion of, 91, 98, 105, 111; export of, 157n44; exports to Germany, 92, 105; global standing of, 105, 108, 110–11, 184n66; impact of El Niño on, 101–2, 107, 110, 176n65; international investment in, 100–101, 175n55; jack mackerel and, 104–5; multispecies fishery, 92–93, 101–2, 105–6, 110; poultry producers and, 57, 158n55; reprivatization of, 111; surplus fish and, 97; translocal connections in, 93; upgrades in technology and vessels, 106, 111, 177n88. *See also* Iquique, Chile; Talcahuano, Chile

Chilean National Nutrition Council, 154n13

Chilean Nutrition Institute, 56

Chillón River, 18

Chimbote, Peru: aerial view of, 62*fig.*; canneries in, 59, 68–69; civil servants in, 70; collapse of anchoveta fishery, 74–75, 110; CRYRZA and, 74; cultural world of, 72–73; *enganchados* (migrants) to, 59, 68, 71–72, 75; environmental burden of fishmeal industry, 73, 122; environmental setting of, 61–62; fishmeal boom years in, 69, 71–73, 75; fishmeal industry in, 13, 59–61, 65, 70–73, 74*fig.*, 162n29, 162n38; industrial development in, 61–63, 71–72, 74, 160n14; industrial fishing in, 69–70, 90*fig.*; living conditions in, 73–74; master plan for, 62; population growth in, 59, 62–63, 68, 71; steel mill in, 61, 63, 68, 160n17, 160n18

Chimú, 20

chub mackerel (*Scomber japonicus*), 128, 131*fig.*

Cieza de León, Pedro, 21–22, 24, 46, 146n55

Clearly, E. J., 61

climate: catastrophic impacts of, 11; extreme shifts in, 124; fisheries regime shifts and, 9, 14; Humboldt Current ecosystem and, 15–16; industrial risks and, 43, 82; isotherms and, 26; Little Ice Age and, 28; lomas and, 21; Peru-Chile coast and, 16, 18–19, 27; sea surface temperatures and, 82; trade flows and, 42; warming/cooling cycles and, 8, 20. *See also* El Niño

Cobo, Bernabé, 22, 24

Cohen, Max, 76, 83

Coker, Robert E., 2–3, 8, 46

Comité Nacional de Pesca (National Fisheries Committee), 65

common-property regimes, 114–15

Compañía Administradora del Guano (CAG), 63–64, 162n29

Coquimbo, Chile, 101*fig.*, 103

CORFO. *See* Chilean Development Corporation (CORFO)

Corporación del Fomento. See Chilean Development Corporation (CORFO)

Cosmos (Humboldt), 26

Costa Rica, 117

CRYRZA. *See* Rehabilitation and Reconstruction Committee for the Affected Zone (CRYRZA)

current systems, 2, 8, 132*map*. *See also* Humboldt Current System (HCS)

Cushing, David H., 4

Cushman, Gregory, 11

Cuzco, Peru, 21

Darwin, Charles, 13, 28

Deustua, Rene, 105

Díaz, Humberto, 98

dogfish (*Mustelus canis*), 128

Dortet de Tessan, Urbain, 28

Dow, Edward, 96

Eastern Pacific bonito (*Sarda chiliensis*), 127

Ecuador, 8, 97–98, 106, 117

Einarsson, Hermann, 68, 85, 169n42

Elguera McParlin, Manuel, 65

El Niño: costero, 113–14; extreme climate shifts and, 124; impact on fisheries, 8–9, 109, 111, 136*fig.*; impact on fishmeal industry, 85, 89, 92–93, 101–3, 107, 110; impact on Humboldt Current ecosystem, 5–6, 8, 11, 113; monitoring of, 82; recurrence of, 18; red tide and, 15; variations in, 11, 113–14. *See also* El Niño Southern Oscillation (ENSO)

El Niño Southern Oscillation (ENSO), 8–9, 111, 113–14, 136*fig.*, 180n8. *See also* El Niño

enganchados (migrants), 59, 68, 70–72, 75

ENSO. *See* El Niño; El Niño Southern Oscillation (ENSO)
Equatorial countercurrent, 132*map*
Exclusive Economic Zone (EEZ), 117–18
Export Fish Meal Association, 42
Exportmar S.A., 103

FAO. *See* Food and Agricultural Organization of the United Nations (FAO)
FAO Fisheries Statistical Series (FAO-STAT), 12, 119
Fernández y Cifuentes, 105
fertilizers: chemical, 30, 119; development of synthetic, 37–38; from fishery by-products, 34–35; industrial manufacture of, 35; menhaden as, 32, 34–35; Peruvian guano as, 31, 35; profitability of manure types, 37
fisheries: biomass data, 12, 114; consumer behavior and, 120–21; exploitative labor practices in, 124; FAO datasets, 12, 119; global food production and, 120; impact of El Niño on, 8–9, 109, 111, 136*fig*.; industrialization and, 4–5; local, 45–46; multidisciplinary approach to, 114; overfishing and, 123; Peru-Chile coast, 3–4, 12, 46–47, 49; regime shifts in, 9, 28, 140n47; tragedy of the commons and, 115; transnational search for, 116; wild-capture, 120; world production, 136*fig.*. *See also* industrial fishing
fisheries management: bio-economics of, 114; cause and effect in, 112; in Chile, 102–5, 176n73; common-property regimes and, 114–15; economic calculations in, 115–16; environmental policy and, 115; Exclusive Economic Zone (EEZ), 117–18; indigenous fisher rights, 124; individual competition and, 114–15; marginal yield and, 115, 182n35; multinational, 117; in Peru, 84–86, 88, 113; rational-choice model, 115, 181n34; regulatory approaches to, 83, 102, 115–18, 123–24; research in, 82; sustainability and, 14, 115, 120–21; world zones, 134*map*
Fisheries Plan (*Plan Pesquero*), 88
fishing, industrial. *See* industrial fishing

Fishing Consortium of Peru (Consorcio Pesquero del Perú, CPP), 81
fishmeal: animal feeds and, 3, 31–32, 38, 40, 42, 44, 54, 57, 110; apparatus for producing, 39*fig*.; commodification of, 10, 13, 32, 40–41, 45, 77; export tax on, 85, 169n43; fish by-products and, 38, 40; fish harvested for, 40; forage fish and, 4, 10, 116, 120–21, 123; global market prices, 86; Humboldt Current ecosystem and, 5; increased demand for, 40–41, 54, 57; Japanese buyers of, 40; Northern European production of, 57; spontaneous combustion of, 43; use of food fish for, 54–55, 57–58, 120, 173n24; use of waste fish in, 38, 57–58. *See also* anchoveta (*Engraulis ringens*); fish proteins
Fishmeal Exporters Organization (FEO), 78
fishmeal industry: agricultural chemistry and, 37; anchoveta and, 5, 10, 13, 60–61, 65, 77–78, 89, 120; aquaculture production and, 109, 121; *enganchados* (migrants) and, 70; environmental burden of, 73, 103, 106–7, 122–23; fish processing, 50*fig*.; global production and, 41–42; impact of El Niño on, 85, 89, 92–93, 103, 107; industrial hazards of, 43, 122; interconnectedness of, 119; international shipping and, 42–43, 153n71; marine technologies for, 5, 106; policy making and, 112; resistance to regulation, 85; special grade products and, 110, 179n1; translocal connections in, 93–94; usage restrictions on, 105, 111, 177n81; wartime shortages in, 41. *See also* Chilean fishmeal industry; Peruvian fishmeal industry
fish oil: aquaculture use of, 91, 111, 121; commodification of, 13, 32; industrial production of, 3–5, 35–36; Japanese production of, 91, 111; menhaden, 34–36; Peruvian production of, 91, 111; use in margarine, 111; use of waste fish in, 57. *See also* marine-based oils
fish protein concentrate (FPC), 48, 56, 120, 157n50, 158n52

fish proteins: international trade of, 40–43; Japanese buyers of, 42, 153n71; nutritional potential of, 56–57; profitability of, 46; salmon aquaculture and, 91, 109; wartime demand for, 41, 49. *See also* fishmeal; marine-based proteins

Food and Agricultural Organization of the United Nations (FAO): agricultural reforms and, 119; on climatological fluctuations, 112; establishment of, 50; fisheries data, 12, 114; fisheries reform and, 119; fishmeal as animal feed and, 157n41; IMARPE and, 85; nutrition campaigns, 45, 55–56, 97; overfishing concerns and, 86; Peruvian fishing sector and, 65; promotion of regional cooperation, 53, 56; study of Latin American fisheries, 51; tensions in accomplishing goals, 13, 51–54

food fish: biomass data, 12; canneries and, 40; Chilean promotion of, 102–3, 105; coastal regions and, 31; fishmeal restrictions and, 105, 111; Humboldt Current ecosystem and, 10, 14; indigenous peoples and, 19; jack mackerel and, 104; menhaden as, 34; nutrition campaigns, 56–57; oils from processing waste of, 34; opposition to use in fertilizer, 40; Peruvian promotion of, 90; processing of, 76; sardines and, 105; use for animal feed, 4, 54–55; use in fishmeal, 54–55, 57–58, 120

food production, 6, 30, 88, 119–20

food riots, 30, 47, 149n1

Fox from Up Above and the Fox from Down Below, The (Arguedas), 72–73, 165n86, 165n87

Franklin, Benjamin, 25

Frézier, Amedée François, 23

Fridthjof, John, 56

Fujimori, Alberto, 91

Funnel, W., 24

Galapagos Islands, 8

General Fisheries Law (Ley General de Pesca y Acuicultura, Chile 1991), 107, 118

General Fisheries Laws (Peru, 1971), 88

General Fisheries Laws (Peru, 1987), 91

General Fisheries Laws (Peru, 1992), 91

General Mills, 89

Germany: agricultural chemistry in, 36–37; agricultural systems, 13; animal farming in, 31–32; animal feed studies, 37; dependence on Norwegian fishmeal, 37, 47, 79, 154n5; fishing partnerships with Peru, 91; fishmeal buyers in, 41; fishmeal/oil import/exports, 81–82; fishmeal production and, 37; import of Chilean fishmeal, 92, 105; industrial ecology of animal farming in, 36–38

Ghio, Marcos, 162n29

Global Fishing Watch, 123

Global South, 77

Gold Kist, 89

Gordon, H. Scott, 114

Graham, George, 56

Gray, Robert, 24–25

guano: Peru-Chile coast, 2, 46, 63; seabirds producing, 2, 31, 46, 63, 85; U.S. agricultural sector and, 35; use in fertilizers, 31, 35

Guano Administration Company (Compañía Administradora del Guano, CAG), 48

Guayaquil, 22, 25

Guerrero Jiménez, Bernardo, 99

Gulf menhaden (*Brevoortia patronus*), 129

Gulf of Arauco, 94–95

Gulf of Mexico, 26

Gulf Stream, 25–27

Gulland, John A., 115

Gunther, E. R., 23

Haber, Fritz, 37

Haber-Bosch Process, 37

hake. *See* Peruvian hake (*Merluccius gayi peruanus*); South Pacific hake (*Merluccius gayi gayi*)

Halley, Edmond, 27

Hardin, Garrett, 115

Heinz, 89

Hellevang, N., 67

herring: abundant populations of, 1; fish oil and fertilizer industry, 36; German imports of, 37, 79; Icelandic, 85, 122; impact of industrial fishing on, 11, 77;

herring *(continued)*
 international trade of, 40, 42; ocean currents and, 47; purse seine fishing and, 5. *See also* Araucanian herring (*Clupea bentincki*); North Atlantic herring (*Clupea harengus*)
Heyerdahl, Thor, 145n40
H.J. Heinz Co., 77
H.M.S. *Beagle*, 28
Hornby's petrel (*Oceanodroma hornbyi*), 129
Huanchaco, Peru, 4*fig.*
Humboldt, Alexander von: Gulf of Mexico study, 26; on isotherms, 26; on sea surface temperatures, 26; study of ocean circulation, 25–27; study of the Southeast Pacific, 2, 12–13, 16–17, 25–26
Humboldt Current ecosystem: anchoveta in, 1–2, 60, 64, 92, 112; biotic-zoological, 3; climate-driven cycles, 15–16, 112–14; fishery collapse, 77; fish populations in, 9; German scientific commissions and, 47; global environmental significance of, 6, 8–9; history of industrialization in, 10–14; impact of El Niño on, 5–6, 8, 11, 114; industrial fishing in, 5, 118; interspecies competition in, 82; nutrition interventions and, 13; oceanic-climatological, 3; Pacific sardine populations, 92; principal reduction fisheries, 87*fig.*; variations in, 84, 111. *See also* Humboldt Current System (HCS)
Humboldt Current System (HCS), 132*map*; characteristics of, 6, 8–9; naming of, 27–28; physical geography of, 7*map*; subregions of, 8, 139n34; trophic web diagram, 131*fig.*; upwelling in, 8–9, 27–28, 84, 114, 131*fig.*; variations in, 9. *See also* Humboldt Current ecosystem

Icelandic herring, 85, 122
IFOP. *See* Instituto del Fomento Pesquero (IFOP)
IMARPE. *See* Instituto del Mar del Perú (IMARPE)
Inca Empire, 20–22
India, 36, 41

indigenous peoples: access rights for, 124; agricultural systems, 6, 18–19, 22; anchoveta consumption, 3, 121; colonialism and, 22, 95; marine resources and, 3, 18–24; net fishing, 19; plant resources, 20; pre-Hispanic resources, 21–22; whale hunting by, 33, 46
individual transferable quotas (ITQs), 107–8, 123
industrial fishing: anchoveta and, 59–60, 64–67, 67*fig.*, 74–75; animal feeds and, 3–4, 138n20; *bolicheras*, 64–70, 89, 162n34, 163n45; in Chile, 3–6, 14, 47–49, 51–53, 98–99, 104–5; crewmembers, 69–70, 164n67; depletion of stocks, 5; farming economy and, 31–32; fishmeal/oil production, 3–5, 174n42; foreign competition in, 104; impact of El Niño on, 109, 111; individual transferable quotas (ITQs), 107–8, 123; infrastructure for, 51–52; interconnectedness of, 119; maritime boundaries and, 97–98, 104–5, 118; modification of vessels, 66; in Peru, 59–60, 64–70, 88–90, 90*fig.*, 91; Peru-Chile coast, 48–53, 97–98; Peruvian nationalization of, 89–90; regime shifts in, 104, 111; research data and, 84–85; risk and uncertainty in, 83–84; scaling back capacity-enhancing subsidies, 124, 186n92; single-species, 60, 65, 92; Southeast Pacific, 11, 46, 58; sustainable measures for, 124; technological innovation in, 58; trash fish and, 43, 58; zones of sacrifice and, 75, 107, 122
Institute for Fisheries Development, Valparaíso, Chile. *See* Instituto del Fomento Pesquero (IFOP)
Institute for Ocean Research, Callao, Perú. *See* Instituto del Mar del Perú (IMARPE)
Instituto del Fomento Pesquero (IFOP), 13
Instituto del Mar del Perú (IMARPE), 13, 84–85
Inter-American Cooperative Health Program, 70
Inter-American Food Production Cooperative (SCIPA), 49

Inter-American Tropical Tuna Commission (IATTC), 117
international commodity markets: anchoveta fishery collapse and, 14, 77; fishmeal and, 57, 86; impact of climate oscillations on, 110; impact of El Niño on, 102, 111; impact of Peru in, 77–82; special grade products and, 110, 179n1
International Proteins Corporation (IPC), 83–84, 89
International Whaling Commission (IWC), 54, 156n39
Iquique, Chile, 29*fig.*, 95*fig.*; divorce resort proposal for, 102, 175n59; environmental burden of fishmeal industry, 106; fishmeal industry in, 98–101; importance of seaport in, 98–99; industrial fishing in, 14, 93, 98; mining in, 93, 96; transition to tourism, 93, 108
isotherms, 26

jack mackerel (*Trachurus murphyi*): Chilean export of, 104–5; in Chilean waters, 93, 104, 108; declining catches of, 111; factory vessels and, 104, 108, 118; food production of, 104; Humboldt Current ecosystem and, 5, 87*fig.*, 131*fig.*; impact of El Niño on, 103; migration range, 118, 129; in Peruvian waters, 91–92; refitting of vessels for, 102
Japan: canned tuna exports, 50; *Clupeidae* fishes in, 36; demand for imported fish proteins in, 42; fishmeal buyers in, 40; fishmeal production and, 32, 42–43; fish oil production and, 91, 111; investment in Peruvian fish industry, 88
Japanese sardines (*Sardinops melanostictus*), 92, 129
Jenyns, Leonard, 29
Johnson, John J., 96
Jul, Mogens, 51, 53–54

Kendrick, John, 24

Latin America: canned goods production, 49; fisheries in, 51; fishmeal production and, 80; foreign investment and, 76, 80; industrial fishing in, 155n24; industrialization and, 45, 119; marine resources and, 58, 79; multinational fisheries management, 117; nutrition campaigns, 45. *See also* Chile; Peru
Latin American Fisheries Council, 53
League of Nations, 45, 50
Ley Merino (Merino Law), 107
Liebig, Justus von, 36
Lima, Manuel, 58
Llagostera, Agostín, 19
Lobell, Milton, 58
Lo Demás, 20
Lübken, Uwe, 114
Ludewig, Carlos, 41
Luna Sauvat, Julio, 54, 157n44

MacCall, Alec, 40
mackerel, 5, 11. *See also* chub mackerel (*Scomber japonicus*); jack mackerel (*Trachurus murphyi*)
Madueño, Arturo, 65
Magellan, Ferdinand de, 2, 138n10
Maggiolo, Augusto, 64
Majluf, Patricia, 121
Mangareva, 20
Mapuche peoples, 95
marine-based oils: commodification of, 33–34; diet and, 118; floating factories for, 35, 150n28; food-fish processing and, 34; industrial manufacture of, 35, 150n28; industrial revolution and, 33–34; menhaden oil, 34–36; seal blubber, 150n18; sperm whale oil, 33, 150n17; whales and, 33–34, 150n17. *See also* fish oil
marine-based proteins: animal feeds and, 31–32, 37, 43; commodification of, 32; diet and, 118; farming economy and, 35; fluctuation of, 111. *See also* fish proteins
marine ecosystem: bioluminescence in, 24; coastal upwellings, 2–3; dynamic history of, 16–17; fishing biomass, 5, 12; global food production and, 120; human impact on, 83, 113; impact of aquaculture on, 121–22; impact of El Niño on, 11; management of, 168n34; regime shifts in, 104, 112; resource management and, 117; sardine-anchovy

marine ecosystem *(continued)*
dominating phases, 92–93, 112; Spanish colonial era and, 25; sustainability and, 112; trophodynamics in, 8, 139n35. *See also* Humboldt Current ecosystem
marine science: 19th century, 16, 25–29; El Niño and, 113–14; Humboldt Current System (HCS) and, 11; Humboldt's contributions to, 25–27; interspecies relationships and, 113–14; ocean circulation in, 25–28; policy recommendations and, 114; sea surface temperatures in, 2, 25–26, 28, 140n38; study of fishmeal production, 64
marine species glossary, 127–30
marine technologies: archaic fishermen and, 19, 144n25; echosounders and, 68; indigenous peoples and, 20, 24; linguistic interconnections and, 144n28; maritime gatherers and, 19, 144n25; purse seine fishing and, 64, 100, 138n24; tuna clippers, 64, 162n33
Marine Trophic Index (MTI), 139n35
Maule River, 21
McEvoy, Arthur F., 11
Meiggs, Henry, 61, 63
menhaden: decline in, 79; as fertilizer, 32, 34–35; as food fish, 34, 54; industrial manufacture of oil, 35–36, 150n28; North Atlantic fishing, 64; oceanographic conditions and, 42; oil of, 34–35. *See also* Gulf menhaden (*Brevoortia patronus*); North Atlantic menhaden (*Brevoortia tyrannus*)
Meseck, Gerhard, 78
Mitsubishi Shoji Kaisha, Ltd., 13, 42–43, 153n71
Moche Valley, 20
Murphy, Robert Cushman, 1–3, 8, 46–47, 63, 94, 113
Murra, John, 72

National Artisanal Fishermen's Confederation, Chile (CONAPACH), 107
National Convention of Fishermen (Chile), 96
National Fishing Society (Sociedad Nacional de Pesquería, SNP, Peru), 81

New England Trash Fishermen's Association, 58
Nippon Gyoryo Kaisha (Japan Fish Products Co.), 42
nitrogen cycle, 31–32, 43
North Atlantic cod (*Gadus morhua*), 10, 128
North Atlantic fishing, 5, 33, 57, 64, 78–79
North Atlantic herring (*Clupea harengus*), 67, 79, 128
North Atlantic menhaden (*Brevoortia tyrannus*), 129
North Equatorial current, 132*map*
North Pacific anchovies (*Engraulis mordax*), 81, 127, 167n23
Norway, 37, 47, 154n5

Oceana, 123
Osorio y Tafall, Bibiano Fernández, 52–54
Otero Lora, Carlos, 64

Pacific Bank of Nantucket, 25
Pacific bluefin tuna (*Thunnus orientalis*), 129
Pacific Decadal Oscillation, 124
Pacific Ocean: climate oscillations and, 110; European scientist study of, 2; fisheries management and, 117; naming of, 2, 138n10; trophodynamics in, 8, 139n35; warming/cooling cycles in, 8, 11–12, 140n38
Pacific sardines (*Sardinops sagax*), 87*fig.*, 92, 104, 129, 176n72
Paita, Peru, 23, 23*fig.*, 24
Patagonia, 19
Patía River, 21
Pauly, Daniel, 120, 124
Peláez Gularte, Wilfredo, 63, 73
Peralta Bouroncle, F. Hernán, 71–72
Peru: agricultural systems in, 120; anchoveta consumption, 121; anchoveta fishery collapse, 74–75, 89, 110; anchoveta protection proposals, 82–83; border disputes, 94, 172n12; canned goods production, 49–50, 77, 155n19; coast-sierra ecosystem, 21–22; colonial encounters, 21–22; distribution of animal proteins, 184n59; early settlements of, 6; exports, 69; FAO and, 51–54, 65; fisheries policies, 88–89; fish

oil production and, 91, 111; impact on international commodity markets, 77–82; Inca empire and, 21; independence of, 25; indigenous anchoveta processing, 3; industrial development and, 45; industrial fishing in, 3–6, 47–49, 51–53, 64–70, 88–91; international fishing partnerships, 91; Japanese investment in, 88; local fisheries and, 45–47, 51, 69; maritime boundaries and, 97, 105, 111, 118; nationalization of fishing industry, 89–90; national sovereignty and, 54, 117; nutrition campaigns, 48; overfishing regulations, 123; poultry consumption, 121; pre-Columbian cultures, 20; promotion of food fish, 90; reductions in biodiversity, 120; salmon aquaculture in, 91; sea surface temperatures in, 28; single-species fishery, 60, 65, 92; state management of anchoveta, 84–86, 88, 113; whale hunting in, 54, 156n39. *See also* Chimbote, Peru; Peruvian fishmeal industry

Peru-Chile coast: abundance of fish species on, 97; Callao Painter and, 15; climate oscillations on, 18–21; competition for migrating species off, 97–98, 104–5, 111, 117–18, 174n29; early marine technologies, 19; environment of, 17–20, 142n12; European scientific knowledge of, 28–29; expansion of US fish processing, 77; fish processing and, 77; guano-producing birds on, 2, 46, 63; human settlement of, 16, 18–20, 142n5; impact of fishmeal industry, 122; industrial fishing on, 48–53, 92–93; local fisheries and, 46–47; major fishing cities of, 7*map*; marine ornithologists and, 2; maritime boundaries and, 97, 105, 111, 118; organism movements along, 16; sea surface temperatures, 2, 26, 28; seismic activity on, 17–19; tolerance zone on, 97–98; upwelling in, 93, 172n6; USFW survey of fisheries resources, 12

Peru-Chile Trench, 8, 17–18, 143n14
Peruvian booby (*Sula variegata*), 2–3, 127
Peruvian cormorant (*Phalacrocorax bougainvillii*), 128

Peruvian fishmeal industry: agricultural commodity production, 110; anchoveta fishery collapse and, 14, 61, 74, 89, 106, 110, 112–13; economic crisis in, 86; expansion of, 60–61, 65, 162n29, 163n41; global standing of, 4, 110; Humboldt Current ecosystem and, 5; impact of El Niño on, 85, 113; international commodity markets and, 77–79, 81; outdated technology in, 106, 111; overfishing and, 113; reliance on anchoveta, 13–14, 60–61, 64–65, 86, 88, 110; reprivatization of, 111; technology lags in, 91. *See also* Chimbote, Peru
Peruvian hake (*Merluccius gayi peruanus*), 128
Peruvian National Bank (Banco Nacional), 89
Peruvian pelican (*Pelecanus occidentalis thagus*), 129
PescaPerú, 89, 91, 106
Pesquera Eperva, 101
Pezet, Víctor, 59, 63
Pfizer, 100, 175n55
phytoplankton, 9, 24, 52, 82, 131*fig*.
pilchard. *See* Pacific sardines (*Sardinops sagax*)
Pinochet, Augusto, 103, 105, 107
Pizarro, Francisco, 21–22, 24
Plan Pesquero (Peru), 98
Poeppig, Eduard Friedrich, 29
Ponce de León, Juan, 27
Popovich, Ivan, 97
poultry: California, 57; Chile, 57, 158n55; fishmeal in food for, 44, 54–55, 57, 80, 98, 111, 119; mass production of, 43; Peruvian consumption of, 121; United States, 57, 158n61
protective foods, 47–48
public health, 45
Pulgar Vidal, Francisco, 83
purse seine fishing, 5, 64, 131*fig*., 138n24, 162n32

Quilcay, 22

Radkau, Joaquim, 115
Ralston Purina, 76, 80

Rapa Nui (Easter Island), 118
Ravanol, Rodolfo, 52–53
Real Compañía Marítima de Pesca, 25
Regional Fisheries Management Organization (SPRFMO), 118
Rehabilitation and Reconstruction Committee for the Affected Zone (CRYRZA), 74
Revolutionary Vanguard, 71, 165n80
Robin, John, 73
Romero, Emilio, 59
Rostworowski, Maria, 22
Ruiz López, Hipólito, 21, 24, 28

Sala y Gómez, 118
salmon aquaculture, 91, 109, 121
San Antonio, Chile, 48*fig.*
Sandoval, Arturo G., 53
Santa River, 18, 61
sardines (*Sardinops*): Chilean fishing and, 105, 111; collapse of West Coast industry, 41–42, 46, 63, 79, 89; dominating phases of, 92–93, 112; fishery collapses, 112; Humboldt Current ecosystem and, 131*fig.*; oceanographic conditions and, 11, 41–42; overfishing and, 11, 63; Peruvian fishing and, 111; purse seine fishing and, 5; resilience of, 123; upwelling ecosystems and, 9; usage restrictions on, 40, 105. *See also* Japanese sardines (*Sardinops melanostictus*); Pacific sardines (*Sardinops sagax*)
Sarquis, Roberto, 105
Sarquis, Sergio, 105
Schaefer, Milner B., 82
Scoones, Ian, 119
Scripps Institution of Oceanography (SIO), 81
Sea Around Us Project, 12
seabirds: anchoveta consumption, 3; guano and, 2, 31, 46, 63, 85; Humboldt Current ecosystem and, 131*fig.*; impact of El Niño on, 8–9, 140n40; location of anchoveta schools by, 68; upwelling ecosystems and, 29
seal hunting, 24–25
sea lions, 1, 24, 46, 131*fig.*
Sechura Desert, 62

Sert, Josep Lluís, 62
Shady Solís, Ruth, 19
Siderperú steel mill, 61, 63, 68, 161n18
sierra (*Thyrsites atun*), 48*fig.*, 96, 129
Siglufjörður, Iceland, 122
skipjack tuna (*Katsuwonus pelamis*), 129
Smith, George, 94
Smith, Harvey, 100
Solar, Enrique del, 64
Southeast Pacific: 18th century exploitation of, 24–25; European scientific knowledge of, 23–29; expansion of US fishing in, 46, 58, 77, 159n66; fisheries development in, 12; fishmeal/oil production, 116; industrial fishing in, 11; Little Ice Age climate changes and, 28; navigating currents in, 22–23, 146n55; seal hunting and, 24–25; sea surface temperatures in, 28, 82; upwelling in, 27–29; warming/cooling cycles in, 11–12, 16, 18–20. *See also* Peru-Chile coast
South Equatorial current, 132*map*
South Pacific hake (*Merluccius gayi gayi*): fishmeal industry and, 54–55, 96, 173n24; Humboldt Current ecosystem and, 131*fig.*; local markets and, 102; overview, 128
Soviet factory fleets, 91, 102–4, 118, 176n74
sperm oil, 33, 54, 150n17
sperm whale (*Physeter macrocephalus*), 130
Star-Kist, 77
Stevenson, Charles H., 33–34
Sulmont, Denis, 71
Supe Valley, 18–20, 143n23

Talcahuano, Chile: Bío Bío River and, 95; environmental burden of fishmeal industry, 106–7; environmental setting of, 95–96; expansion of, 103–4; fish drying in, 97*fig.*; fishermen's cooperatives in, 96, 173n20; fishing infrastructure in, 96–97, 106; fishmeal industry in, 93, 97, 102, 106; fish processing in, 93; impact of El Niño on, 103, 176n65; importance of seaport in, 96, 98; industrial fishing in, 14, 93, 98; jack mackerel harvest, 104, 108, 176n65; merchant

ships and, 95; mining in, 95; small-scale appropriation of fish in, 106
Tallman, John, 35
Tantaleán Vanini, Javier, 88–90
Tarapacá, 46
Terzo, Frederick, 73
Torre, Juan de la, 21
Touraine, Alain, 71
tragedy of the commons, 115, 181n30
trash fish, 43, 58, 124
Treaty of Ancón (1883), 172n12
Treaty of Lima (1929), 94, 172n12
trophodynamics, 8, 139n35
Trujillo, 25
tuna clippers, 64, 162n33
Túpac Inca Yupanqui, 20
Turrentine, J. W., 38

Ueber, Edward, 40
Uekötter, Frank, 37, 114
Ulloa, Antonio de, 23
United Nations Agreement for the Conservation and Management of Straddling Fish Stocks and Highly Migratory Fish Stocks, 118
United Nations Children's Fund (UNICEF), 56
United Nations Convention on the Law of the Sea (UNCLOS), 117
United States: agricultural systems, 13, 35; animal farming in, 32; fishing expansion in the Southeast Pacific, 46, 58, 159n66; fishmeal supply chain and, 57; fish processing in Southeast Pacific, 77; industrial ecology of animal farming in, 38, 40; industrial fishing and, 51; processed food in, 76; restrictions on tuna and bonito imports, 50; use of fish as fertilizer, 32, 35; whale hunting and, 25, 33
upwelling ecosystems, 8–9, 29, 46
US Bureau of Fisheries, 31
US Fish and Wildlife Service (USFW), 12, 48–49, 64
US Fisheries Association, 56
US National Fish Meal and Oil Association, 79

Valdivia, 22
Van Camp Sea Foods, 58, 76, 84, 159n66
Varen, Bernhard, 27
Vecorena Olivares, Cristóbal, 53
Velasco Alvarado, Juan, 71, 73–74, 88–89
Vichama, 19

Walter, Richard, 23
whales: Antarctic quotas for, 54, 156n39; blue whale, 130; indigenous peoples and, 33, 46; as oil source, 33–34, 150n17; in Peru, 54, 156n39; schooling fish and, 9; Southeast Pacific hunting of, 25; sperm whale, 130; sperm whale oil, 33, 54, 150n17
white booby (*Sula dactylatra*), 128, 140n40
Wiener, Paul Lester, 62
Wilbur Ellis Company, 65
wild cotton plants (*Gossypium barbadense*), 20
Wolff, Emil von, 37

yellowtail tuna (*Thunnus albacares*), 130

Zárate, Agustín de, 22
Zeller, Dirk, 124
zooplankton, 131*fig.*

Founded in 1893,
UNIVERSITY OF CALIFORNIA PRESS
publishes bold, progressive books and journals
on topics in the arts, humanities, social sciences,
and natural sciences—with a focus on social
justice issues—that inspire thought and action
among readers worldwide.

The UC PRESS FOUNDATION
raises funds to uphold the press's vital role
as an independent, nonprofit publisher, and
receives philanthropic support from a wide
range of individuals and institutions—and from
committed readers like you. To learn more, visit
ucpress.edu/supportus.

www.ingramcontent.com/pod-product-compliance
Lightning Source LLC
Chambersburg PA
CBHW020810230426
43666CB00007B/949